THE FINAL ONE EIGHTY

The Final One Eighty

A memoir

by

DENNIS DONOGHUE

To Margi,
Happy to share my
story with a fellow teacher!
Best,
Dennis

BOOKS

Adelaide Books
New York / Lisbon
2020

THE FINAL ONE EIGHTY
A memoir
By Dennis Donoghue

Published by Adelaide Books, New York / Lisbon
adelaidebooks.org
Editor-in-Chief
Stevan V. Nikolic

For any information, please address Adelaide Books
at info@adelaidebooks.org
or write to:
Adelaide Books
244 Fifth Ave. Suite D27
New York, NY, 10001

ISBN: 978-1-952570-31-5
Printed in the United States of America

This memoir is a truthful recollection of actual events in the author's life.
Some conversations have been recreated and/or supplemented. The
names and details of some individuals have been changed to respect their
privacy.

To Carla, Beatrice, Apphia, and Justina

&

To the Students and Staff of Salisbury Elementary School

A few years ago the mother of one of my students, with nothing better to do, hid in a rhododendron near the school entrance and videotaped my sixth grade class jogging a couple of laps around the building. I'd taken the kids out for a short break and, being a runner myself, considered the workout a productive use of our time. This woman had other ideas. She sent the video to my principal and the district's superintendent. She inquired as to why these children were not receiving the same amount of *time on learning* as students in other classes. To her shock some ran without athletic footwear. As if that wasn't enough, she was certain I hadn't informed parents about missed instruction time and the risks inherent in vigorous exercise. Subsequently I was reprimanded and told I could no longer take my class outdoors. The superintendent suggested I conduct something called *brain gym* whereby students stood next to their desks and touched their toes. My principal added he would consider allowing kids to run for a few minutes before the start of the school day provided everyone passed in a signed permission slip and wore proper running shoes.

At that point I'd been a teacher for more than three decades and should have been used to anything. But having some fruitcake secretly record my class only to have my supervisors agree with her pushed me over the edge. A colleague who'd uncovered the surveillance from her classroom window understood my outrage (administrators *always* side with parents, she reminded me) and recited her own horror stories to make me feel better. It didn't help. A week later I was still paranoid and unsettled. Who else might be videotaping me? I found myself veering away from parents in the building and casting a leery eye on my supervisors. Had all those years I'd been a part of the school setting, both as a teacher and a pupil, finally caught up with me, addling my brain so I could no longer think straight? Or was I sane enough and simply reacting to an unforeseen and ridiculous circumstance?

For fifty-three years, from the time I entered kindergarten in September of 1961, I'd lived on the academic calendar (with the exception of a six week stint as a UPS delivery man in the fall of 1987 following two years teaching in an alternative high school which left me determined never to set foot inside a school again), rejoicing in June and despairing on Labor Day. Before the start of my last year I decided to keep a journal, to document daily observations and impressions in an attempt to learn something about myself and the profession to which I'd devoted so much of my life. While I'd come across many accounts from first year teachers (and journalists posing as such), I hadn't found any written by someone at the very end of his career who'd been around long enough to witness and reflect on the endless educational trends playing out on his students and colleagues. Yet my aim wasn't to prove a point or take a stand. I had no desire to make sweeping declarations about the state of public education in America. Neither I was out to lose friends or gain enemies. I only wanted to show what it had been like for me, a teacher in his thirty-seven year, as he weathered his final one hundred and eighty days. By June, with any luck, my writing would expose common threads woven into a fabric of sorts. From that fabric conclusions might be drawn, questions asked, opinions staked, and ultimately, a story revealed.

So I began at the beginning, the morning of convocation, when every teacher employed by the Triton Regional School District fought for a parking space in the high school lot, hurried into the cafeteria for a hard Danish and cup of tepid coffee, and strolled upstairs to be fashionably late for the nine o'clock start.

August 27, 2013

In the dimly-lit, cavernous auditorium my colleagues and I sat fanning ourselves with our agendas as the superintendent, a ruddy sixty-eight year old British expatriate, son of a deputy chief constable who brought his dog to work (though we weren't allowed to have anything with four legs in our classrooms), called half a dozen teachers onstage to receive goldplated apples in recognition of their twenty-five years of service. We stood and applauded as the recipients held up their awards. *Another fifteen to go!* someone shouted. After they'd filed off, he updated us on the progress of our progress, noting how the progress we'd achieved only indicated how much more there was to achieve, given the high standards the district had set for itself. He cautioned that if we failed, we were not only cheating the kids but the entire Triton community. How could any of us who called ourselves professionals allow this to happen? I was trying to make sense of that when I felt a tap on my shoulder. *Aren't you glad you're retiring?* someone whispered. I nodded. Of course I was glad. Who wouldn't be? And yet, coming off ten weeks of summer vacation I'd always viewed as a primer for the real thing, and with a balance of one hundred and forty-one dollars in my checkbook, I was thinking about money, the not having it part, about my three kids, one in high school and two in middle school, all of whom might one day express an interest in attending college, of long fruitless days spent searching for a way to augment my diminishing pension. *You'll be fine,* I reminded myself. *Teachers do this all the time.* Temporarily heartened, I turned my attention back to the superintendent who was now encouraging us to work harder and reminded us, as he did every convocation, that this was a pivotal year for the district. He didn't specify why.

Ninety minutes later, after half a dozen administrators had had their say, he escorted them off the stage and out of the auditorium. Before we dispersed to our various schools, Maggie, our union president and the high school band leader, gave a rousing Eugene V. Debs-type speech telling us how corporate America was ruining public education and how for-profit companies pushed bogus research showing how dumb our kids were compared to kids in the rest of the world. Alert and inspired, I was forgetting about retirement already. Around me everyone rose to their feet, cheering, whistling, and clapping as Maggie, who loved us and who we loved in return, finished her speech by telling us to stick together and take care of one another.

Back at Salisbury Elementary, the teaching staff, all eighty-two of us, gathered in the cafeteria. Sitting on a two foot stool attached to a round folding table on wheels, cheek to jowl with fellow teachers, I ate my last free lunch (one per year) provided by the district (tuna roll-up, iceberg lettuce salad, bag of potato chips, strawberry shortcake–no seconds). As I speared a cherry tomato, I realized a year from now I would be somewhere else, the people I'd worked with over the last fifteen years fading from view, the names of the kids I'd meet in two days likely forgotten. A decade ago I'd enrolled in a program allowing teachers with over twenty years of service to pay a higher percentage into their pension in order to shave a few years off their retirement day. Simply put, the state wanted to unload older teachers and our salaries, expertise be damned. Thrilled at the prospect, I had actually jogged to the post office with the application, not wanting to risk the mailman losing it. While I enjoyed the kids well enough, retirement meant freedom, an occasion to explore life beyond the confines of the classroom, a chance to see what it was like to be treated like a grown-up. It wasn't until I received notification last spring stating I could leave by Christmas that it struck me. So soon? What was I supposed to do with myself? I'd absorbed the news by repressing it, proclaiming to anyone who'd listen my unbridled joy at the terrifying prospect of being cast out onto the street while accepting colleagues' handshakes and hugs as if I'd won the lottery. No matter how convincing my bluff, I couldn't shake the idea that the sands around the foundation which had supported me for the last fifty years were washing away.

After dessert, Mr. B., our principal, addressed us on the need for tough love (from him to us, not us to the kids), reminding everyone that even though he tried to be flexible some of us would still let him down. While he didn't mind granting favors such as allowing us to leave for a doctor's appointment twenty minutes before the end of the day, what was he to think when that same person slunk past his window the next morning to get to her classroom thirty seconds before the kids? He paused to let that sink in. Then he told us about a student he'd had back when he taught fourth grade more than a decade ago. Aman was bullied and killed himself after moving to Texas when he was eighteen. Mr. B., now in his mid-forties, still thought a lot about Aman and wished he'd done a better job reaching out to him. I nodded reflexively, having heard the story at the start of previous school years. Like many administrators, Mr. B., who'd taught for a limited time before exiting the classroom, had to recycle anecdotes whenever he felt the need to share a lesson from his life as a teacher.

Later that afternoon, the staff meeting concluded, I organized my classroom desks into precise rows–five across and five deep. I loved rows and never deviated from them, despite endless requests from the kids. As a student myself I'd sat in rows and the arrangement was imprinted on my brain. It felt good to complete this simple task, to see the product of my labor. Reflecting on today, I concluded that so much of teaching elementary school was listening to people tell you what to do or, conversely, telling other people what to do, those other people being your students who might or might not do as you say, and who might very well have a good reason for not wanting to do it but who had to do it anyway because you said so. I was thinking about my last class I would meet for the first time on Tuesday. For once, I wasn't afraid of them. Because this was my final year, I intentionally had no goals or expectations, which I never lived up to anyway. Having none, I reasoned, would benefit all of us. For example, I wasn't concerned about how they would do on the MCAS, our yearly state-mandated high stakes assessment, and so didn't plan on drilling them to death like I usually did. I wouldn't even mention the test until it landed on their desks come spring. Even if the entire class flunked, I wouldn't be around to take the blame. Thus, there would be less pressure on them, and on myself, and that would make for a more enjoyable year for all of us.

August 28

Thirty minutes before I was supposed to leave the house for a day of professional development I was hit with severe stomach pain. Sweating and covered in goosebumps, I staggered outside for some fresh air but managed only a few steps onto the walk before I had to drape myself over the front gate like a human beach towel. I pulled myself off momentarily so my wife Carla could get to her car, refusing her offer to drive me to the emergency room. *I'm fine*, I told her, having no idea. Something was trying to chew its way through my belly button. Since it was her first day with her high school students (she taught in Ipswich, the next town south) I knew she'd be distracted enough to drive right by the hospital. I told her to go. She promised she'd come right back if I changed my mind.

Go, go! I said. *Your students need you. Don't forget your lunch.*

Gradually the pain subsided enough for me to race into the shower. By the time I got to school my colleagues were saying their names, what grades they taught, a book they'd read over the summer. Everyone turned and looked at me.

Why are you so pale? What's the matter with you? You're retiring this year!

The presenter, a representative of the educational company which had sold the district our latest initiative, was energetic and personable and made us feel smart no matter what kind of dopey comment we threw out.

Oh yes, that's an approach I never thought of, she said breathlessly. *I could see how that might work. Excellent observation. Anyone else?*

In the center of each table were red plastic bowls of Hershey Kisses and Jolly Ranchers put there, she confessed, because she knew elementary teachers well enough to know we'd need multiple sugar fixes to get through the next six and a half hours. We laughed and played along and acknowledged she was right. Long ago we'd taken the bit and not spit it out as our more rebellious peers had. We discovered we loved being good and doing as we were told. Why question authority when it was so much easier to go along with it? Now, as we gave her our undivided attention, took careful notes and politely raised our hands, we modelled for a complete stranger just how one should behave in a classroom.

The topic under discussion was writing and how to teach it. Our presenter stressed the importance of transition words, sentence structure, paragraph length, etc. She didn't mention voice or letting kids write whatever they wanted so they'd fill page after page and beg their teacher for time to read their crazy stuff aloud and see writing for what it was–liberating self-expression and not some canned concoction most kids wanted no part of. Still, it was hard to dislike her, as she'd *been there,* she reminded us, both as a teacher and as someone who also once struggled implementing The Initiative's many strategies. I had to give her credit for getting herself out of the classroom and making good dough pushing a product she believed in.

While she scribbled our brainstorming ideas on newsprint with a purple Sharpie, calling on us rat-tat-tat and bobbing her head in approval, Mr. B. and Ms. G., our assistant principal who'd fast-tracked into the position after a couple of years running our classroom for behaviorally disordered kids, wandered in to make sure we were paying attention. We all perked up right then, our hands shooting into the air with more pressing concerns (*Because the only dumb question is the one you don't ask!*). Since the two of them would evaluate us on how well we implemented The Initiative, sucking up was essential. Whenever one or the other offered a remark about what we were doing, we nodded and murmured our appreciation at the depth of their insight. But since I wouldn't be evaluated this year (What was the point? I'd be retired before they could get around to firing me.), I doodled and rolled my eyes, hoping they wouldn't notice because I still feared them even at this late stage of my career.

With two hours to go, the wall clock stopped working. Or so it seemed. Windows shut on account of the feeble AC amplified the heat. With so many of us packed together the air was warm, motionless and conducive to sleep. Components of The Initiative (e.g. how to construct two column notes, summarize, synthesize, find the main idea, create webs, etc.) had been around for as long as I'd been a teacher. But because the district had ponied up a bundle on this repackaged version, our administrators, in their zeal to achieve the results forecast by the purveyors of The Initiative, ordered us to execute the program in the exact manner we'd been shown when they came to observe us in our classrooms. If any of us deviated, choosing instead to teach the way we'd always taught because experience had shown us how to be successful, we would end up with a subpar evaluation in our file. Some of us learned this last year when The Initiative arrived at SES.

Our presenter decided that since we had been so good and worked so hard (*harder than any group I can remember!*) she would dismiss us fifteen minutes early. We chapped and thanked her. She applauded us back and told us how proud she was of us and wished everyone a healthy and productive year teaching The Initiative. Since we still had a lot of questions (*I can tell by the looks on those faces!*) she would be happy to stick around for as long as it took to answer them.

I was the first one out the door, chastising myself for not having called in sick and using one of my accumulated one hundred fifty sick days. I hadn't learned anything new and had missed a beautiful late summer day. This being my last year I'd promised myself I'd ease up on the gas a little. But having been on the school calendar for over half a century, I was coming to the conclusion that I'd suffered significant psychological impairment which prevented me from acting in my own best interests.

September 3

I met my students for the first time and informed them that not only was this their last year at SES (next September they would be off to middle school), it was also mine.

What? What do you mean? Are you dying of something?

I'm retiring.

They sat in rows, scrubbed and expectant, hoping I would let them stay where they were, surrounded by their friends. Many were worried, having never had a male teacher before.

We heard you're mean and make us run.

I told them I wasn't mean but we did run, though it was early in the morning and optional. Otherwise they could stay in the classroom and do seatwork.

Then we'll run then. Were you only just kidding about retirement? Sometimes teachers like to say that.

They expressed their good fortune at being able to tell people they would be my last class ever which meant I would never forget them. Then they forgot about me and asked did I have a pencil sharpener or could they go to the office to have a note signed or what time can we eat snack or you had my uncle's girlfriend, the one with the blond hair. Do you remember her?

To regain their attention I bestowed privileges. No longer would they have to walk in line, eat snack at a designated time, get permission to use the bathroom. They were thrilled at the prospect of such freedoms. Finally they could move from place to place without someone telling them to shut up and march single file, eat when they were hungry and pee when they had the urge. Was this really true? *Yes*, I said. To which a chorus replied, *Then this will be our best year ever!*

For the bulk of the school day we would be together (my colleague Adelle next door taught 6D math and science while I had her class for reading/writing and geography). Of 6D's twenty-one members, sixteen were white, thirteen from dodgy backgrounds (a segment of the population lived in seasonal housing, including campgrounds; one in six of SES's five hundred and fifty kids was homeless; rates of drug use and domestic violence paralleled those of inner cities), and over half exhibited some impediment which affected classroom performance (shaky home life, learning disability, erratic behavior, past trauma, etc.). Every class in the building reflected a similar composition, which meant that as much as we teachers loved the kids (those who didn't departed for easier populations) their needs exhausted us by March and some years by Christmas. We liked to think we were all they had, which gave us a savior complex and in turn made us sick with guilt when we couldn't save them. But as the years went by I learned that it was okay to give up on a kid, even healthy for both the kid in crisis and myself. Trying to save a hopeless case drained reserves better spent on someone with half a chance. Knowing when to cut a kid loose and redirect my energy elsewhere was a skill acquired over time.

Take Charlie, for example, a student I had six years ago. Respectful, pudgy, depressed, with greasy hair that fell over his eyes, he slept all day, rarely lifting his head from the desktop. Whenever I woke him, he grumbled, opened his eyes, looked around to see where he was and dozed right off again. His mother was crazy (she had a habit of railing at passing motorists on the town common), his father a drug addict long out of the picture. Charlie's troubles gave him insomnia and though I liked him well enough I took his snoring personally. Was I that boring a kid could snooze through my class *every day*? The other kids, meanwhile, saw it as a game, pestering me to wake him up and urging a consequence for his napping. This went on for a week or so until, out of ideas, I decided to leave him alone. Sleep was what Charlie needed most, I told his classmates, and the one place he could get what he needed was here. From then on, we let him sleep in peace. That spring he somehow stayed awake long enough to not only complete the MCAS but to pass it. The following September when he visited me from middle school (where I assumed he continued to sleep), I learned he'd enjoyed our time together, even recalling some finer points of discussion which had taken place while he dozed. I was both astonished and pleased that the year he'd spent with me hadn't been a total wash despite my forsaking him.

As part of my first-day-of-school duties, I reviewed standards of behavior. In SES, warnings were posted in the hallways, classrooms, the cafeteria and gym—large white laminated signs with big black block letters like you'd see in a subway or jail advising you for your own safety: *Keep Hands, Feet, and Objects to Yourself; Follow Directions; Give People Space*. These three ironclad rules were the substructure for the hundreds of lesser rules piled upon them, which, we all believed, would allow us to get through the school day. If rules were made for a reason, then the more rules the better, notwithstanding whether the kids understood or followed them.

Relieved it would be my last first day ever having to mention them, I stood before the class and spoke in a conversational tone I hoped might engender some discussion.

We already know them rules, Blaine said without raising his hand. *We've been here since kindergarten. How about we read a story?*

We'll get to it. Please raise your hand.

When then?

Later.

Why not now?

Later I said.

We're wasting time talking about what we already know.

I ignored him. He raised his hand. I ignored him a second time. He said he had his hand up. I said I understood. Then why didn't I call on him then?

You aren't supposed to talk until I call on you.

But how can I say anything if you don't call on me?

He kept his hand in the air while I reviewed the rules they'd been hearing about since kindergarten. There was no class discussion, despite my best effort to couch these directives as user-friendly and a topic which ought to be talked about. They knew better. Blaine propped his arm up with his other hand before giving up. In my head a recording played to an indifferent audience in the same monotone I'd heard every year on this day. Once again I was imploring, *begging,* for their attention and engagement on this crucial matter and they, having done nothing wrong and feeling no compulsion to discuss the matter, disregarded me. I was looking out at rows of blank faces, desperate for a response, when Blaine's hand shot back up. I was thrilled.

He was a personable, good looking kid with grey eyes and black hair who would go on to challenge everything I said. Like many kids at SES, he had a dicey history. The woman he thought was his mother wasn't, a fact that I was told by our social worker to keep to myself. His father had been nearly killed by police in a case of mistaken identity (according to Blaine) and now might be dying of some disease the nature of which Blaine wasn't sure. He'd been at SES for his earlier years, moved away, moved back, moved away a second time and was back for his last year before he went on to middle school. The other kids couldn't stand him. He butted into conversations, never let anyone finish—or start—a sentence, and acted like a know-it-all. Whenever he took a day off we breathed a sigh of relief. But I liked him. Every day he greeted me with a smile and asked how I was doing. He was good about taking his meds, fishing little pills of various colors out of a plastic sandwich bag because he'd been in such a hurry to leave the house he hadn't had time to swallow them. Now he inquired again as to why I wouldn't call on him if he had his hand up.

Your hand is always up. If I called on you all the time no one else would have a chance to say anything.

I wouldn't call on you either, Cheyenne informed him.

She was his foil, and for everyone's sanity I kept them on opposite sides of the classroom. Tall and thin with doe eyes and a smile that made her braces seem too big for her mouth, she was also opinionated, a busybody, impulsive—in other words, the female version of Blaine with a similarly sketchy background.

Managing these two, along with the others, configuring combinations that put maximum space between parties to allow us to get through the day with some degree of consideration of one another was a skill I'd refined through many years of trial and error. I turned every desk into an island surrounded by a No Wake Zone. For some kids, even this wasn't enough, so I planted one desk on the left side of my own desk, another on the right, one up against the back wall, another snug under the paper towel dispenser. What we really needed were office cubicles. They were all for it. *Can you get them for us, Mr. D?*

With twenty-two living and breathing human beings crammed into a typical-sized classroom (including my paraprofessional who had her own desk in the back corner), all of us talking and moving and making noise and shutting one another up and trying to do whatever we thought we ought to be doing, there was no privacy, space or quiet. My job was to keep everyone busy for six and a half hours a day, to maintain a civility which would support proper comportment and to set academic and behavioral goals for us to achieve. But unlike office workers, my students earned no salary and received no benefits package. Many would gladly have been elsewhere, given their struggle to finish even rudimentary tasks and control their manic behavior, both of which elicited much nagging from me. With few if any options available to do anything about the predicament we found ourselves in, we were confined to an over-sized cell and expected to navigate a narrow channel of learning or else we'd hear about it (me from my supervisors, the kids from me). Even though this was just Day 1, considering these obstacles I had my doubts about how well my last year would go, despite my resolution to plan as little as possible.

September 4

On the free stuff table adorned with a *Teachers Only Please* sign outside the office I found a book entitled *Brain Stations* (*A Centered Approach to Thinking Skills*) by Greta Rasmussen, published in 1989. I scanned the introduction: *Most educators agree that the development of thinking skills among children who will be living their lives in the 21st century is of critical importance.* Apparently my colleague who'd dump it here disagreed with the book's premise.

It was slim pickings on the free stuff table this time of year. In June the surface disappeared beneath loads of junk teachers no longer wanted on their shelves. I refrained from taking anything, even this evocative book, as I was beginning to panic about how to dispose of the contents of my own classroom over the next ten months: bins of paperbacks kids no longer read (preferring to download books on Kindles, borrow from our school library, or not read at all), a couple of class sets of ancient dictionaries and thesauri, three tubs of broken crayons (they prefer markers or colored pencils), five cartons of glue sticks, half a dozen racks of kid scissors, stacks of construction paper (I stopped ordering after I noticed I had five drawers full), assorted loose leaf binders on past district initiatives collecting dust on a bottom shelf, a large black eighties boombox with detachable speakers I'd inherited from a retired colleague I used exclusively to play a meditation tape, piles of reproducible workbooks going back decades, two paper cutting boards (the older model the weight of a car battery), a collection of stuffed animals propped up around the classroom (monkey, bear, lion, ostrich, cardinal, alligator, dog, and two large tropical fish push pinned above the whiteboard), a cascading fountain with a broken pump, eight miniature Buddhas arranged in a circle, various teacher guides, fifty or so hanging folders in a file cabinet, each stuffed with lesson plans, and a couple of shelf loads of hardcovers and paperbacks on how to teach everything from diagramming sentences to promoting altruism among middle schoolers.

For starters, I resolved to dump a few items on the free stuff table every day, starting with those outdated binders I'd been afraid to throw away under penalty of reprimand, though just a few items a day wouldn't cut it. The problem was more complex and not easily solved, even with a full year head start. Every teacher guide, reproducible workbook, how-to manual, and set of class texts I had retained with the intention of putting to use again. Having stockpiled for years, I was now faced with the disposal of property I didn't own yet was responsible for getting rid of. Any available storage space in the building had been claimed and filled with the crap of other teachers, many of them long gone. So I was stuck, at least for now, hoping I wouldn't meet the fate of former colleagues more obsessed by the logistics of their clutter removal than by the reality of their impending retirement. Some simply walked out the door and left the detritus for their replacement to deal with, some enlisted friends and family members to cart stuff out by two wheeler on weekends, while others started with the best of intentions and, overwhelmed by mounds of outdated curriculum flotsam and jetsam, simply surrendered. A retiree's ill health over his last year prevented him from jettisoning hundreds of National Geographic magazines he'd been stockpiling since 1982. His successor (me) was forced to recruit a platoon of kids who spent an afternoon stacking the magazines against the back wall of building for trash pickup.

Freeing yourself from what you'd accumulated over the course of your elementary teaching career was impossible to do alone, given the professional connection and emotional overlay you had with nearly every item, and unless you thought it out ahead of time and sought help you could find yourself more and more overwhelmed as your days dwindled.

September 5

Driving home today I crossed the Merrimack River from Salisbury into Newburyport and glanced eastward towards Plum Island. It was seventy degrees, sunny and dry, the best month of the year in

New England. The sky was a deep blue, the water sparkled, pleasure boats tugged at their moorings while narrow docks stitched together pushed out into the channel from both banks. I'd gone over the Gillis Drawbridge twice a day for fourteen years and one thing or another was always being done to it. This morning a line of orange cones protected a cop on detail while a boom truck lowered workers in hardhats and safety vests over the side. Lines of thick cables connected to generators ran along the sidewalk as other workers stepped over them to grab wrenches out of toolboxes in the back of pickups. What was the problem with the bridge that it could never be fixed? I thought of SES, how no matter how hard we worked nothing was ever good enough. In response to this perceived inadequacy, we were ordered to perform frequent district and school-wide assessments which interrupted our daily schedule and stressed us out. Data collected from these trial runs meant time spent not-teaching (substitutes were hired to replace us during the school day) while we interpreted what we'd gathered and decided what to do with it. Harried and exhausted, we griped how we never had time to finish anything in our classrooms. What ever happened to teaching? Our primary objective, we'd come to learn, had shifted to squaring away enough paperwork to show we were attaining the headway our administrators promised us we were capable of. We could fix the kids, they assured us, provided we amassed and analysed enough data. Like the workers on the drawbridge, we did as we were told, our sole purpose to gain approval by showing how industrious we could be.

September 6

Our school day was seven hours long. Of that, twenty minutes were allotted for recess. By the time kids filed down the stairs and out the door that time had shrunk to fifteen (on rainy/snowy days they didn't leave the classroom). For the remainder of the day they had no physical activity, except for gym class forty minutes once a week. Recently our state politicians, outraged over the level of obesity and inactivity among Massachusetts school children, decided to do something about it, mandating a PE period once a day. A bill filed by Kay Kahn (#2634) and passed into law during the 2013-2014 legislative session stated: *In the event that PE classes are not taught daily, all students should have at least 30 minutes of physical activity daily.* Despite passage of the law nothing changed at SES. After the videotaping incident, Mr. B. restricted running to a ten minute time slot before the start of the school day. After I sent home permission slips, eighty fifth and sixth graders returned them. As young as they were they knew enough to understand how rigorous exercise made them feel good and calmed them down, gave them focus and boosted self esteem. And, studies showed, it made them smarter by increasing their capacity to retain information.

There were, of course, loads of research extolling the benefits of physical exercise. So why so little interest on the part of the school, and why weren't my colleagues clamoring to get kids up and moving? I didn't have a definitive answer but I had a plausible theory: like their fellow Americans, many SES teachers weren't in particularly good shape themselves. Because of this they viewed regular exercise as unpleasant and even intimidating and did whatever it took to avoid it. Rather than promote and teach a subject they were uncomfortable practicing, they denied there was a problem, like those kids who struggled with decoding and fabricated every obstacle to avoid the discomfort of having to plow through a reading passage. In the lunchroom I'd hear teachers who paid monthly gym fees complain about never having the time to work out. I suspected there might be another reason.

September 9

One of the benefits of being down to my final 175 days was, as I mentioned, not being evaluated. Last year, when Ms. G. showed up to conduct an observation, 6D was meditating. With the lights out and all of us sitting silently with our eyes closed, she waited at the door for us to finish, likely wondering which part of The Initiative this activity was addressing. The rule for teachers was to pretend your evaluator wasn't there, to act as if he or she was invisible, the thinking being, I guess, that this would promote a business-as-usual atmosphere, despite the fact that as assistant principal Ms. G. was a real person who meted out punishments and called parents and was viewed by the kids as someone to keep a good distance from. Tall, fortyish, professionally attired, with the solemn bearing demanded by her role as law enforcer, she captured everyone's attention as soon as she entered. Proceeding to the kidney table in the back of the classroom, she took a seat and began typing into her Ipad. I broke protocol by introducing her and announcing she'd come to see what we were up to.

After hurriedly splitting the class into groups, I distributed booklets about the continents, drawn from a third grade kit I'd borrowed from a special education teacher. As I stood at the whiteboard jabbering directions on how to set up two column notes, I tried to forget that Ms. G. seemed to be typing quicker than I spoke, which after a few minutes made me break into a sweat as I attempted to interpret whether this was good or bad and decided bad. To compensate, I spoke faster, not so much to keep pace but to impart more information vis-a-vis The Initiative. Was I using proper terminology and phrasing and doing so in the correct order, or was I just bullshiting my way through because in my haste I couldn't remember the sequencing outlined during our professional development in-services? Could she be on to me?

The lesson went okay as far as I could tell, other than my speed talking and the kids' usual reluctance to give me their full attention or anything close to it, though with Ms. G. in the room their focus was sharper than usual. She got up once or twice to see what they were doing, asking a couple of kids to summarize the lesson for her, which of course they couldn't do, at least with what she considered any degree of proficiency. After half an hour or so she gathered up her Ipad and departed with little fanfare. The kids had gone ahead and constructed those two column notes from information they'd gleaned from studying the glossy photographs and reading a four sentence paragraph accompanying each. Their final product was adequate enough, I hoped, to get me by. But later, as I read over her critique of my performance, I saw that she'd highlighted the various ways I hadn't taught The Initiative, along with how I'd flubbed the parts I had attempted to teach. Therefore, the kids hadn't really understood what they were supposed to do in terms of The Initiative's conventions, and thus I was awarded the first *Needs Improvement* rating of my career.

Today, released from the tension of being judged, I decided we would read a play out of *Scholastic Scope* magazine, an adaptation of *Tom Sawyer*. By way of introduction I asked the kids who had done something they weren't supposed to do. Every hand went up. Barrett told us he'd spent all night high in a tree and from his perch observed a search party armed with flashlights shouting his name. Blaine had set off two Amber

Alerts, the second one while he was hiding in a closet in his own house. Nyla had stolen her grandmother's golf cart from a campground and driven the wrong way on a highway in New Hampshire. There were plenty more stories of rash behavior and I hoped they wouldn't find Tom's hijinks boring. Meek ole Tom would have struggled to pass as one of the gang here in 6D though the kids enjoyed his knack for manipulating his way out of trouble.

Though much of Salisbury was working class, it was also a border town and a beach community with a lot of down-and-out types who migrated here from all over the U.S., drawn to the seasonal housing (motels rooms and efficiency cabins) and campgrounds (after Memorial Day when beach motel rates tripled residents moved into tents and campers). Throughout the school year, it wasn't unusual for a kid to show up who hadn't turned twelve but had been enrolled in eight different schools in a half dozen states, and as luck would have it touch down in 6D just in time to take and fail the MCAS, thus contributing adversely to our class average, before decamping for Mississippi or Maine or Montana or some other remote corner of the U.S. This vagabond lifestyle along with their assorted academic, social and emotional woes made it tough to fold any of these students into rhythm of 6D, if indeed what we had could be considered a rhythm. One year a kid who had travelled by bus from Nevada informed me on his first day that his month-long stopover at SES preceded his move to his uncle's cabin in Maine—at least that was where he guessed he and his mom were headed—or else to her girlfriend's mobile home in Virginia. Undersized, polite, pallid and speaking with a Southern accent (he thought he was born in Arkansas), he was deemed the class pet by the girls. While studious enough, he was years behind most everybody else skill-wise. Both myself and the girls did our best to bridge some of his academic gaps, except they wouldn't leave him alone, mesmerized by that adorable drawl of his, and though I liked him well enough I was glad when he left. On his last day he printed a forwarding address in shaky script on a Post-It. We sent off letters but never heard from him again.

September 10

Back when I taught junior high school (when there was such a thing), we had a guidance counselor who'd started a family when he was fifty-four. He could never retire–that's what he told me when I escorted one of my students down to see him– as he was putting his three kids through college at the age of seventy-five. His arthritis made it difficult for him to get out from behind his desk so he stayed put in his office, sending someone to fetch his lunch in the cafeteria. Most kids had little interest in speaking with him, given their sixty year age difference, his gruff demeanor and the manner in which he blew his nose into a handkerchief. I found him friendly enough, despite his complaints about young people's shoddy work ethic, foul language, slovenly dress, lack of respect, etc., especially the non-white kids who, he claimed, didn't try as hard as the white kids. There were housing projects behind the school, blocks of nondescript four story brick buildings with a string of dented metal trash cans outside them, a six foot chain link fence separating the school from the residents, and a gate allowing kids to pass back and forth. He'd gaze out his office window at the place while telling me of the old days when corporal punishment kept everyone in line. There were no discipline problems back then, he contended, and putting away the rattan was a sorry day for education. When he wasn't grumbling, he and I talked sports. He liked to reminisce about his coaching days–signed footballs lined a shelf in his office–and I remember thinking that I, single at the time, might well be in his shoes someday, too old to move around or even think straight.

One January he died of a heart attack and we closed the school to attend his funeral. After the service, we–his colleagues–formed an honor guard on both sides of the casket as it exited the church. I'd never been to the funeral of a teacher, certainly not one who'd died in the middle of the school year, nor been part of an honor guard, or even heard of such a thing. Yet as we stood around in the cold at the grave site, I wondered if this was customary and that perhaps I ought to rethink my plans to be cremated so I might be the recipient of an honor guard too.

With no mandatory retirement as there was for cops and firefighters, teachers could elect to die on the job. Perhaps some of us could still teach effectively at seventy-five though I had my doubts whether I could at fifty-seven. Good teaching was performance art, a combination of manic yet focused energy released over time. Doing it effectively required bundles of humor, creativity, and personality. Seeing those who should have left the profession five or even ten years earlier was like watching Don Rickles or Joan Rivers–you cringed, except with has-been comedians the audience was polite enough to tolerate their outdated antics and laugh at their lame jokes. Not so with twelve year olds.

September 11

The district required us to administer the GRADE reading assessment at the start and finish of each academic year. In September we silently rooted for the kids to do poorly so come

June they would show demonstrable gains. Thus our supervisors could see for themselves how we'd successfully employed the various strategies of The Initiative and note that our classes had achieved *significant improvement* in this assessment when they wrote up our summative evaluations.

By early afternoon the temperature had soared to ninety-four degrees outside and eighty-eight in the classroom. Sliding open a window hoping for a hint of breeze (we had AC in name only), I was met with a blast of warm air, followed by a chorus of groans as I slipped the elastic band off the package of test booklets. Beginning with the vocabulary section, I recited the instructions which told them to choose a word matching the boldfaced one. They sat mute and glassy-eyed, long past being able to summon enthusiasm for any of these types of tests. Later, during Listening Comprehension, I read a sample aloud and told them to choose one of four drawings which matched the paragraph. It was during Passage Comprehension, where they were asked to read random chunks of text and answer the five multiple choices for each, that they wilted. Heads drooping, they sat on their haunches, tugged at their scalps, shifted in their seats, mumbled to themselves and soon began to darken columns of circles at random. They'd had it. They no longer cared a wit, thus guaranteeing their scores would indeed be a good deal higher in June. Around the building, I knew, my colleagues were rejoicing as their classes were performing likewise.

This was the first of many assessments the kids would take throughout the year. Oddly enough, for all our data gathering, the end result hardly reflected our effort. Every year scores on the MCAS might go up–or they might go down–depending on the composition of the class or how a particular kid was feeling on the day of the test. Had he gotten any sleep the night before, eaten breakfast, fought with his father or mother, aunt, uncle, brother? Was he depressed or dyslexic, test-phobic or just plain didn't give a shit? We prepared them as best we could and then waited anxiously until fall when the scores went public. Often a kid you were sure would bomb didn't, other times your aces unaccountably flopped. It was just the way it was with these kinds of things. No kid was a lock or even close to it. But that didn't stop us from assessing, and then assessing some more. Our administrators liked to crow about us being a *Data Driven District* –as if this was a good thing–and I'd gotten to the point where I couldn't stomach data meetings where we reduced kids to test scores and concocted intervention strategies we didn't have the time or energy to implement.

Later, after I'd collected the GRADE, I mentioned the anniversary of 9/11. Only a few kids knew the specifics of what I was talking about. Our school was less than a year old then (we'd moved from Memorial Elementary the previous January), each classroom equipped with a large television set mounted on a wall bracket, a great innovation at the time. Somehow a fifth grade teacher got wind of a commercial airliner crashing into one of the twin towers, turned her TV on, turned it off, then came into my room and told me not to touch the remote.

We're under attack, she said.

From whom?

She shrugged and hurried back to her classroom to lock the door. I continued teaching, distracted and out of sorts, getting information in bits and pieces from other teachers poking their heads into my room, worrying about Carla and the girls but pretending everything was fine, hoping not to alarm the kids who spotted groups of adults congregating in the hallways, some crying and hugging one another, others sneaking out of their rooms to find out what was going on.

Did something bad just happen? Why are they all acting like that out there?

I told them a plane hit a building in New York City, a long way away from SES, and they should continue to do their work. When I knew more I'd tell them, pretending this world-changing event was another story that would come and go. I babbled away about parts of speech, listing examples of adjectives and pronouns on the whiteboard so I wouldn't have to turn and face them, and they, sensing my apprehension, peppered me with questions I couldn't answer, as everyone else in the United States was converging on any television they could find. As 6D's only source of information and having little to go on, I figured the less said the better. This business-as-usual charade was an exercise we teachers had practiced and refined. From time to time someone would be wheeled out of SES strapped to a gurney and inserted into a waiting ambulance (usually one of the behaviorally disordered kids whose removal was for both his safety and ours, though occasionally a staff member complaining of chest pains). For the duration of the emergency, school policy was for kids to stay put and teachers to act as if nothing was going on despite medical personnel racing through the hallways. Except now my own curiosity drove me into the teachers' lunchroom. With televisions in every classroom and not a single one turned on, staff on break crowded around a portable perched on the countertop, an outdated twelve inch model donated after a colleague had cleaned out her attic. Even with its small screen, rabbit ears antenna and fuzzy reception it was more than adequate to confuse and terrify all of us.

Carla, on leave from her teaching job to be home with the girls, called me on the classroom telephone to pass on what she'd learned. I listened without speaking, the kids behind me with their ears perked, hoping to glean a tidbit about this seismic story they knew nothing about, and Carla ending by telling me she'd cancelled a pediatrician's appointment because she didn't feel safe leaving the house.

September 12

Leland brought a chicken finger for snack today—a puffy fried appetizer coated in gooey pink sauce swimming inside a plastic sandwich bag, a leftover from last night's takeout. Other kids produced similarly unrecognizable items which never failed to draw me to their desks to inquire what they were eating as it bore no resemblance to food I ate. Most of what they consumed consisted of processed snacks Americans were always being warned to avoid if their goal was to attain the average life span.

Seven years ago I tried to implement a healthy snack policy after I could no longer stand by idly as they devoured Doritos, Oreos, Gummy Bears, Chex Mix, beef jerky and other assorted foodstuffs which spiked their blood sugar, extinguished their already compromised attention spans, and made them even more impossible to manage. I sent a letter home banning the worst offenders (blue juice, candy, foods whose ingredients I couldn't pronounce when I read them aloud) along with a list of healthy options and a few research articles backing up my reasoning. Though I had no authority to enforce such a policy, a number of parents thought it was a good idea while others protested, mostly the type who rose up whenever a school or teacher tried anything new. Their kids wouldn't eat healthy food and therefore would go hungry, they cried, or they couldn't afford *all natural* foods like carrots, granola, yogurt, nuts and seeds, or they didn't eat *all natural* food themselves so what were they supposed to do, turn their eating habits upside down because of some cockamamie rule? They complained to the principal, to the superintendent, to the school committee. All along I had Mr. B's support and assumed the uproar would die down, that these people would come to their senses and understand the importance of good nutrition. But the issue wasn't about healthy eating. It was about control– theirs versus mine–and they had no intention of relinquishing any of theirs.

For a time afterwards I attempted to monitor what kids ate in class, going on about (and embellishing) my own eating habits and explaining what to look for at the supermarket. I displayed examples of healthy snacks kids brought from home. *This is a pear*, I would announce as I held the piece of fruit aloft and rotated it in my hand while we all stared up in awe. *And this fuzzy brown orb is a kiwi which comes from a far away land called New Zealand and aren't we lucky to have this delectable fruit which tastes like candy?* At first I told myself I was making headway, as with each new day a wholesome snack revealed itself on a desk top, but 6D's penchant for junk food was such that despite my proselytizing, bags of *Fritos* and *Chips Ahoy* and *Cheeto Puffs* continued to spill out of backpacks. They apologized for hurting my feelings and promised they'd try harder. I thanked them for their consideration. *It's not your fault*, I added glumly, without elaboration, a catch in my throat. This was America, the land of corporate food giants piling up mountains of profit producing processed provisions ladened with sugar and fat, the addictive consumption of which resulting in a nation of the overweight and out-of-shape, the infirm and unrestrained, the foggy brained and gastrically distressed. Besides, who was I kidding? I couldn't get my own three children to eat healthy. So I ceased preaching, redirecting my energy to complimenting anyone with something vaguely nutritious (a yogurt/chocolate chip mix, for instance) and tearing up whenever a kid pulled out a plastic baggie of red bell peppers slices or uncovered a container of watermelon cubes. For a while this helped, and other kids, wanting to make me happy, brought in celery and cream cheese, roasted almonds and raisins, clumps of red and green grapes, all of which I pronounced sensational, as if these common food items had been delivered to us from another planet, while the owner sat beaming in the glow of attention as a result of his magnificent foraging.

But in the end I surrendered. Sermonizing about healthy choices made little sense when the food served at lunch wasn't much of an improvement over the junk coming from home. Scoffing down hotdogs and pizza during their brief lunch period, the kids ignored the sad little plastic cups of raisins or pale cantaloupe cubes on their trays, saving their bags of Goldfish or potato chips for later in the day when they would eat them in class, defending these items' nutritional merit because they'd been purchased right downstairs in our own cafeteria.

September 13

Over the summer Lucy visited her grandfather who lived in a small town in Georgia and together they grew a cotton plant from seed. Today she presented the foot high plant to me as a gift. Having never seen such a thing, I held it up and informed the kids the soft white fiber surrounding the seeds was spun into the clothes they were wearing. They regarded me like I was crazy, twisting around and yanking the tags on their clothing.

Can you read the label? Corbin said to Leo after nearly falling out of his seat. *Does it say cotton?*

It was outlandish, this proposition, yet as preposterous as it was, they listened, intrigued, as I explained as best I could the process from plant to apparel.

You mean our clothes are made from that? Brynne said as her eyes bulged in horror.

I walked around so they could touch the smooth green leaves for themselves.

Yuck, no way am I wearing that plant! she declared with a shake of her head. *That's gross! Eww!*

Having had a typical public school education, they had no experience with the sowing and germination of seed, the tending and harvesting of crops, nor any understanding of the complexity and fragility of the six inches of topsoil upon which all our lives depended. As such, this revelation turned into one of those spontaneous lessons I'd grown to love. Whatever I'd been doing forgotten, I found myself lecturing on the history of cotton cultivation, together with the numerous steps required to spin it into cloth, including its less-than-savory role as a commodity during slavery. There were many questions I did my best to answer but I wasn't absolutely convinced at the end, as I placed the clay pot in a sunny spot on the window sill, that they believed what they'd heard. Still, I felt pretty good about my tutorial, having prepped nothing and gotten decent results. I'd utilized a model (the plant) relevant to their daily lives (their wearing of cotton), provided background information, encouraged discussion on why we didn't have cotton plantations in Salisbury, used our pulldown map to have Lucy show us where cotton grew in the U.S., and had them all excited to break this astonishing news about the origin of their clothing to their peers at lunch.

September 16

At our monthly meeting of Triton Regional Teachers Association's Executive Board we (two representatives from each of the five schools, along with Maggie, our president, a vice president, secretary and treasurer–average age early fifties) bemoaned the lack of interest from young teachers regarding our association and collective bargaining agreement, especially with the administration adopting a quasi-business model with the intention, we felt, of using the new evaluation system to target us. As a group, these young teachers were talented, energetic, and committed, yet none seemed willing to run for building representative or offer to serve as a member of the contract negotiation team. What exactly were they afraid of? Lots of work in return for a measly stipend? Even more meetings to attend? Having to confront their bosses on their colleagues' behalf? Being called a pinky-ring-wearing union thug? Okay, fair enough, but surely they understood their salary, benefits, and tolerable working conditions resulted from the sweat and toil of their older brethren–and that all three were under assault every time a new contract was negotiated. Perhaps their tepid support was tied to the bashing of teachers' unions, a popular talking point not only on conservative media outlets like *FOX News* but more left-leaning publications like *The Boston Globe.* Much was reported on how we stood in the way of student progress by refusing to work longer hours (for little or no pay), resisting charter schools (where teachers had less rights, worked longer hours, and were required, in some places, to wear the same unflattering uniforms as their students), bankrupting districts with our fat contracts (starting salary in our district for someone with a master's degree was around $40,000), protecting our incompetent colleagues, etc.

And you might believe it until you compared your paycheck to someone with your qualifications in the private sector, or witnessed the patience your colleagues displayed in getting a point across their students, or counted the number of times these same colleagues dug into their own pockets for classroom supplies and party snacks. Anti-teacher union propaganda apparently was effective enough to keep the younger crowd away from leadership roles in an organization whose sole purpose was to protect and promote their interests.

September 17

To commemorate the town of Salisbury's 375th birthday, a local bank sponsored a coloring contest, a drawing of an antique carousel that for years had operated on Salisbury Beach before the boardwalk became a hangout for stoners and other deadbeats. A bank committee planned to leaf through the five hundred or so submissions and determine winners. Earlier we'd been warned by the office that this activity was to be done at home, as coloring had no place in today's sixth grade classroom.

I distributed the sheets anyway. Every kid of every ability loved to color. Not only did it reinforce fine motor skills, develop an eye for rich and subtle color combinations and strengthen focus, it chilled everyone out. Some kids hummed or sang, some bobbed to an internal melody, some sat stock still and silent, lost in the undertaking. When a crayon fell to the floor it got picked up. Snacks were shared, small talk exchanged, compliments delivered. Coloring turned us into people who enjoyed being around one another. Although employed in a myriad of therapeutic settings, in public schools at this grade level the pursuit was shunned as having no value as *real learning*, despite bringing out a more empathic side of the kids and revealing facets of their personalities evident by their choice of bold colors or muted pastels. Even the most fidgety kid sat quietly, contemplating the right choice to shade the horse's curried tail, the ornate saddle, the flying mane and prancing hooves.

Once finished, the entire class was anxious to display their work on the whiteboard, names on the back so no one would know the artist.

Pick the winners, Mr. D.! demanded Blaine.

Okay, but since I was no judge of art the ones I didn't choose might well be better than the ones I did.

Just choose already!

So I did, examining the color combinations and delicate texture of each composition with the enthusiasm of someone with zero artistic background, tossing out a compliment on each and selecting the top three. No one complained. In fact they agreed with me. I did have an eye for art after all.

You should teach art, Mr D.! Nyla said.

They thanked me for allowing them to color in place of *real work,* knowing they weren't supposed to be doing this proscribed activity as they'd been reminded since they'd left first grade that coloring was for babies. Except they couldn't suppress their desire for it. Art of any kind was considered a frill at SES, something without legitimate value, even if every kid found in it joy and contentment and would gladly do it in place of anything else, and even if research indicated art made them better overall students and boosted their self-esteem. In response to this need, the district allocated a forty minute class once a week. But since I was retiring I could do art every day all year long.

September 18

I turned fifty-eight today and according to my Massachusetts Teacher Retirement Board Creditable Service Estimate I have reached 78.66% and by Christmas I'll hit the maximum 80% mark, which means I can collect 80% of the average of my last three years' salary every year for the rest of my life (though I elected to go with another option, giving me 66% in return for ensuring that when I die Carla will get two-thirds of that amount for the rest of her life. Conversely, if she expires before me, I'll pop up to 80%). Though the payout wouldn't keep pace with inflation, it might be adequate so long as I got a job and didn't survive beyond the average American male's lifespan. But I had no business complaining. Without having to lift a finger, I'd get a check every month for the rest of my life. The deal was so good, in fact, I didn't even have to exist for the tap to continue to flow, albeit with a bit less pressure. In a sense, then, I was being compensated at a higher rate simply for remaining alive. It was a heady prospect, this impending freedom along with a monthly direct deposit into my checking account, even if my standard of living would drop like a stone once the girls started college.

No sooner had I informed Mr. B. of my intention to stay until June (*For the kids' sake*, I said, clinging to my savior complex) then I wondered what was wrong with me for agreeing to work another six months while forking over eleven percent of my salary into a pension system. Okay, so I wasn't the first teacher to continue working after he'd had accrued enough time to retire. And yes, I was afraid to leave. Terrified, actually. The outside world, lacking morning announcements and mandatory lockdowns, monthly assemblies and supervised recesses, loomed as a wild and unforgiving place. How would I survive out there when those I told what to do had the option of not doing it? On top of that, who would enforce the rules I'd been following with stoic conviction for the last fifty years? At least if I stayed until the last day of the school year, I could pretend I was leaving for the summer like everyone else.

In April 2013, the rules changed regarding retirement for new Massachusetts public school teachers. No longer could we go out before the age of sixty. In addition, rather averaging the final three years of our salary, the law now required averaging the last five, thus reducing the size of our pension. Yet teaching–or at least teaching here at SES–fell in line with the zany showmanship required of street performers. Maddening, exhausting, exhilarating, it was especially trying when many if not most in your audience would rather be somewhere else. To remain fresh and inventive decade after decade was difficult, if not impossible. Every day you had to remind yourself you were an entertainer, though not necessarily by choice, and that your ability to reach those before you required a performance that might well take the life out of you. The more authentic and innovative your act, the more appreciative and respectful the audience and the easier and more gratifying your work. Yet who could maintain this type of vitality six and a half hours a day five days straight, over forty weeks stretching from September to June? While some managed better than others, all of us showed our wear once we hit our fifties. I certainly found it tougher to make it through the school day. By noon, having taught for three and a half hours with nearly as much time to go (the two breaks allotted by the contract were a forty minute planning period and a twenty minute lunch, both regularly encroached upon by kid-related matters or meetings with administrators), I sometimes found myself standing before the kids rubbing the bristles on my chin, scratching my head, glancing down at my shoes, all while contemplating how to cope with the daunting prospect of instructing all afternoon without a break. No one was going to hand me an intoxicating curriculum. I didn't know any magic tricks and couldn't juggle. There were no guest speakers from reality television on the agenda. And to top it off, I wasn't allowed to take the kids outside of the classroom. The notion that it was all up to me to preside over them in this confined space for this extended timespan was a phobia I struggled to repress, even when I had something I thought they might like. I dreaded afternoons—we all did—and fervently prayed that when Mr. B. formulated our schedules in August he would give us our lunch and planning periods as late in the day as possible. Mornings were a cinch—anybody could teach with the kids fresh and semi-alert. It was afternoons that killed us.

Are you okay, Mr D.? asked Mia. *Why are you just standing there like that?*

September 19

The results of the GRADE assessment ranged from a 2.4-8.0 grade equivalent for both my reading classes. Of the group of forty-one kids, ten read on a third grade level, eight on a fourth, and six on a fifth. Of the students on IEPs, four required a scribe. Nine had been diagnosed with ADHD. Most of the rest, not to be outdone in terms of educational stumbling blocks, struggled with impulse control, motivation, organization, and just plain old getting along.

Remedying these deficiencies and bringing everyone up to—or closer to—grade level was up to me, along with my paraprofessional Sheila, and a special education teacher who took anywhere from one and four kids at a time out of the classroom for small group instruction forty minutes a day. My task was impossible, of course, as evidenced by the abysmal scores of these kids who had been in our school for seven years and still couldn't read. Why couldn't they read? I wasn't sure. Having more teachers would have helped but perhaps it was the method itself which stalled progress. My favorite writer on American public education, James Herndon (*The Way It's Spozed to Be; How To Survive In Your Native Land; Notes from a School Teacher*) claimed reading was a skill no one could explain but which everyone could do:

And yet if you can't do it, you must have been prevented from doing it. Most likely what prevented you was teaching. For one thing, if you get taught the same "skills" for seven years over and over again, you probably get the notion that it is very difficult indeed. But more important, the "skill" involved in reading is at once very simple and quite mysterious. Once you look at C-A-T and get the notion that it is a clue to a certain sound, and moreover that very sound which you already know means that particular animal, then you can read, and that is certainly quite simple, even if the ability of humans to do so is opaque. What you probably need to do then is read a lot and thereby get better at it, and very likely that's what you will do, again, if no one stops you. What stops you is people teaching you skills and calling those skills "reading", which they are not, and giving you no time to read in the school without interruption.

Certainly there were interruptions. We disrupted reading time to assess the skills or lack thereof, having kids put down books to answer questions on a random piece of text they had little interest in. Yet someone with supposedly dismal skills— Tanner, for example—would return from library class with books he'd checked out because they'd looked interesting. I'd scan his selections and suggest he find something easier (never being able to figure out a courteous way of telling him he couldn't handle the level according to his latest assessment) and in response he'd defend his right to choose whatever books he wanted. *Okay, fine,* I'd say, and have him read a page to prove I was right. He would then grind his way through a couple of paragraphs with nary a grip comprehension-wise. Or so I thought. The next day as soon as he arrived he'd race to my desk to show me how far he'd gotten and recite everything that had happened up until then, exclaiming he'd gotten no help with any of it.

And what do you think of that Mr. D.?

I'd congratulate him, thrilled with the news. Whether he'd made much headway or not didn't matter. He'd carried the book home, gained confidence as he advanced from one line of prose to the next, in due course turning the page and seeing laid out before him another country waiting to be conquered. No problem, he told himself, as he now had the time and drive and quiet and no one like me around to tell him he was in over his head. He kept at it, he was game, staying up long past midnight to prove me wrong.

September 20

For my seventh grade daughter Justina's thirteenth birthday she invited two middle school friends who were in my class last year to her party/sleepover. Three years earlier, when her oldest sister Beatrice did the same, a former student would come bounding downstairs in the morning and there I'd be drinking coffee in my pajamas. *Good morning, Mr D!* the kid would say. I'm not sure if seeing me dressed like that mattered to her but it did to me. As it was Saturday morning I had no intention of putting on a collared shirt and a pair of slacks. Once Apphia started seventh grade, however, having former students in my house became part of the routine. Even so, I toned down the silly stuff fathers do around their kids so it didn't get back to my present students. But sometimes it did.

Avery was at your house this weekend and she overheard you say we drove you crazy, Thad informed me Monday morning. *And here's you drinking a beer.*

I glanced at his phone and sure enough there I was holding a frothy mug to my lips as the rest of the class hurried over for a look.

You drink a lot of beer? asked Brielle.

I did drink beer, I told them, and liked it, and by law was permitted to, as I was above the legal age by nearly four decades. That was okay with them then.

Have you ever been drunk? Thad asked me as he raised his phone up so all of 6D might have a look.

I paused, debating whether to concoct a lie or tell the truth, though of course with a moral attached forever lamenting why I'd done such a foolish thing.

Of course he hasn't! a startled Mia blurted as I shooed them back to their desks. *He's a teacher!*

My own sixth grade teacher, Mary Florette, always had the perfect response whenever put on the spot. A member of the Sisters of Saint Joseph order, she spent her adult life in three adjacent buildings– grammar school, convent, and church. By 1967, nuns' habits had seemingly vanished over-night, the wimple replaced by barrettes, bobby pins or nothing at all, debunking our theory that our teachers not only shaved their heads but polished them too. Like me, Sister Florette was at the tail end of her career and showing it. Scatterbrained, soft-spoken, as frail and nimble as a sparrow, she taught every subject, including music, to the forty-two of us, a number that seemed impossible until I counted every face when I came across a glossy black and white class photograph taken on the front steps of Saint Brendan Church. Just before the photographer clicked the lens, she'd positioned herself on the right side, leaning in as if she expected the frame might not be wide enough to accommodate her, or maybe because of fatigue, no doubt exhausted after herding her formidable flock down the hill from the school and yanking us by the elbow to arrange us height-wise, the boys in ironed white shirts and clip-on blue ties, the girls in plaid pleated jumpers and navy knee socks.

I don't remember much about that year, other than that she was agreeable and harbored no desire to make our lives miserable. Paul Hennessey and I, seated by the door in the back of the classroom, regularly ducked from our seats and raced into the boys' room where we hung out for no reason, knowing she'd never miss us. One day, though, she must have done a head count. As we leaned against the bathroom sinks wondering if it was possible to spend an entire day there conducting an informal scientific experiment on the limits of human endurance, she came flying through the door. Hennessey, who I loved because there was no jam he couldn't talk his way out of, was ready for her.

What is the meaning of this? she demanded to know.

She stood in front of the stalls holding a piece of chalk while brushing white dust from her sleeve with the other hand. The nuns applied a certain kind of talcum whose scent without fail put me on edge.

We saw something shiny roll by the door, Sister, he replied, *and so we chased after it.*

She looked at him, then me. The retort was total bullshit, of course, made more absurd by his tone of phony earnestness years of parochial education had refined in us as a defense against constant reprimand for venial transgressions. But Sister Florette didn't fall for the line like I would have, remonstrating over flouted trust, belaboring the point until my eyes watered and my mouth went dry. She didn't even raise her voice.

All that glitters is not gold.

And that was it. She turned and left. We followed her out, chastised and feeling ridiculous. We never left the classroom again.

That sage advice has done a lot for me over the years. Attributed to Shakespeare, it serves as a safeguard against every kind of enticement. I regularly recommended it to 6D, reminding them the bright dangling lure was often a trap, and that which appeared mundane and demanded hard work might well turn up a more gratifying reward. Once I even overheard a kid use the line on a classmate who planned to dump his birthday loot on a pair of flashy overpriced Nikes as the two stood by the coat cubbies getting ready to go out for recess.

No one else has a pair. I'll be the first.

They're a total ripoff.

Maybe to you. I gotta have them. I'm going straight to the mall after school.

Just remember— all that glitters is not gold.

The next day I saw the sneakers myself, on the feet of the kid who couldn't resist temptation.

September 23

Though tedious and spirit dampening, worksheets reinforced basic skills and kept the kids busy (in fact, the term *busywork* derived from the book *Plans for Busywork,* published in 1901 and edited by Sarah Louise Arnold, emphasizing that the best classroom management tactic was to keep a healthy supply within arm's reach). Though I sometimes felt a tinge of guilt distributing them (a more creative teacher would have considered this practice a cop-out), given the length of the school day, the physical confines of the classroom, and my limited energy, I relied on the practice to keep the kids quiet and on task, like any office manager who feared that his workers, without something to keep them occupied, would have time to contemplate the futility of their station, organize themselves into a cohesive unit, mutiny and lock him in a supply closet. I wasn't unaware that by doing so I was requiring them to sit for extended periods, thus providing ideal training for a lifetime of meaningless employment (e.g. data processing) in the American workplace. Having been conditioned from earlier grades, 6D expected worksheets to come their way and didn't raise much of a fuss about it when they did. Some even thanked me and a few found perverse joy in racing to my desk with the finished product, thus undermining the whole concept of busywork. As a reward for their efficiency they demanded leisure time which meant doing whatever they wanted to do, and so disrupting the atmosphere of everyone else doing their busywork. To prevent this I had to keep an endless reserve handy, stacks of copies addressing various skills ready to be distributed. Because of the time and effort required to make such copies, occasionally a kid (or the entire class) would proclaim to have already done such-and-such a worksheet (whether this was true or an attempt at task avoidance I could never be certain). In response to this outcry I would counter that I *was* keeping track (I wasn't, at least not consistently) and they in turn would insist I was mistaken.

We've already done this one already! Why are you making us do it again?

To which I would end the debate by saying if that was the case then the second time ought be a cinch so why were they complaining in the first place?

When I did get around to returning them, scored with edits or comments and a grade of some sort (letters, checks or numbers), half the class stood up and deposited the worksheet I had spent my valuable time assessing into our blue recycle bin. Showing neither interest in what I'd written nor exhibiting any flair for the dramatic–no balled-up wads fired in disgust or paper airplanes zipping through the air–they expressed the same emotional attachment to their work as if they'd picked up a scrap of paper off the floor without looking at it.

A few kids, on the other hand, kept everything I passed back, sliding *each and every paper* into their binders or desks, not to bring home at some point, but to safeguard like legal documents until their binders exploded and desks wouldn't close, thereby necessitating an intervention by me. Having never figured out how to deal with the pathology of hoarding, I would sit beside them during classroom cleanup, extracting one sheet after another, while the recipient of my generosity sat arms folded in detached resignation as I drained the life blood from his veins. His curious behavior, a byproduct of stress and anxiety as well as a method to control the chaos resulting from the machinations of all of us jammed into a cramped space, provided a sense of comfort and security. My actions, on the other hand, filled him with terror. As he sat stoically I rambled on about how much better he would feel with everything organized just right so during class he could locate whatever it was I was requesting (*Please take out your* _____.) without having to plunge head and shoulders inside his desk and rummage around for five minutes while I twirled an Expo marker and fumed along with everyone else. As the overstuffed desk was an affront to my hard work in keeping the flow flowing, I took the insult personally, as if the culprit had some nefarious objective in mind other than to help himself get through the day.

Squalor, at least as far as the shallow confines of the hoarder's desk allowed, provided solace. It drove me nuts.

September 24

I read aloud a couple of chapters of *When Zachary Beaver Came to Town* by Katherine Willis Holt. Winner of the National Book Award, this young adult novel set in the early seventies covered love, death, divorce, friendship, family, community, and what it's like to be poked fun at while earning your living as a morbidly obese adolescent starring in your own one person freak show. The antagonist, a fifteen year old orphan named Zachary Beaver, spends his days in a cramped aluminum camper hauled around by showman Paulie Rankin. When Paulie abandons Zachary in the small town of Antler, Texas, while he ventures off in search of other acts, Zachary attracts the attention of the locals. Toby Wilson, the main character (whose mother leaves his dad to pursue a singing career in Nashville) along with his buddy Cal (whose brother is killed in Vietnam), are at first horrified by the sight of Zachary and put off by his boorish behavior only to discover they have as many issues as he does.

As I read there wasn't a sound–no chair legs screeching, desktops slamming, water bottles crinkling, pencils snapping, etc. If I didn't glance up I'd swear I was alone in the room. The intensity of their listening gave rise to an eerie silence, a subtle force of intense absorption with every ear attuned to the sound of my voice. Now and then I had to peek up to make sure 6D hadn't vaporized into thin air while praying my fly was zipped. A tingle of stagefright shot through me until I reminded myself that what they wanted was the story and I was simply the conduit delivering it to them. Hitting my stride, I put everything I had into it, modulating my tone to match the tension of a scene, pausing to reflect for a second or two on what I'd just read, turning a page with a slow shake of my head as if I couldn't believe the power of the words in front of me, through it all feeling like some televangelist ministering to his spellbound flock. It was a potent stuff.

September 25

Last night was my last time greeting parents for our annual open house. They wandered into the classroom and glanced around before squeezing themselves into their kids' desks, sitting up as straight as they could manage while I stood before them to provide an overview of the sixth grade curriculum. These sort of speeches always made me nervous though I'd done them countless times. Summoning enthusiasm for the benchmarks of the Common Core while being regarded by rows of fatigued faces wasn't easy. All around the school teachers were giving similar talks after handing out district brochures summarizing what we were supposed to cover each month from September to June. But how did any of us know what exactly we would end up teaching and when? Was it even possible to predict the length of time required to get across one set of skills to twenty or so kids with a range of needs before charging on to the next set? Would anyone ask a surgeon the number of operations he anticipated performing over the next ten months, the complexity of each, how quickly the patient would recover, or demand of a lawyer how many parties he planned to sue, the duration of the court proceedings, the outcomes of those suits?

In any case, what these parents really wanted to hear was a few words about their kids. Theoretically, I wasn't supposed to tell them anything, this being strictly an open house where my job was to disseminate general information and elaborate on expectations for the class in general, but as a parent myself I liked hearing any anecdote about one of my own kids, how she stood out for one reason or another, maybe her brains or quirky personality, her flair for the dramatic or sensitivity toward her classmates, though at times—and here the teacher and I would share a laugh— it wasn't always easy dealing with her. So when approached, I did my best to accommodate them. Usually the parents reciprocated, going on about how the kid had come home with something I'd mentioned in class, or how he or she could finally go to the bathroom when he had to pee and eat when he was hungry. Perhaps it was my paranoia but over the last few years I'd heard fewer compliments about what I was doing. Part of this I attributed to the way teachers were portrayed by the media—our fat contracts and reluctance to work longer days (and school years) stifling student achievement, etc. It was hardly news our vocation no longer held the status it once did and that a sizeable lot of the public resented us. Then again, perhaps my style wasn't as seamless as I'd once thought, given the age difference between the kids and me.

You're older than my grandfather! Sierra informed me last week when I told her my age.

Grumpier too no doubt.

September 26

The purpose of our teachers' association's monthly executive board meetings was to discuss potential violations of the collective bargaining agreement which teachers had forwarded to their building representatives and then decide what to do about them. Each of us tended to be long-winded regarding topics which pertained to our particular buildings and colleagues, the injustices obvious to us though maybe not so to others in the room. Today the high school reps went on about certain dismal particulars while the rest of us listened, or pretended to. They questioned the efficacy of quarterlies and how there wasn't enough time to plan their content, in spite of the fact no one believed in using them. I wasn't sure what quarterlies were and didn't care enough to ask. Somewhere into the third hour it was brought to light that administrators had their own copy machines and even their own secretaries but high school (or were we talking about the middle school now?) teachers had to run down the hall to a copy center only to find the machines out of order, thereby requiring the teacher to waste her time procuring the services of someone to fix it, if she could even find someone, only to have it break down halfway through duplicating the packets she'd needed for an essential trigonometry lesson. We all agreed a complaint ought to be lodged with the principal who might or might not have a way to remedy the problem, or who might not even care. It was six o'clock by the time we'd finished debating this less-than-ideal situation and we still had a few items remaining on the agenda.

I'd taken the position of building representative four years ago, recruited by Fay, now retired, who had taught next door to me.

You'd be good at it, she said. *Plus we need a body.*

Carla was all for it.

It'll improve your listening skills, she said.

My father had been a union man. I pictured myself as SES's Lech Walesa, lifting the helpless proletariat (teachers) up

54

by the bootstraps while dodging the slings and arrows of the oppressive state (administration).

Just keep everyone happy, Fay told me when I asked about my responsibilities. *And don't piss anyone off.*

It hadn't been that easy. In fact, the opposite seemed to be happening. For starters, I was operating solo. Ideally there were supposed to be two of us per school but since Fay had departed in June, I'd failed to recruit a partner. Perhaps my colleagues sensed something I didn't, or else found settling kid disputes enough of a headache. As for grievances, there were plenty enough (for example, having to relinquish your planning period to attend an IEP meeting, or feeling you were entitled to more maternity leave). To prepare myself, I studied the contract. I intended to give both sides a fair shake as I abided by the letter of the law. I would be the insightful, disinterested judge whose concise and clever solutions surprised both parties. Except mediation wasn't what I'd expected. My jokes fell flat. Taking umbridge seemed to be the order of the day. I had all I could do to keep the conversation going while each side waited for the other to blink. It wasn't easy asking people to give up some of what they had in order to get some of what they wanted. I had empathy for car salesmen.

The final item on today's agenda had to do with, ironically, time, as in the keeping of it. Would we ever consent to the installation of a punch clock in the place of our present honor system, where we arrived sometime before our first class and departed at some point after the conclusion of our last? It was our bosses' opinion, we were certain, that we could never arrive early enough or stay late enough to please them. A punch clock would remedy that, along with getting those in line who came and went with the kids, making the rest of us look bad. But would our bosses use this device unfairly, standing next to it every morning, writing up Teacher X who questioned his policies and was two minutes late getting her own kids to school one day a week, and not Teacher Y, his golfing partner, who was ten minutes late every day? By the end, we agreed a punch clock was not a good idea. Better to keep it handy as a bargaining chip during negotiations when things got sticky.

September 27

The email Mr. B. sent me had a red ! beside the subject line and summoned me to his office. Because of my role as building representative, he felt compelled to update me on his step-by-step strategy when dealing with a teacher with whom he had a problem. For this latest infraction (a parent had called to complain about Marcia's frank manner during a phone conversation, during which she'd questioned her son's motivation), he would write a summary of the conversation and place a note in her file. His other option was to calm the parent down, speak to Marcia directly and be done with it. But for the last couple of years tension had been building between Mr. B. and Marica over her teaching style. While her customary refrain was that she'd acted in the interest of the kids, only to be informed later that she'd stepped over some arbitrary line, his response was that she ought to have known better.

Judging whether someone was fit to teach depended not only how the teacher conducted herself but also how her evaluator felt about her. Of course, there were obvious indicators that someone had to go (chronic absenteeism or neglect of duty, drug/alcohol use, behavior endangering staff or kids, etc.) but beyond that assessing a teacher's ability with the potential outcome of termination of employment was both complex and subjective. Needless to say, it paid to stay on your supervisor's good side, to be handy with a compliment or volunteer for administrative tasks which did not directly benefit you or your students. If you decided you had enough to do as it was, or believed sycophantic behavior was beneath you, your lack of diligence could come at a price.

Given any concern about a new hire's competence, however, a principal had plenty of opportunity to terminate her. For the first three years of employment in a Massachusetts public school, a teacher had provisional status with no due process rights and could be fired over any issue, no matter how trivial. But for whatever reason, some principals were reluctant to dump those whose style, skill set, or personality they found incompatible with the school's philosophy. On the first work day of her fourth year, a teacher was granted professional status and thus had some job protection. She could still be fired but the process entailed providing opportunities to correct whatever it was her evaluator found subpar. But by allowing such provisional teachers to hang around, principals often ended up facing problems of their own doing (or the doings of previous administrators) once that teacher was awarded professional status. Disinclined to blame themselves, they criticized the union for protecting its members.

Mr. B. had told Marcia about the complaint and now he was telling me. I indicated I understood. He nodded in return. There wasn't much more to say. Since taking the position of building representative, I left these encounters with a headache that lasted until the end of the day. Marcia had been at SES for more than a dozen years and no doubt in Mr. B.'s mind there'd be further issues to face throughout the ensuing months. Would those same transgressions committed by another teacher, say, for example, someone with a more accommodating personality or who shared Mr. B.'s love of Boston sports or had kids the same age as his, have resulted in memos deposited in her file? I couldn't say one way or another. I was just relieved I wouldn't be around by the time the decision came for Marcia to receive her pink slip.

September 30

During our after school data meeting we analyzed the GRADE reading scores, a task we'd already completed on our own. Instructed by Mr. B. to double check our work, we sat for seventy-five minutes in the library and did what we'd already done. Tired, bored and irritable, we lamented how we had better things to do, like come up with plan lessons, organize our classrooms and call those parents whose kids were driving us nuts. During his early years at SES Mr. B. didn't hold data meetings—or any staff meetings for that matter—thus making us the envy of the district. Instead he sent emails or called a teacher into his office whenever he had something to say to her. Lauded for his insight, he understood that after a long day of instructing, staff meetings were counterproductive, draining what little energy we had left and insuring none of us would do any school work once we got home. Agenda items tended to be redundant, or applied to a handful of people (I once sat through a twenty minute discussion on toilet training protocol for preschoolers, a topic relevant to a half a dozen of the sixty or so teachers present). Eventually, Mr. B. (pressured, went the rumor, by our new superintendent who demanded he get us in line) instituted this spirit-zapping exercise and compelled us all to attend, going so far as to have us sign an attendance sheet. So once a month we sat around after school and analyzed data.

But since I was retiring I skipped today's meeting and went home.

October 1

Janelle was a new teacher on our team who had taught in Ohio before moving here in August. Thirty, good-humored and creative, she gave off a steady enthusiasm about the kids and the profession I was always trying to match. Today after school she dropped into my classroom, wandering over to inspect a bulletin board of comic strips kids had done featuring characters in a story we'd read. Was it okay if she borrowed my idea? I responded with mild surprise at the prospect of a young teacher I admired interested in anything I was doing. But that was part of her appeal. She wasn't afraid to ask questions and gather ideas from colleagues. She would have succeeded in any line of work and I wondered, given her financial straits, why she'd chosen teaching.

Having only a BA and no money to pursue a master's degree, she was stuck on the low rung of the pay scale, her years of experience not translating salary-wise here because of a glitch in coursework she'd been unable to correct in time. Her husband worked from home and cared for their active fourteen month old, the three of them living in a small apartment as both incomes weren't sufficient for anything larger. After only a month she was anxious about covering the material she was expected to teach, overwhelmed by the demands of the curriculum maps and the needs of her students. She had her own ideas, lessons she'd successfully used in her previous school, and asked me whether it was wise to risk trying them at SES. As a new teacher with provisional status she could be terminated any time during her first three years, and so despite her background she was in no position to do anything other than what she was told to do. Whenever I passed by her door at the end of the day, no matter what time it was, she was busy pinning student work on bulletin boards or correcting stacks of quizzes and homework. Her classroom was a bright inviting place where kids collaborated at work stations, an arrangement I couldn't manage with 6D without a dissolution into chaos. But Janelle's influence came from not just from her affection for them but her knack for seeing the world through the eyes of a twelve year old. At recess one day she raced the fastest boy across the outfield and beat him (she'd been a sprinter in college). Astonished to see her take up the challenge and even more astonished to see her edge out ahead of him, I realized she was the type of teacher kids bragged about having. After the race, the girls surrounded her to offer high fives. She was certainly worth twice her salary and then some but her search for some creative leeway allowing her to teach the way she wanted was likely to turn out to be fruitless.

October 2

I took half a personal day to take my freshman daughter Apphia to an orthodontist appointment. When I arrived to school mid-morning, I couldn't hear a sound. Where was everyone? Had the building had been evacuated in my absence? Was Seabrook, the nuclear power plant just a ten minute ride north of us, melting down? Certainly I would have heard the 121 emergency sirens, capable of sending an alert as far as ten miles (as I did whenever the station dry-ran its emergency notification system). Anxiously I hurried from the parking lot over the crosswalk and along the sidewalk next to the preschool classrooms. Finally, to my relief, the murmur of young voices through window screens!

On this warm and breezy Indian summer day, puffy white clouds backlit by the sun eased across a pale dome of blue sky. Along the boundary fence, tips of maples flared red, yellow and orange. Designed for a calendar cover, this New England day was one of those gems that came along maybe a dozen times a year. Stepping indoors made you feel off-kilter, as if you were defying a law of nature and would pay for it (all that clean air and autumnal beauty proven stress reducers), yet not one of the five hundred and fifty kids was outside enjoying it. Confined to their desks, they toiled away, from time to time gazing dreamily out the window at those brilliant maples, stirred by a primal longing for fresh air, tall trees, green grass, and open sky, through no fault of their own contributing to the obesity epidemic widespread among children in the United States. Public schools could at least guarantee their method of instruction was boosting one score: the body mass index of every kid from ages 6-18.

October 3

Raelynn, a sweet, dark-eyed kid with straight shoulder length black hair streaked a cobalt blue, came into class this morning and informed me her mobile home had burned down, the dwelling a total loss.

Just like that, she told me, snapping her fingers. *We got out but our cat died. I rescued my ferret.*

I asked her whether they'd managed to save anything else.

These, she said, tugging at her clothes.

Did she want me to mention the fire to the class? She hesitated. She'd think about it and let me know. Off she went to her seat. She seemed fine, though after carrying on for a while, pretending to be just as normal as everybody else was pretending to be, she'd stopped coming to school, or would put her head on their desk and go to sleep, or turn surly, or request permission to visit the nurse six times a day, or disappear into the bathroom until I found a female staff person to haul her out. There was a time when I thought kids could put trauma behind them, wiggle out from under it or dig a hole big enough to bury it, that supported by the school routine they could click to autopilot while coming up with a coping strategy or two. But outside forces being what they were, it didn't happen. The notion we could fix kids was something I'd bought for a long time—all that talk about *advocating for yourself,* a line we threw around at meetings as to what troubled kids ought to do to improve their lot. I wasn't even sure what *advocating for yourself* meant. Of course it was impossible for an eleven or twelve year olds to rise above the shitstorm of their lives, whether advocating for themselves or not, and so we created terms like this to help ourselves feel better. For sanity's sake we told one another our intervention was their only chance.

For a while Raelynn went about her work with the usual grit. I shifted her desk next to mine, the proximity allaying my guilt and I hoped comforting her too. The slide had begun before the fire, her unsettled life leaving her wan and glassy-eyed. It was tough to watch a kid slip away without being able to do much to arrest the decline. I clung to the thinking that maybe she'd pull out of it this time, she being the exception, and our conversations, which got to the point of being forced in my effort to keep her talking, might be enough to achieve that end. If I kept her going on about nothing in particular and steered clear of the sensitive stuff (which she didn't want to go near and would instantly clam up) I might keep her distracted, which was better than nothing and maybe allow her to hold herself together a bit longer.

October 4

Though the MCAS scores from last spring had been out for a few weeks, I was afraid to look at them. Early last year I'd been part of a meeting with the parents of Leah who'd received a Warning on the fifth grade reading assessment (a polite way of saying she'd flunked). The couple was understandably furious and expected me as her new teacher to do something about it. Years of Title 1 services (which, for some reason, terminated in fifth grade) hadn't helped and I remember thinking *Oh shit, it's up to me now.* That afternoon I glanced around the conference table as the experts (Title 1 teacher, reading specialist, assistant superintendent of curriculum) promised the parents that Leah's deficiencies would indeed be addressed and remedied. Then they turned to me, her new teacher, whose job it was to do that addressing and remedying, all three promising a different outcome this year. On the spot, I nodded along, biting my tongue. How could I buttress that promise? I certainly knew less about the methodology of reading instruction than those present and didn't want to expose myself as an ignoramus by opening my mouth. Because I was friendly with the parents (Leah and Justina played on the same soccer team and I sat with them on the sidelines), if her score didn't improve I'd have to find a way to avoid them for the rest of my life.

Finally today I worked up the courage to look. Somehow she'd gone from Warning to Proficient with a Student Growth

Percentage of 99%. I was stunned. I hadn't done anything out of the ordinary other than provide extra help now and then but nothing I hadn't also given the other kids. I'd talked with her about the books she was reading, jotted comments on her written responses like I also did with everyone else, etc. So what accounted for the jump? All I could come up with was that I'd gotten to know her because of Justina. Whenever Leah came over to the house for a playdate– a frequent occurrence as she and Justina became best friends– we grew comfortable around one another. In this atmosphere free from the tension and spectacle of school we chatted and joked about nothing in particular and in the process built something deeper than the usual teacher/student relationship. My hunch was that this connection had carried over into the classroom, allowing her to relax enough to become a more competent reader, which had translated into a better test-taker.

Monday, October 7

At 10:20 I went down the hall to monitor the other two sixth grade classes during indoor recess while my colleague Adelle took care of hers and mine. Rain slammed against the window while I sat with a pile of quizzes I didn't feel like grading. The girls organized themselves into twos and fours for board games. The boys, unable to organize anything, swatted a beach ball around the classroom. One kid sat off by himself slamming his palms on a table top. He had no idea what he was doing, or else found it relaxing, this table pounding, as he took in the goings-on with the trancelike expression of a tribal drummer. *Boom, boom, boom.* No one cared about the noise except me and I felt obligated to do something about it. But what? Who was he bothering? But it wasn't okay to pound tables in a classroom and here he was putting everything he had into it. *Boom, boom, boom.* I waved him over and asked if he play percussion in the band.

What? What do you mean?

He came out of his spell long enough to remind me that his sister, now in the tenth grade, had been a student of mine. Did I remember her? He was skinny, medium height, a pasty redhead with a feral stare, knobby elbows and a mop of hair he couldn't get a comb through. I'd heard his name from various teachers since he'd entered school, a notorious wild man who, they claimed, was sorely in need of medication for his reputed ADHD. He seemed normal enough, though I didn't have any day-to-day dealings with him. Could he please go back to his drumming? He folded his spindly arms expectantly while I considered his request, then thought for a moment of all the times he'd spent in front of teachers like me, waiting it out while being addressed on one behavior or another.

You aren't supposed to do that sort of thing in school.

Why not? It's recess. We can do what we want.

Jump out a window?

I'm just drumming. It's recess. It's supposed to be our free time.

Here he was being reprimanded for a behavior he hadn't even realized he was engaged in, never mind that it might be against some purported rule or other, and now he wanted some explanation for *my* behavior.

What's wrong with it?

Unlike many kids he wasn't pushing me for the sake of a challenge. Maybe he'd been warned before and forgotten, or had scrutinized the student handbook for a bylaw forbidding table pounding and found none, or figured since it was his free time he could do whatever the hell he wanted. There was no rule, per se, but I as teacher could create and enforce one on the spot without having to provide a reason, if there even was a reason, given the noise level in the room.

Never mind, I said, too exhausted to continue. So off he went back to his seat to pick up where he'd left off.

Tuesday, October 8

Every day after lunch the kids sat with their books or Kindles, reading or not reading while in the outside world few if anybody read novels anymore, or much else for that matter. Given the option to read whatever they wanted, some kids elected to read nothing at all, and so I had to insist everyone read for pleasure, *demand it,* all the while preaching the merits of this worthy pastime, the joy and insight it would bring to their lives. During our thirty minute silent reading period (officially designated school-wide as *Sustained Silent Reading,* the *sustained* implying not so much a diversion as a chore, an application of physical effort, akin to the folding of laundry or the weeding of flower beds), whenever a kid looked away from page or screen, I would glare at him until he returned. Daily I struggled to foster a library-like quiet to encourage a relationship with the written word. On top of that, I had to scrounge up material to entice the lowest readers who wanted to draw instead, thereby putting me in the awkward position of having to ban art in favor of reading. Whatever books I found, either the content interested them but the text was too difficult, or the text they could manage but the content was babyish. And nearly all had ADHD and so couldn't sit still long enough to get anywhere unless I sat next to them. I'd hunt for a book I thought a kid might not only like but be able to read independently, get him started by listening to him grind through a paragraph, both of us agreeing this was the book he'd been waiting for his whole life (his concurrence because he wanted to make me happy). I'd send him off to his seat, only to see a minute later the book lying closed on his desk. My reglare would be answered with a nod as he found his place and pointed to the page to show me how much he was enjoying the book I demanded he read.

Since those of us who read for pleasure comprised a dwindling number of the population, I saw it as my duty to sit behind my desk during Sustained Silent Reading and model how to engage oneself, holding a hardcover in my hands, wetting my index finger before turning a page, nodding in satisfaction and smiling contentedly for them to witness as I engaged the text, all the while collecting a salary to do what I had little time to do outside of school. I sat, I read, I smiled and nodded some more, I turned a page, a physical display of delight as if I were an animated mannequin in a department store window. *This is what reading can do for you!* What would be the role of the teacher when students stopped reading altogether? My own three kids hardly read, preferring to stare catatonically at their cell phone screens, sliding from one image to the next, despite having two teachers as parents who fell asleep with open books atop their bed covers.

Wednesday, October 9

During read-aloud today my voice gave out, cracking and whistling, then seizing up before floundering into a hoarse whisper and stopping altogether. Clearing my throat, I managed to jump start it, a wheezy old motor sputtering and spitting along, out of rhythm and without power. I couldn't speak for more than a few minutes without pausing to sip water and apologize to the kids. Over the past few years this problem had been starting earlier and I could only guess what kind of damage I'd inflict on myself by the time June rolled around. As a young teacher I could yodel like Tarzan across the expanse of a ballfield or playground to summon the kids, never once considering this precious commodity needed protecting. In no profession did you rely on your voice as you did teaching elementary school. I'd known teachers who'd retired with their voices permanently impaired, reduced on physician's orders to whispering into a portable microphone over their last year or two. Whenever my own went, I drank from my water bottle and drew up saliva while the kids waited patiently as the one device I relied on more than any other flagged and faltered. It was frightening to stand before them exposed like that. Once I resumed reading, my battered vocal cords, pushed to their limit, fought on for a few more minutes. Another sip, more gullet clearing, more apologies. Clear, sip, apologize, restart. What power did a teacher have without his voice? And as my biggest strength was reading to them, an exercise I'd perfected by doing it twenty, thirty, forty minutes twice a day, year after year, to the point where they would sit and listen for as long as I elected to continue, I found the little power I did have–my ability to captivate them with words– deserting me. Desperate, I'd considered audiobooks–some colleagues suggested I switch as they had done before I injured myself too severely– but my voice even in its battered condition had more to offer, I felt, than a audiobook. Hopefully it could limp along in this condition until June when I could finally rest it.

Thursday, October 10

Gwen, a fourth grade teacher, confessed to struggling with the demands of The Initiative. Having kids take construct two column notes, hunt for the main idea (*Impossible to discern in nonfiction narratives!* she protested) and summarize paragraphs wasn't the only way to teach reading. Why couldn't she be trusted to instruct the way she'd always had, when she got kids excited about the subject rather than dread it? With over twenty years under her belt, she knew what she was doing, or thought she did until she was told she didn't, the reliable old way of doing things now replaced by this flashy new way. At this point in her career, she should have been used to this sort of upheaval. Had she herself become the problem? Would she ever be able to teach in the manner expected of her? I assured her she was a fine teacher, that others felt as she did, and maybe she'd find some consolation in that. Though resigned to the present state of affairs, she reminded me that like all initiatives, this one would run its course—the typical lifespan, we figured, was three, maybe four years. Until then she'd have to gut it out, though there was always a chance the next initiative that caught the fancy of our administrators would be more difficult to implement and less helpful remedying deficiencies than this one.

Friday, October 11

After reading to the class an adapted version of *The Tale of the Headless Horseman*, I defined *corporeal* versus *spirit*, holding up the book as an example.

This is real. Corpo-r-e-a-l.

I slapped the whiteboard behind me. *And this is real.*

From his seat Blaine pointed to his groin. *This is real.*

For his contribution to our discussion I threw him out of the room. In the hallway he made faces, prompting me to go out there to address the issue of his behavior only to have him refuse to apologize. Why should he if he was just pointing to his stomach?

You weren't pointing to your stomach, I said. *I saw it with my own two eyes.*

What did you see?

I saw you point to your crotch.

Why were you were looking at my crotch?

I was looking in that general direction.

It wasn't my crotch, it was my stomach.

Don't tell me it wasn't your crotch.

It wasn't my crotch.

From now on, do not point to yourself or any part of yourself for any reason whatsoever. Understood?

I raised my voice to emphasize my point about not pointing. Meanwhile, the rest of them were going crazy, craning their necks, leaning out of their seats, busting to see how Blaine would worm his way out of this one. In response to my request, he offered a blank stare, the same one I'd seen countless times over the years, and always with the same message: *Are you finished yet?* Our confrontation left me with a headache and the realization that Blaine would continue to point despite the promise I attempted to exact from him. He would continue to mouth off too. And I, after thirty-six plus years, would continue to allow myself to be drawn into exchanges like this which led nowhere, bending down so we were eye to unblinking eye, only to see that he'd set me up, while also discovering how powerless I was after all *his* years of experience with people like me. He paraded back into the classroom, his status a good notch higher, and I followed, mine a good notch lower, trying to remember what the hell I'd been doing before all this, trying to figure a way to get us back on track.

Monday, October 14

Today I started reading *Maroo of the Winter Caves*, a novel by Ann Turnbill about a girl and her family living in France near the end of the last Ice Age. Because the book was out of print I'd kept a class set patched together with clear packing tape, using the same set year after year and insisting the kids treat the book like the rare manuscript it was. Sometimes as I read aloud a book would deteriorate further, a page or a section slipping its binding, the kid quick to alert me to the problem and delicately reinserting it for mending later on, as our goal was to keep alive and healthy this novel we so dearly loved.

The theme–how a family led by matriarch Old Mother managed to endure because of the pluck and wits of her four-teen year old granddaughter Maroo – generated discussion of life 12,000 years ago. What was it like to live out of doors, to identify and gather edibles, to read the sky and track an animal, to trust your sense of direction, and have in your possession a repertoire of survival skills, to be in top notch physical condi-tion? The kids questioned their own lives and why they were forced to sit in a classroom all day and regard nature through panes of glass. They would all die, they assured me, had they found themselves lost in the woods during the cold–or not so cold–months in New England.

How come we don't learn the things Maroo learned how to do? asked Derrick, a lanky, poker-faced kid who rode snowmo-biles at his father's Maine camp on weekends and who'd once tried to explain to me without success the specifics of valve clearance. *Why don't we know anything about what's outdoors?*

I had no answer for that, not feeling like elaborating on why I was forced to teach x and not y, even if y was what they wanted to know about, and even if I agreed it was important for us to know about *y* too. Once winter arrived, I suggested, we could build a snow house, except I had no idea how to construct one myself, as I also possessed zero survival skills, having been educated in a similar fashion, and when the snow fell kids were instructed to stay away from it per school rules, to pretend it wasn't there, not pick it up or walk on it during recess as they'd been warned about its dangers and what could happen if they did, as if we residing in New England had no experience with such inclemency. Moreover, to build a snow house required permission from the office to venture out into that dangerous snow, first sending home permission slips explaining what we would be doing as well as detailing the potential hazards involved in erecting such a structure, along with the risk to students of being exposed to temperatures potentially below freezing, necessitating they dress in specific types and layers of clothing and also alerting parents to the risk inherent in utilizing tools required for the job (shovels). All of which made me not want to do what I'd promised and hoping when the time came no one would remember so I would not have to deny saying it.

Two years ago I did get Mr. B.'s permission to bury a time capsule. By the front door we excavated a hole with my post hole digger. All of 6D was mad for a turn, lining up for a chance to slam the curved steel jaws of the odd implement into the soft earth, to manipulate its long wooden handles, pulling them apart to extract a clump of clay the size of a softball. It was tough going but we were all eager and jabbed away until our palms blistered and arms throbbed. After twenty minutes of hard labor we stood proudly over a three foot deep hole. Standing in a circle we proclaimed some optimistic and solemn aspirations (*On this day, we, the class of 6D, do hereby wish the people of the future congratulations on finding this capsule. May they consider those persons long since dead who placed it here.*

Hopefully what's inside will tell them a thing or two about the lives of said persons who lived in the fair town of Salisbury in the year 2011.) Inside we'd stuffed notes we'd composed about our daily habits (*Somehow I'm always late even when I leave early!*) along with keepsakes we brought from home (e.g. *Hello Kitty* keychain). When the capsule was dug up a century from now would anyone be able to identify our mementos or possess the technology to decipher our handwriting? Would they think the crumbling foundation next to the hole had been that of a prison or would schools continue to be built the same way?

All of this made me wonder why I hadn't become an outdoor education teacher. Of course, the few jobs there were in the field paid next to nothing because those in charge of public schools in America saw outdoor education as a non-essential, as serving no real purpose in the lives of those they compelled to spend seven hours a day indoors. And besides, I wasn't sure I had the moxie to lead wilderness hikes and rappelling trips in the Adirondacks Mountains with amped-up adolescents, to forge white water rapids on the Penobscot with a raft load of paddle-wielding twelve years, or will myself to fall asleep on the floor of a forest clearing without obsessing about groups of kids having sex in their tents or fleeing into the woods to smoke dope and then have sex. Those were *real life* teaching skills which performed marginally could get someone injured or even killed. There was no faking your way through that kind of instruction.

Tuesday, October 15

Columbus Day—no school.
I became an educator by chance, taking a semester off from my sociology major in the spring of 1976. Brandeis University

offered K-8 certification in exchange for eight weeks of student teaching and the completion of a couple of education courses. Enticed by the prospect of a marketable skill along with my liberal arts degree, I soon found myself stuffed into a lime green AMC Rambler station wagon with a leaky exhaust along with five other trainees, all of us sleep-deprived from the racket in the dorms, travelling twenty minutes across town to the Cabot Elementary School in Newton. We carried in our briefcases a red ball point pen, a spiral notebook, folders of student work and a box lunch placed on our breakfast tray consisting of a roast beef sandwich on Wonder Bread, a package of vanilla Hostess cupcakes, a Red Delicious apple as hard as a marble, and a can of Coke wrapped in tinfoil.

For much of my time at the Cabot I stationed myself at a low table near the coat cubbies and observed Mrs. Hanson at work. A twenty-five year veteran, competent and in control, she seemed, once she'd introduced me, to forget I was there. As I awaited the chance to prove myself, I took in the proceedings and doodled in my notebook. From what I could tell, teaching sixth graders didn't look any more complicated than getting a dog to fetch or roll over. Besides, I was a twenty year old college junior who already knew a thing or two about what made kids tick, having a twelve year old brother and an eleven year old sister I bossed around and threatened with physical harm if they didn't do what I said. But when my turn came, the class ignored me, having had student teachers since first grade and knowing how to deal with them. When I tried to win them over by bribing them with fun activities like *Charades* and *Simon Says*, they rolled their eyes and ignored me, a harsher insult than if they'd threatened to leave the room. At least then I could have blocked the exit. Rather than listen to my instructions, they rummaged through their desks, combed their hair, needled one another and refused to look in my direction as I stood before them in cranberry polyester bell bottoms, a cream Banlon shirt, and a pair of crepe-soled loafers with block heels I'd purchased at Mal's for seven dollars. My armpits saturated, I desperately sought the right moment to jump in, to *take control*, having been told or deciding for myself that this was the one tactic at my disposal. Issue a command and demand compliance. Show them who was boss. If anyone refused, re-issue more forcefully before laying down a consequence. Isn't that how real teachers did it?

I ordered them to pay attention. That went nowhere. I raised my voice and raced through a description of my project idea of publishing an early American newspaper I called *Colonial Times*. Despite their indifference I pushed on, getting my words out by talking over them. If I was loud enough, I figured, they'd *have* to listen. Wasn't that how information got conveyed to crowds in train stations, ballparks and airports? But after just two minutes, I was stunned by how ineffective I was. How was it conceivable for an entire class to behave as one in their disregard of me, as if some autonomic response kicked in every time a student teacher opened his mouth? Flustered and terrified, I wanted nothing more than to go back to my dorm room, close the door and sleep for the rest of the day.

Just as I was attempting to assign the roles of editor and reporters, Mrs. Hanson, eavesdropping via the PA system, interrupted me. At first I had no idea where the voice was coming from and thought I'd lost my mind. The kids, apparently used to this sort of thing, turned to face the wooden speaker box above the clock. I did too, feeling not so much like a deranged man as an emasculated one. She went on to remind them that if I ever planned on becoming a teacher I needed their cooperation. As I was new at this, she added, I had no idea what I was doing. *And that means you, Randy.* There was a bit of static as she hung up the mouthpiece. Randy then proceeded to ask me in front of the class if I knew what an erection was, modelling one by slowly unfurling an index finger and arching it upward. In response, I demanded he put his arm away, whereby he lifted his desktop and shoved the limb inside, then asked me wasn't I relieved Mrs. Hanson had been tuning in, as who knew what kind of chaos would have ensued?

In the end I earned a grade of B for those eight weeks, while my fellow Rambler passengers received A's, the deduction a result of my calling Randy a rotten little bastard after he told me on my last day that I was the worst student teacher in the history of the school.

And that's saying something, he added. *The worst, bar none.*

He'd squealed to his parents and Mrs. Hanson, to whom I denied saying any such thing when she called my dorm that night. Unconvinced, she relayed the insult to Professor Munson, the head of the education program whose windowless office reeking of cigarette smoke occupied a corner on the bottom floor of the social sciences building.

There's nothing to tell, I said when he asked me to describe what happened. *He claims I called him a rotten little bastard.*

Did you?

No.

Professor Munson broke the ash of his Pall Mall into a paper coffee cup and cleared his throat.

Teaching elementary school isn't for everyone. Kids can be merciless. They have a knack for hitting your sore spot and can make you say things you'd never say to anyone— a colleague, a roommate, even a spouse for that matter.

He's lying, I repeated. *He made the whole thing up.*

Be that as it may. Just remember that whatever comes out of your mouth you're responsible for. You're also responsible for whatever kids think you said, even if you didn't in fact say it.

A few minutes later he saw me to the door.

Consider this a lesson. One that's not in the textbook.

Over the summer, my Massachusetts K-8 grade teaching certification printed on an IBM card arrived in the mail. I placed the card in a cedar cigar box on top of my dresser along with my passport, a few silver dollars, a tie clasp my brother had given me for being best man at his wedding, and a roach clip with faux eagle feathers I'd purchased at an Indian reservation. Still shaken by my lack of self control, I concluded teaching was the one profession I was completely unsuited for. But in September, with no better prospects, I found a job as a classroom aide and enrolled in graduate school, earning a degree in special education because that was where the jobs were.

For eighteen years I worked in the field before taking a fourth grade classroom position, all along never quite sure what I was supposed to be doing. No sooner had I gotten the hang of one method of instruction when another came along to take its place. Binders detailing teaching strategies collected on my classroom shelves, each in its turn having been anointed as the master plan to remedy any and all assortment of student deficiencies. Keeping pace with educational trends left little time for what really mattered–to get anywhere you first had to make a connection with a kid. Simple enough, but given what I'd said to Randy, was I even capable of that? And what teacher had time for *connecting* when there was so much *stuff* to get through? What kind of teacher just sat around getting to know his students?

Wednesday, October 16

Some years ago I volunteered to be on a textbook committee. Our curriculum superintendent decided we teachers ought to chose the sixth grade geography text since we would be the ones using it. In Central Office we gathered in a walnut panelled conference room around a large oval table, ensconced in thick armchairs that swivelled and rolled over the plush carpet, wondering why we had no such seating behind our own desks. In these surroundings we listened as she explained how she'd expedited the process by culling the lot to half a dozen selections.

Oh, we thought, *then what are we doing here?*

We examined each one, thumbing through the textbook and checking out accompanying workbooks, chapter tests, auditory tapes, videos, teacher guides. Her single requirement was that the texts be challenging. We nodded that we understood, happy to be away from the kids to enjoy some peace and quiet for a couple of hours. Left to decide among ourselves we reached the same unspoken conclusion: our kids would struggle to read any of her choices. Who among us dared to admit it was *our* particular class who couldn't read the texts and offend our boss after the hard work she'd done? Rather than risk embarrassment, we kept our opinions to ourselves. In the end, we picked the one with the brightest graphics and most interesting photographs, figuring every kid regardless of his reading ability could at least get something from the visuals.

Over time we worked up the courage to reveal the truth to one another. We hated the text. The print was small, the chapters long, the subject matter–geography, economics, government, social issues–compressed into dense paragraphs. The kids despised it immediately, flipping cover to cover, fanning the pages, stunned at their number, astounded at the length of those words they were expected to pronounce. The fact that the entire geography of the earth and the ethnicities of its inhabitants, present and past, along with chronicles of their exploits, were contained in this single volume, well that was just too much for them. *Are we supposed to read this whole thing! This book belongs in a college!* Harnessing their attention for more than a few paragraphs exhausted me. After a year I gave up, electing to rummage around for more accessible substitutes (atlases, magazines, easy-to-read booklets on continents). Now the ponderous volumes taxed a couple of shelves over the coat cubbies. Last year the lower shelf collapsed and narrowly missed burying a kid who'd gone to get a snack out of her backpack. Since the materials cost the district a bundle, to alleviate some of my guilt as a taxpayer I had the kids take them down from time to time to examine a map or read one of the few folktales or check out a photograph (they loved the one of the guy in sunglasses and red bathing suit floating on his back while reading a book in the Dead Sea). The heft of the textbooks made them ideal for slamming on desktops, triggering a sound like the report of a cannon and scaring the hell out of me every time.

Thursday, October 17, 2103

I ran into Aileen, a third grade teacher, downstairs where I'd gone to use the photocopy machine (the one on the second floor was either being used or was out of order). Sweet and soft-spoken, she was one of those people who laughed at everything I said, her good nature such that I always enjoyed her company. Today, though, she wasn't laughing. A week ago she'd been evaluated and it hadn't gone well. Rather than teach with the ease and experience of a seasoned veteran, she found herself stumbling over The Initiative's sequencing and terms, confusing both herself and the kids. As her building representative, my role was to offer guidance and reassurance but I wasn't sure what to say, given my own less-than-stellar performance with it. Throughout my career, I'd found initiatives an inconvenience at best (*A pestilence visited upon us at regular intervals*, as a veteran teacher had once described them to me), the implication being that we weren't doing our job, or doing it well enough. Since we weren't measuring up, a new approach was called for, one costing a lot of money and requiring hours of training to fix whatever our administrators considered broken. Though I had nothing against initiatives per se, the lack of choice irritated me. I couldn't, for example, opt out by citing evidence of student progress or by poking holes in the initiative's rationale. Neither was I allowed to extract what I found useful and discard the rest. To make matters worse, I was subsequently evaluated on how well I executed a program I didn't believe in or had little use for. My assessment would then be compared with my colleagues', all of us competing for that *proficient* or *exemplary* rating, all of us sucking up and stressed out, wanting to get it right, to execute the details precisely the way we'd been shown during our professional development sessions, feeling like children ourselves, forced to do what we were told to do and facing a consequence for not doing it, or not doing it the way we were supposed to do it, rather than professionals with minds of our own, which was hardly a recipe for creative and relaxed instruction.

Friday, October 18

As I called out their times at the finish line, panting milers sprawled on the cement apron in front of the main entrance as parents hauling their kids into the preschool stepped around the writhing bodies, wishing they could have done this sort of thing in their day. Wasn't it fabulous kids had the chance to race around the school until they collapsed whimpering in pain and struggling to breathe, chests heaving and legs cramping, as they burned off all that energy that only got them into trouble later in the day?

Mr. D! gasped Corbin. *I think I'm going to be sick!*

Isn't that the greatest feeling in the world? I asked.

I guess so.

You're fine. Congrats on your time.

Why, these parents asked me, wasn't every teacher outside pushing her students to the limit until they thought they would die?

Restricted since the videotape incident to a ten minute allotment before the start of the school day, I tried to squeeze in as much physical exertion as possible. On Friday mornings we ran a timed mile— fifth and sixth graders lining up three deep and charging three and a half laps around the building. Initially they'd been terrified by this unimaginable challenge on par with the rigors of scaling Everest or trekking across the Sahara. But every week the distance grew more manageable and to some even too short.

What about we run two miles next week? asked Leo.

I told him it was a fabulous idea so long as we could do it under ten minutes and be standing at our desks in time for the Pledge of Allegiance.

Now those milers, radiating accomplishment that came from dashing this formally formidable distance as quick as they could, exclaimed how they'd improved their times from a week ago but planned on going even faster next week.

What's the world record in the mile for twelve year olds? Sierra asked me.

No one wanted to go back inside but the coveted Dum Dums pops earned as a reward awaited in a Tupperware bowl in the bottom drawer of my desk. Once everyone recovered, the pack, now fully recharged, stormed through the lobby and up the stairs, taking two at a time, hooting and stomping, under the influence of fresh air and secreted endorphins, mad for those pops and mad to tell all who cared to listen how they'd improved their times from last week. Teachers in doorways frowned and shushed them, shaking their heads at me as if I was one of the kids. School had just officially begun though all anyone was doing was wondering where the racket was coming from. There was jubilation in the hallways and something had to be done about it. Requests for silence were unheeded by me also as I'd taken the troublemakers out of their classes (all troublemakers loved to run) and felt those teachers owed me a favor and ought to shut up themselves. After the kids crowded around my desk and received their Dum Dums they raced off to their classrooms while I tucked my stopwatch into my top drawer where I would always know where to find it.

Monday, October 21

During our weekly team planning time Martha, our school's reading/writing/data specialist, informed us we were to administer a district-wide writing assessment this week. *What? When?* We freaked out. There was too much to do as it was. The prompt told kids to read two short stories by Cynthia Rylant and *based on your knowledge of character, plot, and setting, write a letter to your teacher explaining which story you would recommend and why, utilizing evidence from the two stories to support your answers.*

Could we read each story to the kids, so poor readers would have some idea what to write? Was it even possible that one kid, never mind four classes worth, could summon a degree of competency close to addressing the prompt? Who came up with it anyway? And who was going to read and assess all of it? Not us! But we would, of course, because we'd been ordered to even if none of us (teachers, kids) understood what we were supposed to do. What mattered above all was that we amass a pile of material from which to gather data. And from experience we understood that once amassed, this data would be analyzed and argued about, and out of that debate proposals would ensue about what to do with it all. In the end (if there ever was an end) we would struggle to arrive at a consensus on which tool to employ to remedy the deficiencies exposed by our analysis. But by that time we would have moved on to other assessments which would furnish us with additional data. Substitutes would be brought in so we could convene during the school day to review pages of statistics, hoping our intervention might change those statistics in future assessments. Those dreadful meetings stoked my desire like nothing else to be back in the classroom and I would return grateful to see the kids and to be able to teach again.

Tuesday, October 22

A sign up sheet was posted on the door of the unoccupied classroom next to 6D, with its dozen computers and Smartboard, to allow us to reserve slots to show videos or give the kids computer time or use that Smartboard, except when district administrators show up and commandeered the room. Today three people from Central Office sat in a tight circle in the middle, plucking away at laptops they'd positioned, of all places, on their laps, and not even bothering with those computers or that Smartboard at all! What was up with that? Could they just go somewhere else and give us the damn room chock full of technological equipment we were so desperate to use, brazenly ignoring a colleague's name scrawled half-legibly by a kid instructed to do, and not one of us feeling the slightest bit guilty about doing it? The sign-up sheet regularly disappeared too, stuck as it was to the glass by a single piece of cellophane tape, falling off and drifting away or else being torn off and crumbled up. Without it, use of the room became a free-for-all, first come first served, one class overstaying its thirty minute allotment while a second waited at the door. No teacher wanted to share, her own needs more pressing than those of her colleagues, and so would ignore that crowd milling outside or else come out to plead for more time.

Please, I know my turn is up but I'm at a critical point in my lesson on metacognition. Could you all just come back later, say in ten minutes or so?

Now, a few of us, thoroughly frosted, collected in the hallway, rolling our eyes and mumbling less-than-respectful comments at those administrators, ducking out of sight whenever one glanced our way, the pecking order in public schools as clearly delineated as that of any military organization. We knew our place and had one of us had dared suggest asking them to relocate she would have been hauled away by her colleagues for her own well being.

Wednesday, October 23

Yesterday Colleen Ritzer, a twenty-four year old Danvers High School math teacher, was found murdered in the woods behind the building. The suspect, a fourteen year old who'd come for extra help at the end of the day, followed her into the bathroom where he stabbed and sexually assaulted her. The news numbed us as we spoke in the hallways, not believing our ears, wanting to know how to address the issue with the kids who would surely bring it up. What were we supposed to say? How to even begin? Our job was to make them feel safe and now we felt powerless, overwhelmed, frightened, and incapable of ensuring anyone's safety, including our own. Danvers was a thirty minute drive south of SES and though the proximity didn't matter since violence against teachers was rising nationally (a forty-six year old high school teacher in Sparks, Nevada, had also been killed by one of his students just a few days ago), the short distance made the threat seem closer and more real. All of us had stories of kids pushing limits, the unanticipated desk-flipping or throwing of whatever happened to be within arm's reach, the physical contact which left us shaken and bruised, questioning why we did this line of work, or worse, blaming ourselves for setting the kid off, as if we could have prevented the outburst with a different look or rephrased word. What was wrong with us, we wondered, that we hadn't been able to read a kid's intention before he acted? But this case was obviously something far different.

Ritzer's photograph showed a smiling, beautiful young woman who loved her work and hoped to make a difference. Teaching was her dream job, all she'd ever wanted to do since she was a little girl.

It's not just strangers wandering into the school we have to worry about, said Sam, our technology teacher, as he and I supervised the lobby during dismissal. *It's the kid sitting right in front of us.*

Thursday, October 24

I woke up at 3:07 thinking about Colleen Ritzer, the Danvers High teacher stabbed to death by one of her students who was later identified on videotape wheeling a recycling bin containing her body through a hallway. Over the summer the alleged assailant had moved from Tennessee. The media reported he was upset about having to relocate to Massachusetts. Was anyone there aware of his fragile state of mind? What about the paper trail? Why was he alone with her in her classroom after school? How many other kids with severe mental health problems beyond the skill set of a teacher were sitting in classrooms across America?

Kids regularly showed up from another town or state ahead of their paperwork, the sluggish pace of bureaucracy weeks or even months behind the moving van, the teacher maybe getting a sense about her new arrival, maybe not, having only her intuition to guide her. Would she act on that intuition when he turned peculiar or belligerent and subsequently request help, or would she second guess herself, provide the benefit of the doubt, understanding that her role was to deal with every student regardless of privation, to do whatever it took to accommodate his needs, even if she had to compromise her own well-being to do it?

One time a student with an IEP mandating two hours a day of individual counseling was placed in my classroom. He'd just arrived in town and despite diagnoses of PTSD, bipolar disorder, and ADHD, he wasn't on any medication. After the IEP was rewritten and adjusted to fit our manpower specifics (a common practice in schools whenever a new kid showed up), he received no services other than a behavioral checklist designed by his SPED teacher with a reward of five minutes of free time at the end of the day. I was assured he wasn't the same kid he'd been in his previous school and that I shouldn't worry. He was older now, calmer, more mature. As I was told not to worry, I didn't. Or tried not to. He turned out to be likeable enough, charming and eager to please, and after a while I couldn't imagine him doing anything diabolical, as familiarity made it easy to dismiss those diagnoses. He was an averaged-sized twelve year old, impulsive and less than intimidating. And maybe that was the problem – after a while you were lulled into thinking you'd figured kids like him out, that you'd uncovered tricks other teachers had missed. You banked on the assumption you'd found a connection everyone else had overlooked. But how could you gauge headway if the kid was conning you, if you didn't know any better, which made you believe he was someone other that who he was? This false sense of confidence might well lead you to let your guard down. Carla had her own stories, how she'd gotten to trust a kid when a simple request sent a desk over or a book flying across the classroom. Perhaps years of experience might tip you off to a subtle rising tension putting you on edge and intuiting you to act for your own well-being. Unfortunately, Ritzer hadn't had the benefit of that.

Friday, October 25

During a writing exercise, Tanner glanced up from his work.
Mr. D., do owls have two legs or four?
Two.
He nodded, confirming his hunch, and returned to his story.

Monday, October 28

Every autumn we travelled to Sargent Center in Hancock, New Hampshire, to spend the school week at a residential outdoor education program run by a guy named Larry, a stocky story-telling harmonica-playing native Texan with an impish grin and plain-spoken demeanor who not only grabbed the kids' attention but kept them spellbound. This morning, not long after we'd exited the coach buses and deposited our electronics into a recycle bin for safekeeping for the week, we gathered in the community room, kids on the floor, teachers and counselors on folding chairs behind them. Before he addressed his audience, Larry blew a few riffs on his harmonica and waited for everyone to shut up. He confessed he hadn't gotten much sleep, such was his anticipation over our arrival. Leaning forward, he swept his gaze from one side of the room to the other. Returning his stare were sixty-five gung-ho twelve year olds (fifteen kids had elected to stay back at SES) awaiting their marching orders. Judging by the grin on his face, their readiness for what lay ahead suffused him with delight. First he touched on the can't-miss events in store for them. Then he promised this would be the best week of their lives. In fact, he guaranteed it. With bottomless patience, he proceeded to answer every question as if he couldn't wait to hear what the kids had to say. His passion for outdoor education wasn't hindered in the least by the fact that the program was threatened annually from lack of funding. I'd been here a dozen times and watched kids roam the seven hundred wooded acres in all types of weather, led by their alt post-collegiate hippy instructors who lived in weatherbeaten dwellings on-site for paltry wages and who after every meal donned outlandish homemade costumes to perform skits, dressing up kid volunteers to join in their pantomime, everyone singing corny pun-laced songs geared to educate about the environment.

The camp curriculum was built around developing team exercises, conducting scientific observations, learning survival skills, negotiating a ropes course and scaling a climbing wall. Kids slept in squeaky bunks on thin mattresses and ate family style, ten to a table, passing around platters of link sausages and buttermilk pancakes, bowls of green beans and plates of fried chicken, trays of spaghetti and meatballs. Out of plastic pitchers they poured either milk or water. A single glass of grape juice was allowed at breakfast. Food waste, called *ort*, got collected and weighed in a white five gallon bucket after each meal. By the end of our stay, if we ate everything on our plates, that bucket would be empty. After meals kids did chores and travelled in a two-person buddy-system so no one got lost in the woods, all the while reciting the program's theme, the Four C's–caring, cooperation, communication, commitment– drilled into them by Larry and their instructors.

As for my colleagues and I, we were the most blessed of creatures, teachers without classrooms, free to wander woodland and meadow, to nap after lunch, to tag along with a group of kids and their instructor when we felt like it or not at all. We put the kids to bed at night and got them up in the morning, believing them when they told us they'd brushed their teeth, saw them again at mealtimes and during Wednesday movie night (*Honey I Shrunk the Kids*) when we passed out popcorn (their instructors, having the night off, dashed off to the nearest pub).

In a wilderness classroom there was plenty of room for everyone to move around. Noise and weather were not an issue. If you wanted to howl at the moon or dance in the rain, you got only encouragement.

Whatever makes you happy, pointed out instructor Simone, who preferred to be called Running Deer.

Tuesday, October 29

Blaine was a problem. He planned to roast acorns over an open fire he'd started with his Bic lighter. While on a day hike somewhere north of camp, he'd alerted his group to the fact that Wayne, their instructor, did not have their best interests in mind, then took it upon himself to recruit volunteers to hightail it into the forest to fend for themselves. Wayne, at the end of his rope, radioed for help. With no time to spare, I raced out of the lodge, down a trail, over a hill, and located the beleaguered party in a clearing on the other side of a swamp. I confiscated the lighter and hauled Blaine back to the lodge. There I scolded him and coerced promises I knew he couldn't keep. He, of course, had no idea why I'd taken him away from the rest of the group.

 —You had a Bic lighter, I began. *You lit a fire!*

 —That's what it's for. I always carry one.

 —You can't have it.

 —Who said?

 —Me.

 —You told us yourself a lighter is the most important survival tool to have in the woods. Remember saying that?

 I nodded before changing the topic.

 —Why were you leading your group into the woods?

 —I invited Wayne but for whatever reason he wouldn't agree to come.

 —You have to stay with your group at all times. Period.

 —I did. Wayne didn't. We were going off together then he got mad and called you. That's why I don't understand why I'm in trouble.

 At that point I gave up, or at least stopped talking. Later I called his father to let him know what was going on, ending our conversation by saying he might have to drive up to Hancock and take his son home if he didn't behave.

I've got cancer! he exploded. *I don't have a car! I got no warning about any of this!*

I reassured him that Blaine could just as likely make it through the week if he shaped up. But he was, I reminded him, exhausting all of us. His father understood, then lowered his voice and suggested I pass on some advice.

Tell him 'Be a man'.

I liked that. It was lame and straight out of the fifties and of no help whatsoever but I found it endearing, a heartfelt expression from a contentious father to his desperate-for-attention son.

My role here at camp was to supervise the kids whenever they weren't with their instructors, which, Blaine aside, was easy and gave me time to think. Outdoor education played almost no role in public education in America, and certainly none at SES, despite its significance in the lives of anyone who ventured out of the house for any length of time. But since no one was going outside anymore, preferring instead to inhabit the dark confines required to stare at a video screen, outdoor education could be brushed aside even more easily as having no purpose in the lives of young people. In that respect, it was similar to physical education. Just as more than a few teachers and administrators were intimidated by exercise and had no desire for it to play a role in schools, many were also afraid to venture beyond the borders of a town park. Twelve year olds, on the other hand, had no issues with hylophobia. They longed for the wilderness, the wilder the better, desperate to satisfy a primal urge for running, climbing and hiking, for screaming, howling and singing at the top of their lungs, for constructing survival structures, foraging for edibles and fording gushing streams, for coating themselves with cold mud and silken ash, leaping over roaring campfires and sleeping under a broad sweep of stars. At their age this longing hadn't yet been civilized out of them, though public schools were doing their best to keep them away from nature and by doing so creating an anxiety and fear born of ignorance.

Wednesday, October 30

I spent five hours at Monadnock Community Hospital with Cory who sliced his leg open sprinting down a narrow rocky trail. The skin over his knee cap snapped back like a window shade, exposing a pinkish-white inch wide gap requiring twenty stitches to close. The physician, a guy my age, had spent his career working the nightshift in small hospitals. Easy to talk to, humble and gentle, with a wry sense of humor which put Cory at ease, he was skilled at what he did, distracting him throughout the procedure by talking about sports and video games. He told me he'd always liked community hospitals where he got know his patients and their families. To him that was the best part of the job. Now, in this age of specialization, he lamented how young doctors opted for prestigious and lucrative positions. Patients were strangers, people met once or twice for fifteen minutes and never seen again. He, on the other, was recognized by everyone in town. His opinion made me feel good about having spent the past fourteen years in an elementary classroom in a struggling town, getting to know the community. Cory studied our faces, forgetting about his knee, and I wondered what he thought of our conversation, two old guys reminiscing about how we'd spent our working lives.

A few hours later his father arrived at camp to take him home in a twelve year old Buick with mismatched fenders. They lived together, the two of them and another brother, the mother God knows where. Cory was respectful and sweet, a bright student and a good athlete. Though he loved his father, there was a sadness about him, evident in his eyes, as there was in kids separated from their mothers. His father took up the slack as best he could, loved his kids, volunteered by making signs for the school whenever we had a fundraiser (he was a sign maker by trade) and was grateful for the attention and care we'd provided his son. Later that night they headed home, a bed with a pillow and sleeping bag arranged by reclining the front seat, the Buick banging its way out of the dirt parking lot, its suspension rattling over potholes before it turned right onto the paved road which led to Peterborough and Route 101 and back to Salisbury.

Thursday, October 31

For our last night each group of campers performed a skit as part of the talent show. The participants, simultaneously exhausted and amped up, sat cross-legged on the floor of the dining lodge before a fieldstone hearth framing a roaring pellet stove. Their performances reflected both lack of effort and rehearsal time, with most of the dialogue incoherent, lines either screamed or mumbled. Many kids forgot what they were supposed to say or do but we all clapped and cheered anyway. While one clutch of performers bowed and raced off the makeshift stage, the next sprang up to take its place. In this out-of-control but allowable-under-the-circumstances atmosphere the kids' joy was offset by the headaches of the adults who had to sit through the acts. Exhausted ourselves, having stayed up late and gotten up early for the last four days, we were numb to the delirium and just wanted to go home. At nine o'clock, after the grand finale (a counsellors' skit involving the confusion of the words *banana* and *bandanna*, whereby one unfortunate actor ended up with an overripe banana smeared on his face rather than the bandanna he'd requested, eliciting howls of laughter), we escorted the performers back to their dorms. Along the way we teachers exclaimed how we were unaware of the theatrical acumen of our students, at least the part involving an actual stage, and that Hollywood should be given fair warning. They shrugged. It was nothing. Who couldn't do what they'd done? What was the big deal with acting anyway?

As it goes with these overnight adventures, we were as excited to depart in the morning as we had been to arrive, anxious for a decent night's sleep in our own beds and something to eat other than camp food which elevated our intestinal psi to painful levels. I missed Carla and the kids and having me away meant extra work for her. Next year, of course, I'd be home, though my colleague and friend Fay who'd retired two years ago returned to camp last year as a volunteer, such was her desire to see kids savor the outdoors. I couldn't see myself doing such a thing, for as much as I loved coming here, it took me a week to recover.

Friday, November 1

After lunch we met as a group for the final time before boarding our buses for the trip back to Salisbury. When Larry asked the kids for feedback on their last five days, Rickie raised his hand and told us, *I learned that when you fail at something you regret it for the rest of your life.*

Yesterday poor Rickie been unable to complete the ropes course, jerking to a stop midway, twenty feet above the ground, stranded on a single line strung between two trees while grasping another line above his head, wobbling wildly, searching in vain for equilibrium which would allow him to inch himself forward to the safety of the platform. He shook, he cried, he teetered and tottered, lurched and trembled, moving a baby step and jerked some more before screaming for help without seeming to hear any of us down below chanting his name and cheering madly, imploring him over and over to believe in himself and not give up.

You're doing great! Just edge another tiny step forward! You can do this! We love you!

Except he couldn't and with the cooling afternoon temperatures, fading sunlight and queue of climbers growing behind him, he was lowered to the ground by a couple of capable and endlessly patient instructors. Back on earth his color returned and his breathing eased. We tried to console him but there wasn't much to say. And if I knew Rickie like I thought I did (although he wasn't in my class, we'd had numerous run-ins in the hallways) I worried he might eventually consider illicit drugs as a way to keep his subpar effort from haunting his dreams.

A few other kids who also hadn't completed the ropes course empathized with him, while others recalled how they'd been bailed out by remembering the Four C's and were determined to carry what they'd learned back into their other lives, the ones many of them were trying to forget and would soon be thrown back into. Blaine, to my surprise, rallied after the incident in the woods (likely constrained by my threat to send him home) and appeared, by the end, to have gotten as much out of his time here as any of the kids. He didn't want to leave and to make the transition easier found a brochure listing summer camp offerings like wilderness trekking and rock climbing he was sure his dad would go for.

Dudley Sargent, a pioneer in physical education at Harvard, founded this secluded forest camp a century ago with the motto *Where the weak come to get strong and the strong stronger* (apparently he hadn't considered that if both goals were met the strong would still end up dominating the weak). After five days of observing kids engaged in outdoor learning with an enthusiasm I rarely saw in the classroom, I wondered why we didn't do more of this– ship kids into the woods for a month or two to learn how to orient themselves among the pines, oaks and maples, start a fire with flint and steel, forage for tubers and berries, construct survival structures, make observations and draw conclusions. On Monday I would struggle to gain their attention as they watched the last of leaves floating onto the baseball field. I'd listen to them reminisce about the rustic beauty of environmental camp, the sense of belonging and shared responsibility instilled in them by their counselors, how they'd discovered a part of themselves they hadn't known existed. I'd hear them perseverate on the adventures and interactions which had changed them forever brought about by their time in the woods. Some day, they all vowed, they would return to this Eden. They would bide their time. They'd find the money and hitchhike there if they had to. Until then the dream of returning would live in their hearts. Finally I'd have to tell them enough was enough–we had a curriculum to get through.

Monday, November 4

I plugged in my portable ceramic heater and set it beside my desk. The kids called the heater, always set to its highest setting, *our wood stove* and warmed their palms over it as if we were stranded in a cabin in the White Mountains. The draft from the windows found its way into my bones no matter how many layers I wore. According to fire department regulations, I wasn't supposed to have a portable heater but I couldn't teach without it. Why was there no heat? The construction of SES, a school just fourteen years old, had been awarded to a bidder who'd installed a furnace lacking sufficient thrust to push warm air all the way up to 6D, as we occupied a second floor corner room which snagged northeast winds, the frames of our large windows no match for the nippy current finding its way into the room. Rays of early sunlight hopscotched over desktops before departing to the other side of the building.

The chill was a problem but so too was the wearing of jackets to ward off that chill. Kids pulled them over their heads, hid cell phones in the pockets, played with the zippers, etc. School policy forbade coats in class, along with accessories like hats, gloves, scarves, the reasoning being that such apparel would soon or later be used as a toy, weapon or place to hide from the demands of academics. Oddly, once winter arrived, lots of kids continued to wear tee shirts. Always too large, they doubled as pup tents, allowing arms to be retracted while the wearer sat and shivered and regarded me with loathing whenever I presented a task requiring the use of hands. Other tee shirt fashionistas, seemingly immune to the frosty flow, went about their business as if it were a summer day. This choice of fashion puzzled me. Why not sport a flannel shirt, sweater or sweatshirt? The only conclusion I could draw was that tee shirts were cheap to purchase and perennially in vogue (though any proclaiming the merits of booze, drugs, weapons, or profanity were prohibited, the owner ordered to visit the nurse's closet for a change of attire) and thus many wearers were willing to suffer through the discomfort for the sake of trendiness and economy.

Tuesday, November 5

I'd accumulated over a dozen pair of large scissors over the years, formidable in size, sharp as steak knives, forged from stainless steel and stored in a box in my desk for safekeeping. Excited to prove they could handle *teacher scissors* and promising they'd be careful, the kids pleaded to use them in place of the smaller blunt-nosed *baby scissors* to cut copy paper into flashcards for vocabulary words. With great concentration, they followed the pencil lines they'd drawn, demonstrating they could manipulate this tool without spilling blood or wounding a classmate. In SES an instrument as insignificant as a pair of scissors shared the same status as a chainsaw in the outside world. Kids were prohibited from engaging in any activity offering the slightest risk, even under supervision. We had no shop class and teachers hovered over kids so they wouldn't hurt themselves performing simple tasks. The paper cutting board in each classroom, for example, was off limits. Whenever I mentioned the need for one a kid would bolt over to the shelf to get it, balancing it over his head and setting it down with a clap on the kidney table before volunteering to shred every piece of paper in the classroom. As I was always pressed for time I was grateful for help—*please make sure you have all ten fingers when you finish*—whenever I had to prep for an art project or other activity required various sizes of paper.

It was ironic we provided kids so little chance to prove themselves when outside of school they engaged in risky behavior on what seemed a daily basis—staying out late into the night, climbing fences to trespass on private property, riding bikes down the centerline of Route 1, jumping off buildings, bridges, etc. One year a fourth grader climbed a tree and got stuck at a height beyond the range of the Salisbury

Fire Department's ladder truck. Assistance was required from Newburyport whose fire department had an extension ladder tall enough to rescue him. A sneaker stayed wedged between trunk and limb as a reminder of his perilous stunt. While I'm not suggesting kids ought to do this sort of thing during recess, preventing them from moving from one part of the building to another without an adult escort, from carrying out simple tasks with any degree of independence, keeping them so *contained and monitored*, only contributed to that pent-up energy which drove their perilous after school adventures.

Whenever bestowing the privilege of using a pair of those *teacher scissors*, I would first lecture about safety and responsibility, even while knowing the kid drove a Bobcat around his grandfather's gravel pit or that she'd minded her baby sister while her parents went away for the weekend. The kid, in turn, understanding how school worked (it having no connection to the real world) would nod and play along. Opportunities for supervised risk-taking were not part of our curriculum in any sense, even though for this particular age group, research showed this sort of activity was crucial for healthy physical and mental development.

Wednesday, November 6

While my class was in gym, I spent my planning period attempting to assess essays written by kids who weren't in my class. The product of our district-wide sixth grade writing assessment, the sizeable stack in front of me was to be sorted with the help of a rubric. My job was to rate essays from 1 to 4, though having this odious task dropped on my lap, I griped to Mr. B. about what I considered a violation of working conditions as outlined in the contract. My colleagues, however, didn't understand what

I was torqued off about. Elementary teachers, at least the ones at SES, never questioned their mushrooming workload, even when additional demands ate up their planning time. Our high school colleagues, on the other hand, weren't afraid to stick up for themselves, having figured out our bosses, having no classes to teach, felt obligated to drum up tasks for us to do in addition to what we were already doing (i.e. teaching and planning to teach). As Central Office shared a main corridor with the high school, perhaps this proximity had something to do with it. You couldn't walk by those interior windows without glancing in and wondering what was going on in there. Even when you knew, you'd shake your head in disbelief. Two years ago, for example, a memo circulated out of CO stating that the term *field trip* was no longer to be used, replaced instead by *field work*, the idea being that *trip* connoted leisure, a fun and relaxed atmosphere, whereas *work* indicated, well, work. Henceforth we were required to use *field work* both orally and in writing when referring to *a field trip*, thereby changing the tone of what we did on these ventures from one of enjoyment and exploration to one of tedium and drudgery. The notion that our administrators sat around and debated this nonsensical issue fried the hell out of me, but none of my SES colleagues were nearly as piqued as I was.

Thursday, November 7

At an IEP (Individualized Educational Plan) review meeting Tanner's mother expressed concerns about whether he'd be ready for middle school. On what grade level, she asked me, would he be reading by June? Did I teach spelling too? What were the topics of the research papers I had planned? He didn't live with her and sometimes the non-custodial parent arrived with a page of notes and a certain angle meant to demonstrate that they were more on the ball than the custodial parent, that they cared more about the kid's social, emotional and educational well-being, and wasn't it plain an injustice had been served which had resigned them to their secondary role?

What specifically are you worried about? I asked her.

Well, you're mailing it in. Retiring, right? How is he supposed to get what he needs with you as his teacher?

Lost for a response, I looked at her before clearing my throat. Here was a question unrelated to Tanner's ability to access the curriculum and how we all might help him. Rather, it addressed *my* purported lack of focus, *my* inability to do the job by simply not giving a shit.

That's hardly the case, I stammered, failing to disguise the hint of annoyance in my voice. The meeting coordinator and special education teacher, also caught off guard, ventured nothing in my defense, not a word about me being the kind of teacher who would never *mail it in.* The woman's ex-husband stared at the table top and had nothing to contribute either. She'd cornered me at Open House back in September, requesting I send her duplicates of Tanner's report cards and progress reports, call her if he wasn't toeing the line, etc. I promised I would and added that Tanner seemed to be enjoying himself this year.

I hope that means he's learning something.

One and the same, I said, trying to lighten the mood.

She pointed two fingers at her eyes and turned those fingers toward me.

She was in her mid-thirties, in a low cut blouse and tight jeans, a cross around her neck. To keep Tanner on task, I told her, I'd moved his desk next to mine. When he was focused, his work ethic, I added, was off the charts. So too was his ability to get along with others. And I'd just found out he loved birds! I kept going, my fawning compliments I hoped enough to win her over. Now, six weeks later, it was obvious my tactic hadn't worked. Perhaps she'd meant it in the general sense, the biding time bit, figuring any teacher in my position would go through the motions as he approached the end of his career. At least she had part of it right—I *was* trying to survive the year. Who wasn't? But had I checked out without realizing it? Maybe. Yes, I had. No, not entirely. Still, I chafed at her insinuation in front of colleagues that with a year to go I was dogging it. She had no proof to back up her allegation, even if it might be true.

Friday, November 8

What was it like to be on an IEP at twelve years old, to be extracted from the classroom for small group instruction by a different teacher, only having to re-enter with no idea what was going on (your *real* teacher having to explain it to you in a hasty condensed fashion which in your embarrassment you didn't hear a word)? The implementation an IEP, perhaps worthy in theory, extinguished any remnant of self-esteem a child might cling to after being officially labelled *special needs*. Once designated, the label stuck forever, like a footprint on the moon. Everyone knew who was *special needs* and never let them forget it. So what to do with those the school deemed other than *normal*? How to spare them the misery of being taken away in the middle of whatever they were doing and delivered to some small airless room to receive *specialized instruction* from the *special education* teacher? The inclusion model didn't work—kids on IEPs couldn't follow what was going on in the *regular class* despite *modified work* (further humiliating the kid who received it, everyone reminded once again who the dumb kid was, the one whose work was different from everyone else's, the one with that teacher who came and went and none of the other kids really knew. Had everyone been working on a variety of material suited to his ability level, then of course there would be no *special education* and thus no dumb kids.).

The one prototype ignored by schools was to have those who understood what was going on instruct those who didn't. Most kids were born teachers and eager to show off what they knew so it was easy to recruit candidates. The recipient, more at ease with peers than teacher, did not view such assistance as stigmatizing. Without having to endure the soul zapping setup inherent in *special needs* instruction, the kid receiving peer help could retain his dignity. And the favor could be reciprocated. One time I'd watched a kid on an IEP instruct a classmate on how to draw a map of Australia freehand. The two sat together at the back table, heads nearly touching, the IEP kid, who happened to be an artist, pointing out every inlet, river and peninsula in a patient voice, instructing the regular ed kid to take his time (*Watch Collier Bay. It's tricky!*), understanding that quality work can't be rushed. He was more encouraging and less critical than I would have been. The toughest part for me was minding my own business by not pushing another method (i.e. my way) of doing it, to free myself from the anxiety of observing a twelve years old teach more effectively than I could.

Monday, November 11

Veterans' Day–no school.
On Friday we wrote to service people in Iraq and Afghanistan (a box full of letters from fifth and sixth graders would be sent off to be randomly distributed).

What should we write about? asked Ivan.

Anything.

Anything?

I won't read them.

You won't?

No.

Okay then.

Awed by the prospect to discourse on any topic, not a word of it censored, they set to work. If there was one characteristic 6D shared it was the burning desire to tell their stories to anyone who would listen, even if they had no idea who the person was. With more to tell than opportunities in which to tell them, and liberated from the burden of brainstorming, using graphic organizers, adhering to grammatical conventions and all the other requirements that made writing such a chore for them, they embarked on the good deed of unloading to strangers stationed halfway around the world.

Just a few months ago, I told them, my mother had returned to me a letter I'd written in 1966 to my Uncle Ted, a Marine stationed at an airbase in Vietnam. Just sixty-two when he died, he'd struggled since the war with alcohol addiction. Somehow he'd kept my letter in the same pristine condition as the day my eleven year old self had written it at the kitchen table, describing the hot dogs and beans I had for supper, how Tony Conigliaro had belted another homer over The Wall and would lead the league for the second year, and how I intended to be a Marine someday but only if I could fly jets.

Your letter could end up like mine, I told them. *Treasured by someone for years.*

My uncle's a vet, Rylie informed us. *He tried to kill himself driving the wrong way.*

The others stopped writing and pressed for details, of which Rylie wasn't sure. And besides, she told us, it was nobody's business but his. I figured that was the end of it until she added he'd tried to get help but couldn't, went on using drugs, overdosed, recovered, robbed a convenience store to pay for more drugs, overdosed a second time. She spoke in a straightforward manner, as if updating us on a relative's job promotion or move to Vermont. I listened, chilled by her frankness.

They took away his license so he can't work. He has no money and can't leave the house because of this thing he has to wear on his leg.

An GPS monitoring device, interpreted Thad.

Then why don't anybody help him? Nyla asked her.

Once you're discharged, Rylie informed us, *they don't care what happens to you.*

How come we don't write letters complaining to politicians then?

Another day, I said.

Tuesday, November 12

Despite the draft from the two sets of windows behind my desk, they offered a nice view of the woods beyond the baseball field as well as the vernal pool directly below, not twenty feet from the building. The pool was surrounded by a high chain link fence to prevent kids from doing what kids normally did—stomp in the mud, toss pebbles into the water, search for mole salamanders and wood frogs when the level rose in spring and spread in places beyond the fenced boundary. During recess they balanced themselves over the water's edge or hopped on partially submerged stones until teachers gave them hell and told them to move away. The depth was all of a foot, maybe a bit more during a rainy week in April, the fence indicating a place of danger, not exploration. In spring I'd watch from my window as a first grader curled his fingers around the chain link as if he were at a zoo, his eyes zeroed in on a painted turtle slipping off a log, a young maple leaf spinning across the surface, a bullfrog plopping from a stone into the mud. The vernal pool sustained me the same way it did turtles and salamanders and first graders, providing a place to go in my head when I needed a break from the craziness and couldn't leave the classroom. I'd swivel my chair around and stare out the window and there it would be, an oasis protected by tall swaying pines, its circumference not much more than that of a large puddle until it swelled with snowmelt and spring rain but always providing something interesting to look at, be it a sideshow of downy woodpeckers or manic crows or bustling squirrels in those pines just feet from my window, or perhaps small ripples generated by a November breeze nudging a twig along the surface. In winter the pool froze to a chalky white, the pines groaned with the cold, and a lone squirrel in its gray winter coat scampered among the branches. So long as I could turn around and escape to that pool whenever I had the urge I was able to return to the kids recharged.

Wednesday, November 13

Our guidance counsellor Dan retired today on his sixty-third birthday. A burly guy with a bushy beard and a hearty laugh who played offensive guard at Bates in the early seventies, he hobbled on rickety knees from the parking lot to the lobby and from there rode the elevator to his second floor office. Before he limped out the door of SES for the last time he told me he would never set foot inside a school again. He was fond of the old days before administrators became business managers, when teachers decided for themselves what was best for kids since they were the ones teaching them.

Do you remember the time long ago, he would ask me with fond recollection, *when kids were allowed to move around?*

We would joke about that, laugh the kind of laugh when you didn't know what else to say because it was so shameful. Both of us had been around the block a few times and as young teachers were convinced we were part of something revolutionary, a new beginning where students and their instructors would engage in a creative environment with lots of choice and resources, learning from one another as we went along. It would be an entirely fresh way of doing things, the start of a new day for elementary education. Unfortunately, our prediction had not come true.

The staff took up a collection for Dan the week before, dropping fives and tens into a manilla envelope when a couple of kids showed up at our door. At a potluck breakfast held in his honor in the library, he acknowledged our dedication and said what a great school we had and how much he'd miss us. I'd always envied his job, his office stashed away in a small corner room where he invited troubled kids to have lunch with him and having those same kids check in later in the day or else teachers coming to him for suggestions on how to deal with kids driving them nuts. He had no papers to grade, no assessments or report cards to fill out, no teacher/parent conferences to sit through. What he loved most was simply sitting there and listening to what kids had to say, ensconced like a buddha in his armchair and them spread out in front of him either sitting or lying on the rug. He didn't talk down or raise his voice or demand they do such-and-such, leaving the kid to decide for himself whether to heed his advice and discovering when he did he was better off for it. As a result, they clamored to see him, his office a busy place with shelves of chess boards, decks of playing cards, drawing pads, crayons, markers, and small toys to manipulate as a way to avoid eye contact as they opened up to him.

Dan was also blessed with an intuitive sense about people and their motives. One time during a contract negotiation, when the administration presented an offer which surprised us with its generosity, he brought us back to earth.

Beware of Greeks bearing gifts, he warned. And he was right. Negotiations slogged on for weeks.

Early in his career he'd been an Outward Bound instructor and now his three grown sons were seeking adventure in far flung corners of the globe. With technocrats in control of public schools, Dan warned me, an existential crisis loomed where young people, disheartened and alienated, would graduate without knowing how to think critically and act in their own behalf. Who could argue with that theory? I'd miss his insight for sure. Both of us had spent time in Ireland and wondered why the pints of Guinness over there went down so much smoother. Rumor had it stout didn't travel well. It was Dan's plan, once he got his knees done, to return to Ireland and chase down whether there was any truth to that rumor.

Thursday, November 14

My blood pressure soared to 130/90, the highest it's ever been. I'd gone to have my shoulder looked at, fed up with the ache that kept me up nights. My physician leaned toward a torn rotator cuff diagnosis and prescribed Xanax for anxiety. I filled the prescription but was afraid to take it, fearing side effects, addiction, etc. My biggest worry, though, was becoming someone with no anxiety at all. What would that person look like? Would anyone recognize me? How could I walk away from a disorder that had been so much a part of me for my entire life? Would I surrender my right arm just to see what it felt like? Carla, married to someone with Generalized Anxiety Disorder whose symptoms thanks to his impending retirement had escalated beyond what a tolerant person could be expected to endure, needed as much help as I did. After sampling one of those blue pills, she kept the prescription bottle tucked inside her sock drawer, readily available and hidden from the kids. More than satisfied with the results, she insisted they were fine, just fine, that I had nothing to worry about and to please try one for her sake and see. Her insistence and enthusiasm weren't enough to convince me, because though they might work fine for her, I countered, I was another person entirely and who could predict what might happen with my particular blood chemistry, which then caused her to regard me in a new light, as someone even crazier than she'd thought after all these years.

Next year my salary would tail off by over by thirty percent, spiralling downward every year in futile battle to keep pace with inflation. Thus I was dependent on COLA, which would, provided the cost of living index rose enough, provide me a 3% raise on my first $13,000 next year, which I calculated to be $392.00. With no marketable skills to speak of other than teaching twelve-year-olds—or I should say *managing* twelve-year-olds, since I no longer had confidence in my ability, given that what I was required to teach and what I thought twelve-year-olds ought to learn resided in different universes—I could, if faced with no other options, venture over the border into the wilds of New Hampshire to teach in the town of Seabrook where there always seemed to be job openings. The kids there were just as needy as those in Salisbury, the pay less, the town home to a nuclear power plant whose license was regularly on the verge of getting revoked (in the event of a meltdown one road led out of town). Though the border was just a five-minute drive north, I had little intention of exercising this option unless I found myself unable to function away from the confines of a public school, which I considered a definite possibility.

Friday, November 15

Leland had been wearing the same clothes (hooded sweat-shirt, jeans) all week. Sheila, my paraprofessional, pointed this out to me. Had I noticed? Then what should we do about it? The nurse kept a closet full of pre-owned shirts, pants, and jackets kids could borrow if they tore what they were wearing or needed a coat for recess. What she didn't provide was a rotating wardrobe for anyone with one set of clothes. Besides, addressing the subject ran the risk of embarrassing him. He was a bright kid though not tuned in socially, and the peers he spent time with, as Sheila also pointed out, wore the same clothes too, though not with the same frequency (i.e. every day). Should we leave well enough alone? What if we pulled him aside for a private conversation and tactfully mentioned the obvious? Say we went ahead and procured apparel from the nurse, would he wear a style that conflicted with his taste and had once belonged to someone else? Did we even have the right to tell him to change his clothes, never mind make him wear donated ones? Unable to come up with a solution,

I passed the buck by telling her I'd mention the issue to our social worker Greta (*What do you expect her to do about it?* she asked). Because Leland wasn't unhygienic, this allowed us to believe in the possibility that he might be laundering those clothes with some regularity. If they were clean, if he didn't smell, that made it okay, didn't it? We would let it go for now as we had more pressing matters to deal with. Odor was the bottom line. In that case, we would be forced to act.

Anyway, he was one of those types who needed me only when he wanted my permission to leave the room, buzzing through his illegible work before bugging me for a chance to visit the cafeteria to collect drinking straws. From there he would mosey over to the art room to coax the teacher into handing over pieces of coated wire which combined with the straws he fashioned into odd-looking little men who resided in his desk and took orders directly from him. His parents swung between users and ex-users, working and not working, living together and living apart, having a car and not having one, renting an apartment and getting evicted. He lived with his father on weekends except he hadn't seen or heard from him since he'd been hospitalized a week ago. I told Leland he could call the hospital from the classroom phone.

He won't answer, he said.

Leave a message. Tell him you're thinking about him.

I already did that.

The best I could do was offer was a few minutes in the hallway to talk about his situation so both of us could get through the rest of the day. His case worker informed me last week the family file had been closed for some reason even she didn't understand.

That's an excellent hospital, I went on. *They'll take good care of him.*

Yeah, he said. *He's real sick.*

You can try again later. Maybe he's sleeping.

He promised me a new cell phone.

He mumbled responses barely audible in sidelong glances with zero eye contact. Maybe I'd increased his anxiety by putting him on the spot. He generally didn't take me up an offer for a private conversation–some kids were like that and I'd learned not to be offended by their rejection. I wasn't sure why this time as he always seemed to be dealing with one crisis or another. Maybe he was genuinely concerned about his father's health and needed to unload. To his credit he wasn't angry his dad had let him down a million times, only worried he was in tough shape and might die, which made me think no matter how down and out you were your kid could still love you.

Monday, November 18

I took a half personal day to take Justina to the orthopedist where she had a cast placed on her sprained wrist. When I walked into class at 11:30 the kids quietly greeted me. The substitute, a genial older woman named Eleanor with a kind soft face, cat-eye glasses on a chain and bright green eyes, surprised me by saying she would sub again anytime.

Who wouldn't want to spend the day with these beautiful children?

I held my tongue before uttering something sarcastic, figuring she must live alone cut off from all human contact. Her handbag sat on my desk, one of those large deluxe models older women lugged around in the event somebody needed anything from a breath mint to a defibrillator. The sight of it there, along with the idea of her making herself at home with the personalities of 6D, gave me a warm feeling. In the few minutes we had to chat I got the impression the kids had had a fine time with her too. She apologized for not getting through all the material as she'd spent time listening to them expound on various topics, including Darwin's theory of evolution. They'd pointed to our photograph of the facial reconstruction of an early human who'd roamed the African savanna, one I'd cut out from a National Geographic magazine and stuck in a frame after informing the kids it wasn't a monkey though they insisted it was. (I sometimes lectured apropos of nothing how early humans ventured out of and away from trees because our unique pelvis allowed us to stand upright and ambulate while watching out for predators. Unlike our primate cousins, we grew adept at covering longer and longer distances on two legs, our sweat cooling us in the heat, our efficient physiques allowing us to outrun any animal on earth. The kids didn't believe me at first, exclaiming how older family members got winded climbing a flight of stairs.). Eleanor told them how much she loved the *monkey photo* to which the kids cried out *That's not a monkey, that's us!* She got a kick out of that and even took out her phone and snapped a photo of our photo. In these crazy times, she asked me, with creationists insisting the world was formed three thousand years ago, that we were descended from Adam and Eve, and that somewhere between then and now Noah had saved us all at the last second with his ark, was natural selection still being taught? I told her I certainly hoped so, then added that only once had a mother complained to Mr. B. that I'd let her son in on the fact that he was descended not Adam and Eve but from fish. An evangelical Christian who supported everything else I did, she requested to be allowed to leave class whenever the topic came up. That was the one time anyone challenged me outright, though I was careful not to go on too long about evolution least word got out that I was teaching science in a public school.

Tuesday, November 19

I stayed up until midnight watching the Patriots lose to the Panthers on a non-call as time expired, a penalty flag thrown in the end zone and then picked up as the referees ran off the field. I waited for an explanation, got none, went to bed, tried to sleep, and had what Carla and I call *teacher dreams.* In the dream, I'd lost my balance in front of the class and couldn't stand up. I kept falling down, getting up, falling down again. My feet refused to stay put under me. The kids got up and came over. *What's wrong? What's the matter with you?* I told them I was fine, that I'd find my balance soon enough. I just needed a few minutes was all. To help me they should return to their seats and continue doing their work. That was the important thing, that they keep doing their work. *Should we call the office? Can we help you stand up?* They gathered around me. A hand reached down. Then another. *Let us get you up! Let us help you!* I shooed them away. For whatever reason I was stuck on the floor, my legs all rubbery and my inner gyroscope gone wonky. Instead of looking *over* them as they sat at their desks, I was looking *up* at them. The room was the same, not rolling, pitching or spinning, the kids the same, predictably using the excuse of me lying supine and terrified as a ploy for not doing their work. They insisted on staying with me, my well being their only concern. After a few more minutes of struggle I gave up. From the linoleum I studied the water stain on the ceiling tiles, the one that looked like Florida, telling myself it was okay when I knew damn well it wasn't okay.

It's fine with us if you just want to lie there like that for the rest of the day.

If you really want to help me, I reiterated, *please do your work.*

So long as they were in their seats and kept busy, I told myself I was fine. So long as the fire alarm didn't go off and we didn't have a lockdown, I was good. As far as I knew nothing in the contract stipulated a teacher couldn't teach lying on the floor. I was doing what I was paid to do. At some point I'd get up. It was a matter of wait and see. Once the kids were back at their desks I gave directions. In turn they leaned out of their seats and said they had no idea what they were supposed to do. It was business as usual. After a while lying on the floor just seemed like a normal part of any other crazy school day. I wasn't at my desk or at the front of the room but I was still teaching. What was the big deal anyway?

Once retired, I hoped I would no longer be subjected to these disturbing dreams which grew out of my bottled anxiety and the feeling of powerlessness I felt during the school day.

Wednesday, November 20

How was school today? I asked Justina.

Boring, she said as she dug cheese ravioli out of the colander.

Since preschool she'd never wavered, not once, intuiting at an early age that nothing about her education would change. Her profound stance, a steadfast resolve, unaffected from one grade to the next, both impressed and rattled me. She wasn't some kid in my class whose disaffection I could pay lip service to (*Yeah, that's how it goes sometimes*). She was my own daughter with whom I attempted to sort through this dilemma.

What was boring about it?

Everything. School sucks. It's not like I have a choice. I have to go.

Debating this non-choice only gave her a headache. She was expected to get through high school (house rules) which meant six more years of incarceration. Then, having served her time, she would be granted her freedom (no early release for good behavior). She wasn't happy, she didn't understand why she had to go, and I had no explanation for her. She had a solid ally in a good friend of ours, who like Justina detested school from the minute his mother let go of his hand on his first day of kindergarten some sixty-five years ago. By the time he'd gone off to college he'd hatched the idea of suing the federal government for involuntary servitude in a class action suit and wondered why no one had thought of it before he did.

Since I was part of the problem (as a teacher) I couldn't address the issue without sounding like a hypocrite. School was boring and boring was school. You sat all day. You followed orders. You ferried lifeless textbooks that put you at risk for scoliosis. You took assessments to reach benchmarks to ready you for high stakes tests, then did it all over again, year after year. The routine never changed–not only for you but your teachers too.

Before she'd begun kindergarten, Justina had hung out at playgrounds, read picture books she'd chosen, sang songs, did in arts and crafts, gone on nature hikes, swum at the Y, visited museums, aquariums, zoos. She'd been under the mistaken impression her school days would be more of the same. Carla and I waited, figuring she was a late bloomer. Sooner or later, her curiosity piqued, she'd applied herself and discover the virtue of study. No dice, she told us. If school interested her, she *would* apply herself, just as anyone with a passion for something delved into it more deeply. It was tough to debate an eighth-grader with unshakeable logic regarding her education. She knew the score and no amount of discoursing would change her mind.

Thursday, November 22

Fifty years ago today I was in third grade when the principal visited each class to break the news that President Kennedy had been shot and we were being sent home. I told the kids this as we read a story in *Scope* magazine about the assassination.

Teachers could beat up kids back then, Ivan informed us.

Not really, I said.

And kids walked to school in those days, he added.

That part is right, I said. *And since there was no cafeteria, I walked home for lunch too. With all that back and forth I travelled three miles a day, strictly transportation, and if I ran home I had more time to eat.*

I would love that, said Ryder, a bright artsy kid who sometimes came to school dressed in costumes he'd made himself (*Robin Hood* was my favorite) and who insisted on doing his work standing up, shaking out one leg and then the other as if he was warming up for an athletic contest. Other times he jogged in place or hopped from foot to foot. He'd been in trouble in earlier grades because his teachers had insisted he sit down. *Won't happen,* he'd informed them. He wasn't being rude or defiant. Sitting was simply something he was incapable of doing. When I'd tried to get him to sit myself, not knowing any better, he politely declined in the same matter-of-fact tone as if I'd asked him to fly around the room. *Sorry, no can do. Not possible.* So he stood all day, leaning over a table, squatting, bending, arching and rotating his spine to stay limber. His desk was kept neat and clean and used strictly for storage, his chair elsewhere since he had no use for it. Thus he could do his work anywhere, and sometimes would sprawl out on the linoleum in the back of the classroom and I would wonder where he'd gone and ask if anyone had seen him until I heard him say, *I'm back here on the floor, Mr. D.*, an arm shooting up and waving.

Now in America we had specifically designated *Walk to School Days*. Arrangements had to be made, cops notified, traffic rerouted. It was a big deal because schools–ours was one–were so far from neighborhoods kids couldn't walk to them without crossing highways, bridges, and busy streets. Sidewalks were a relic–there were none along Route 1 leading in either direction to our school. On weekends SES, situated at the end of a long driveway and hidden from view, become an isolated place despite its playground, baseball field and basketball courts. Kids were warned not to hang out or go there alone. Our old school, Memorial Elementary (we'd moved to the newly named Salisbury Elementary School fourteen years ago) was plunk dab in the center of downtown next to the town common, the public library, the post office, a Laundromat, convenience store, gas station, pizza joint, Chinese restaurant, pharmacy and barber shop. Neighborhoods surrounded us. The area teemed with life, older folks killing time on benches, young mothers pushing baby strollers, people coming and going on errands. Nearby was an assisted living facility where one afternoon a week we visited to play cards and board games with the residents. Now we were a mile away and couldn't walk there for want of sidewalks.

Even youth sports programs (in which my three kids were part of) were more an extension of the school day than an opportunity for free and creative play. Coaches lectured on fundamentals in a structured setting while young athletes stood around pretending to listen after a long day of not listening at school.

Friday, November 23

At the end of the day I let the kids play board games–chess and checkers, *Boggle, Scrabble, Battleship, The Ungame* (created during the sixties, it was a game designed to have no winners I inherited from a retiring colleague. It turned out to have no players either as the kids pushed it aside). This game playing allowed me to rest my voice which was faltering again, catching and hoarse, forcing me to clear my throat multiple times (and grossing the kids out) as my salivary glands shut down. You could lose your mind in this profession but if your voice went you were finished (I'd once known a guy in the early stages of Alzheimer's who'd somehow managed to complete the year teaching eighth grade. As a special education teacher at the time, I assisted in his classroom and witnessed the decline. As bad as he was–he repeated himself, forgot kids' names, didn't return from the bathroom–right up until the last day of school he maintained a stentorian tone which provided a measure of control despite his fraying mind.). How the kids perceived you depended on your timbre, volume, and frequency of use (the less the better). Shout and you exposed yourself as someone without restraint. Speak softly and they ignored you. So how to get their attention? First, wait for it like an actor walking on stage. Stand in front of them, confident and loose limbed. Rub your hands together and nod, let slip a smile to draw them in, as if what you have to say you've been holding onto all day, the next big secret you can't wait to let them in on. Catch them off guard by saying the opposite of what they expect to hear.

—*What makes you think you're in trouble?*

—*You mean we're not?*

—*There's this riddle I heard.*

—*What? What riddle? Tell us!*

—Are you listening?

—Yeah! Shut up everybody. Tell us!

—What did the preacher say when the skunks walked into the church?

—What? We give up!

—Let us spray.

—Haha! Good one! Haha!

If they've done something to piss you off, compliment what they did right and then dissect the problem in such a sombre tone it'll take them a minute to figure out you're talking about them. When they do, they'll come to their own conclusions about what buffoons they'd been. Never ask for an apology. Bring them to the point where they'll offer one.

As kids formed their groups and set out game pieces, I sat at my desk and drained my water bottle. To soothe my vocal cords and avoid a recurrence of a kidney stone I was drinking more than a quart of water during the school day. A drawback to teaching elementary school was having to discipline your bladder. You couldn't go to the bathroom, at least not when you had to, so you learned to hold it, sometimes for hours. I was at the age when I had to go more often, especially given the volume of water passing through my renal system, and was less able to hold it, so at times I would slip out of the classroom without informing the kids, thinking it better not to alert them to the fact there was no teacher in the room and hoping for a few minutes they wouldn't notice (Sheila, my paraprofessional, splitting her duties among three classes, never seemed to be around when I had to make a run). Hurrying down the hall, I prayed no one was in the staff bathroom, otherwise I'd have to jog to one at the other end. While urinating I would chide myself for this surreptitious emptying of my bladder, which because I'd waited so long took forever, and while I stood there images of the ensuing chaos once my absence was noticed filled my brain, a kid by now bleeding and unconscious. It occurred to me that I could become the target of a lawsuit and possibly even the recipient of a prison sentence. Why was I being so cavalier? What the hell was wrong with me? Then I reminded myself that I had every right to go to the bathroom, that doing so was covered under the aegis of basic human freedoms, and how the hell could I be prosecuted for that?

Whenever the kids were out of my sight (strung out ahead of me in a hallway while I paused to speak to a colleague, for example, or left alone in the classroom while I pulled the phone cord outside into the hallway for a private conversation, or bolting ahead of me on a field trip as I listened to the docent's instructions), I obsessed on the potential for disaster, leaving me unable to listen to whomever I was speaking. My temples throbbed as rivulets of cold sweat trickled from my armpits. I simply didn't trust the kids, not because they were devious but because they were prey to any and all impulses. It was only when I was back in their midst that my pulse eased and I could think straight again. My own anxiety contributed to this heightened state though every SES teacher grew edgy and distracted whenever she was away from her class for more than a few seconds.

Monday, November 25

Every Monday morning at 8:20 we met in the staff lunch room for half an hour of team planning which for years had been promised in the contract but never delivered because of language about how the administration would *strive* to provide this allocation to elementary teachers. Anyone who has ever done any contract negotiating knows whatever is strived for won't occur, as the striving party is under no legal obligation to provide whatever they claim to be striving for. Once the language was tightened in the next contract (*will strive* replaced by *shall*), Mr. B. consented to this planning time but rather than leave us alone, he elected to attend himself to observe us speaking to one another, his record of our conversation potentially ending up on our formative evaluations. So while we sat around the table pretending to discourse like normal people, he sat in an armchair by the window typing on his Ipad.

Last night I'd stayed up to watch the Patriots battle back from a 24-0 halftime deficit against Peyton Manning and the Broncos.

Did you guys believe what Brady did last night?

A couple of head nodded.

He's amazing. And don't you feel bad for poor Peyton Manning? Boy, does Belichick have his number!

Silence.

And how about our defense? Bend but don't break!

More silence.

I was desperate to talk about the game for a few minutes, mention the comeback as any partisan football fan would to his co-workers, but they, cognizant their boss was not only eavesdropping but documenting, ignored my commentary by engaging in a stilted discussion about math assessments and an upcoming field trip to see *A Christmas Carol* and which kids might not be able to come up with the thirty dollar bus and admission fee. In affected professional tones they outdid one another in the presence of Mr. B. who seemed to be typing word for word, scaring the hell out of everyone except me, the one person in the group retiring and thus not being evaluated who was free to express himself in any way he saw fit. I knew my colleagues were as rabid about the Patriots as I was, that they'd stayed up to watch too, but they, each of whom I loved and respected, wouldn't take the bait, as they were understandably more concerned about covering their own asses than listening to anything I had to say.

Tuesday, November 26

In the high school gym at the end of the day I found my oldest daughter Beatrice along with groups of kids, mostly girls, decorating the walls above the wooden bleachers with banners for homecoming tomorrow. A radio blasted hip hop as they went about their business without a teacher in sight. An indifferent custodian pushed a dry mop, corralling balled-up paper, candy wrappers and plastic cups into a corner. Kids came and went, organizing and carrying out tasks in a fluid unschool-like way, contributing what they could before hurrying off to other commitments or else arriving here from previous ones. Beatrice was at work in the sophomore section, along with some former members of 6D, painting a banner in school colors—navy blue and white—and I thought about how once the day ended kids loved being in school, whether for intramural sports, activity clubs, even extra help sessions where a teacher could relax and get her point across as if a pressure valve had opened. Kids could mosey around or just sit and do nothing and be in no hurry to do it as the tension of the day drained out of them. A teacher might crack jokes or talk about her own kids or ask what a student's sibling were doing these days. By being herself, she would be revealed as a real genuine person now that the day's obligations were dispensed with, no longer some distant figure at the front of the classroom unknown to her students.

After school you didn't have to worry about this or that duty or someone coming through the door to evaluate the way you did this or said. It was a time to teach the way you wanted to teach, to relate to the kids without having to be someone other than yourself, to shoot the breeze without feeling you weren't doing your job. And the kids, because of this, could relax and be themselves and had no need to playact. It was the best time of the day.

Wednesday, November 27

Today was my last Williams Bowl, our annual intramural flag football and field hockey league championships named after a retired PE teacher and held in the gym on the morning before Thanksgiving break. The bleachers strained under the weight of kids, parents, grandparents, uncles, aunts and anyone else who felt like wandering in and sitting through two and a half hours of elementary school athletic competition. Those electing not to risk the overtaxed stands lined walls and plugged doorways. Recent SES graduates who'd skipped class at the middle school converged here to show us that they were indeed skipping school, thinking we might care on this half day before the holiday. A team called Infinity won the field hockey championship, the Patriots the flag football component. Both football teams had a couple of girls on their rosters but no boys competed on the field hockey teams. In fact, I'd never seen a boy play field hockey though had one been interested he would have been more welcomed by the girls than the football players had been in accepting teammates of the opposite sex. The female players found themselves stranded on the edge of the action, e.g. wide receivers rarely thrown the ball or blockers at the tail end of the line. When a girl did make a catch everyone went wild, and running the ball she deked and pivoted, showcasing moves as good as the boys, which seemed to further discourage her teammates from getting the ball back into her hands.

In this cramped festive atmosphere of posters and face-paint and the SES band blasting fight tunes, in front of me sat Vance, one of my former students, a college sophomore majoring in environmental science who looked the part (full beard, red flannel shirt, cargo pants, untied work boots, weatherbeaten Red Sox cap on backwards). We shook hands and during a lull in the uproar reminisced about the year he'd spent in my classroom. With his shy grin and easy manner, he'd gotten along with everyone but his illegible handwriting and hatred of having to scribble even a single sentence made school a miserable proposition. The summer before he became my student I tutored him, hoping to alleviate some of his writing angst. Together we wrote stories, scrawling paragraphs as fast as we could, sliding a pad of paper back and forth across the table, our characters caught up in one bizarre escapade after another so that we were tugging the corner of the pad to get it back so we could see what might befall them next. Our pens raced through scenes we ourselves couldn't believe we'd produced.

Where did that come from? he would ask as I read his version back to him. *Did that come out of me?*

Yeah, I said.

Then I need help. Something's wrong with me.

You're a writer. It's a good kind of crazy.

Though I wasn't sure the technique resolved his uneasiness, we produced pages of prose and by the end he did not seem to hate it so much, marvelling at how bonkers he was, shaking his head at what he'd written. I wondered how his writing was going these days, up against those annotated term papers and five-page essays and all the rest. Apparently he'd found a way, tackling the task himself, having his girlfriend do it, or buying his papers off the internet with his work-study cash.

From time to time I ran into kids like Vance who'd struggled with rudimentary skills and years later were succeeding at a four year university. All along I'd underestimated them, reasoning if a kid couldn't read or write with a degree of proficiency on my watch he'd never do it. A natural enough supposition but a biased one which kept him from progressing without me realizing it. Some kids caught on later than others, were late bloomers, though it was tough for a teacher to look into the future when, attempting to get his point across, he was met with a blank stare. A blank stare meant–what? Lots of things, though usually interpreted as insouciance, a lack of focus or even outright defiance (kids diagnosed with selective mutism, for example, responded to requests with a stony gaze, their underlying social anxiety preventing them from returning eye contact and engaging verbally, and so the teacher, not knowing any better, interpreted this behavior as uncooperative, thus contributing to an adversarial relationship doomed from the start). If a kid wasn't getting it, I reasoned, he never would, so what did that say if he went off and succeeded *after* he'd left my classroom? I consoled myself by imagining I'd provided some underpinning or other which had led to that favorable outcome but the truth may have been he'd simply matured and figured it out on his own. That conclusion was hard to swallow, as what teacher wanted to think he was the reason a kid hadn't learned what he was supposed to?

Monday, December 2

Perfect attendance despite a number of kids out building-wide with head colds and stomach viruses. The day was overcast and chilly with periods of rain. I'd opened the windows in an attempt to kill germs and now thanks to my foresight I along with everybody else was sneezing and shivering in spite of the heater. While the kids grumbled and fumed over their worksheets I sat protected from them behind my desk and considered ways I might supplement my pension. Would I ever, out of desperation, disjointed reasoning, or both accept another teaching job?

A couple of years ago a retired teacher in the district ventured over the border into the wilds of Seabrook to take a position as a paraprofessional. His job consisted of trailing an autistic kid class to class, helping him with note-taking, organization, social interactions, etc. That was it—no papers to grade, unruly kids to subdue, staff meetings to suffer through, administrators to grovel to, etc. As he knew his way around an elementary school the job was easy enough, and like me, having been part of the institution of public education for so long the outside world must have seemed like an uncivilized and hostile place. Why gamble when he could stay where he was, safe and secure inside the walls of a classroom, even if it meant taking orders from a teacher half his age and working for a fraction of the salary he'd earned the year before?

In June, less than twelve months after he retired, he was diagnosed with cancer and was dead by fall. That terrified me—not so much the cancer and dying as his going right back in again, convinced it was the only line of work he was capable of doing, his shaky self-worth preventing him from undertaking anything other than what he'd done for the last thirty-five or forty years. Maybe that wasn't the reason, maybe he just loved being around kids and the routine of the school. If that was the case, why had he retired in the first place?

Tuesday, December 3

Twenty years ago today I met Carla at the B&L Laundromat in Medford as she sat with a folder correcting papers on a rainy Friday night. I assumed she taught at Tufts University, as the campus was a short walk up the street.

No, she said without looking up, *I don't.*

Where then?

Pause.

High school.

What grades?

Pause.

Freshmen and seniors.

That can't be easy.

Slow nod.

Despite her reticence, I pressed on with little fear of embarrassment, as we were the only people in the place, keeping our distance by holding down the end chair in a row of orange plastic seats. The previous week she'd moved into an apartment a mile away, along with her dog Riley, a Jack Russell terrier. I told her I loved dogs, that someday I intended to have a few. I would have said the same thing about rattlesnakes. A decade earlier she'd done her student teaching at a Jesuit high school in Boston where she'd found a number of the all-male population coarse and obnoxious, along with a few of the teachers, uncomfortable at the sight of a capable and intelligent young woman in the hallways and classroom. I'd gone to that same high school but knew if I revealed that fact any chance I had would evaporate. We talked about our jobs, complained about the workload, confessed we liked the profession enough to stick with it. When the dryer buzzer went off I pulled my clothes into a canvas cart and wheeled it over to the folding table while she sorted her laundry at the other end. With some effort I kept my eyes on what I was doing so there was no chance I'd glance at her underwear and be dismissed as a pervert, though it wasn't an easy thing to do. Every time I spoke I measured my words, my tone, my mannerisms, desperate to sound–how? Like someone other than who I was, or who I thought I was, a better, more confident person, a guy she might be drawn to. With her looks, she was a stretch, and had there been anyone else present I wouldn't have uttered a word. As she gathered up her laundry basket, I spit out something about the two of us having coffee. She gave me a look– a smirk or a frown I couldn't be sure–then scribbled her phone number on the back of a dog grooming coupon she has taken from a stack on the window sill. I still had that coupon around the house somewhere though I needed +250 reading glasses to see what she'd written on it.

Now she was teaching advanced placement English at Ipswich High School. I wasn't smart enough for a position like that though it didn't stop me from crowing on a regular basis how it required uncommon talent to contain the free spirits of 6D, how it took a real mastermind to spur them to achievement, and how my best efforts often went unappreciated, making me sound as annoying as one of those students at the high school where she'd done her student teaching.

Wednesday, December 4

Mr. B. sent an email about what to do about kids who couldn't pay the thirty bucks for the field trip (I couldn't get myself to call it *fieldwork*) to see *A Christmas Carol* at the North Shore Music Theater. He wanted the parents of those kids to call or email him for the money.

That's the least they can do, he said. *I'll never turn them down.*

These were the ones always strapped for cash whose kids wore the same clothes and never had a snack or pocket money or even a notebook. So why not just pay the fee and leave the parents out of it? Why make them beg? He agreed finally, though all of us were guilty of harboring resentment when it came to these families. Were they really being straight with us? Then how come they could afford cigarettes, tattoos, cars, movie tickets? Had they been on public assistance so long they expected the school to pay for everything? And why couldn't they go out and work for a living like the rest of us, damn it, and stay home and take care of their kids? There was a fair amount of grousing over the idea that families on the dole enjoyed a gilded life while the rest of us worked night and day to put food on the table. You'd think after seeing the woeful state of these kids and the parents and grandparents who accompanied them to school events that we wouldn't be seduced so easily. But from the nature of our work we were suspicious and insecure and could never shake the feeling we were being taken advantage of. Nothing set us off like some kid claiming he couldn't go on a field trip because he didn't have the money.

Thursday, December 5

I distributed copies of Shirley Jackson's *The Lottery* and read the short story aloud. When I finished the kids looked at me with their mouths open. *What? What just happened?* We discussed tradition and ritual and Old Man Warner warning the villagers never to give up the lottery or else: *Lottery in June, corn heavy soon.* Yes! Now we get it! I found a couple of old videos on Youtube, not knowing if I was overdoing it, if they were too young to handle the content, then I thought to hell with it. They were riveted and that was good. And the theme of *The Lottery*, I realized, was a bit like a teaching career. Every year the profession lost good young teachers because attrition had been going on forever and that was the way it was, a tradition not to be messed with. Except leaving the field wasn't decided by something as random as a lottery. Teachers departing for other careers had sound reasons. I'd known many and envied their self-preservation skills and felt embarrassed when they approached me in the hallway, asking how I tolerated having kids with a wide range of needs dumped into my classroom, administrators burdening us with paperwork and writing up unfavorable evaluations because you'd exhibited a bit of flair that fell outside what they'd expected to see, and overbearing parents running to the principal or superintendent or school committee because you'd undertaken something you considered in the best interest of the kids. I had no answer to any of these questions and would stand there like a dummy, as if someone had just tipped me off to the fact I was being bullied and what did I plan to do about it? Those who chose to leave the profession were sharp, motivated and refused to be pushed around. Armed with these traits, they always did well wherever they ended up.

Friday, December 6

Raelynn asked if I drank coffee as she wanted to get me a pound for Christmas. She'd been living in a motel room since the fire, along with her mother, eight-year-old brother and an aunt just out of rehab. A couple of times a week she brought her brother into class after lunch to give his teacher a break. The siblings sat together at the back table where she helped him sound out his letters and, following her lead, got him to recite one syllable words. For some reason he'd never been to school before this year and just showed up one day. His social and academic skills were in line with those of a four-year-old, he didn't speak, at least to me, and yet his presence had a salubrious effect on the kids who gathered around him, peppering him questions, passing him little treats, congratulating him on taking a stab at those vowel and consonant sounds and especially those tough two syllable words.

That's a real big book you're reading Jamie! We're so proud of you!

When he held up the book with a penguin on the cover, we all cheered. He smiled and nodded and pointed to a word and mumbled something or other, then moved his finger on to the next one. He was just so adorable, so everyone exclaimed, and wouldn't he make a perfect addition to 6D?

Just look how happy he is, Mr. D! said Desiree, a kid who wore work boots, had six cats, and loved to write her name in blue, red and green swirls on the whiteboard. *Can we keep him? Please? We can teach him all his subjects! He can just stay here! And anyway how come he never came to school before this year? Where the heck was he this whole time?*

Monday, December 9

An annual .504 meeting was scheduled in Ms. G.'s office to review Leland's progress and discuss whether he needed the same classroom accommodations he'd had for the past year. Ms. G. and I waited, guessing his mother, father, or both might be tied up in traffic until we remembered neither owned a car. We made small talk about our kids, my retirement, the weather, expecting the parents at any moment to hurry by the office window. They'd told us they were coming and we believed them. Maybe they'd had to arrange for a ride or call the local taxi service. Maybe they were walking or rollerblading. Twenty-five minutes later we were still waiting. We'd give them another five minutes. A school could mandate kids attended every day–dispatching a truant officer to collect them if necessary–but it couldn't make the parents show up no matter how many phone calls were placed, even for the signing of a legal document providing a year's worth of services tailored to their kid's needs. For seven hours we looked after them, while parents, or those who passed for parents (grandparents, older siblings, aunts, uncles, neighbors, the guy living above the garage down the street) had them the rest of the time. Working with a kid with an erratic home life was like hauling around a perforated bucket, the water draining out as fast as it went in. Early in my career I was big on suggestions on how to navigate life's hairier straits (steer away from trouble, confide in a trusted adult, come to school, avoid drugs, alcohol, etc.). Right when a kid was about to make an unhealthy decision, I pictured my stern face with a wagging finger flashing in his head. But how could I understand what he or she up against from one day to the next? How could I control what happened *outside* the school when I could barely control what happened *inside* the school? Still, I couldn't shake the habit of dispensing paternal platitudes on a regular basis, like some classroom Fred MacMurray.

Tuesday, December 10

I asked Mr. B. for a reference today. What kind of job I can get at fifty-nine? Would I hire someone like me given the option? Age discrimination was different from other forms. People my age were more sickly, less energetic, crankier and poorer dressers than those decades younger. Okay, so maybe possessing wisdom compensated for some of those drawbacks but since when was wisdom in demand in the American workplace? I'd likely be reduced to accepting a form of menial labor if I planned to supplement my diminishing pension and contribute to my kids' college tuitions. In my thirty-six plus years employed as a teacher, the financial cushion I'd built by saving frantically had the thickness of a piece of cardboard. My retirement plans didn't include a river cruise on the Danube, rounds of golf in Myrtle Beach or volunteering at a cat shelter. I had to work, and keep on working, into my eighties and maybe beyond, like those red-vested octogenarians who greeted me at Walmart and reminded me to smile every time I walked through the automated doors. They were a happy bunch, and welcoming customers seemed a rewarding job as I always felt better when a stranger said hello to me. I wasn't a smiler but did smile for those elders whose upbeat attitude never seemed anything other than genuine. If I could stay on my feet all day and maintain some degree of emotional equilibrium by not obsessing over Walmart's outrageous profit margin at the expense of workers like me, that would be a gratifying job, saluting the forlorn folk pouring into the Seabrook store anxious to spend their money on cheap imported goods to distract them from the weight of the world.

Today I read aloud another couple of chapters of *Tuckeverlasting* by Natalie Babbitt. Winnie Foster, the novel's main character, lived a life much like the kids of 6D, in spite of her pampered existence as an only child residing in a mansion. Ignored by her parents, nagged by her grandmother, and restricted behind the iron fence of the front yard, she chafed under the demands of a cloistered existence until one summer morning when, having had enough, she escaped into the woods next door where she happened upon the alluring Jesse Tuck drinking from a magic spring.

We discussed the novel's theme: it wasn't how long you lived, it was how well. Would you drink from a spring that kept you changeless, fixing you exactly as you were for all of eternity (If you took a sip now you would be twelve forever! But wait—would you hold off until you were sixteen so you could drive, or until you were twenty-one so you could buy booze?). Then you could run away with beautiful Jesse who had drunk the water himself when he was seventeen, without knowing of its power, and thus he remained seventeen forever. Now he was begging you to have a sip and travel the world with him, promising there was nothing, *nothing*, the two of you couldn't do together? *Well, would you?* And what about The Man in the Yellow Suit who planned to swindle the Fosters out of their land so he could own the spring and bottle the water which he could then sell for a fortune?

Who wouldn't want to live forever? The Man in the Yellow Suit asked.

Not us! we concluded after going back and forth for half an hour. To a person we were adamant about wanting to grow old and gray, feeble and absent-minded, to fall victim to the ravaging diseases of the aged, to wither away and die, soon be forgotten. Anything was better than being fixed on the wheel of life as Jesse's father Angus Tuck lamented as his family's eternal fate.

I'd read the story so many times the lines flowed out of me as if I was an actor on Broadway or a drunk on a street corner. The only sound in the room was my voice, the kids holding their breath in anticipation of how Winnie would deal with this astounding knowledge of the magic spring. *I love, love, love this book,* Lucy told us. Her comment made me wonder how I could duplicate this job satisfaction in my retired life, to have an audience of twelve-year-olds in front of me begging me to keep reading even when it was time for recess.

Wednesday, December 11

By my calculations, I could leave after Christmas vacation though I told Mr. B. I'd stay until June. How many other teachers would work an extra six months while forking over eleven percent of their salary into a retirement fund? Exactly zero. No one was that dumb. The reason for my decision was that, with no idea what to do with myself other than sit around the house all winter wondering how far I could lower the thermostat before the pipes froze, I was terrified to leave. So I generously offered to stay for the kids' sake, which pleased him to no end as he wouldn't have to plug an untested trainee into 6D and deal with the inevitable havoc. Remaining at my post was a big price to pay but at SES I had a place to go, a routine to follow, a connection to people. Around the kids I felt like a skilled person, a needed person, someone viewed as a guy who knew what he was talking about, even if he wasn't sure himself. Fearing departure added ballast to my theory that there was something wrong with me. Other retirees circled the exact day on the calendar when they could walk out the door and never look back, perseverating like felons about their pending release dates. It didn't matter whether the day fell in September, February or May; it was all they talked about. They'd performed their duty and were so drained from the experience of working for a living they couldn't go another minute, nevermind forfeiting a hefty hunk of their salary by doing so. In my case, I didn't utter a word. I pretended the day wasn't coming. When asked about my plans, I brushed them aside. *Retirement? Haven't given it a second thought! My focus is on the classroom!* One of life's biggest steps, demanding thought, planning and emotional balance, was happening to someone else.

Thursday, December 12

The kids were dismissed at 11:40 because of report card conferences. Each parent got fifteen minutes to view and discuss the first trimester report card, a three-page document which looked as if it was published by the IRS. The district report card committee, made up of teachers who regretted having volunteered for it, along with an administrator who oversaw the proceedings, had been up and running for years now and still the document was considered a work-in-progress. A brochure explaining this latest edition accompanied the report card, though parents ignored it, hunting for grades the way parents have done since the inception of public schools in America, hoping to spot something familiar, like one of the first five letters of the alphabet. Finding none, they looked to me to interpret the meaning of all those little boxes and numbers accompanying the many lines of obscure language.

We are in the process of aligning our report card to the Common Core, I began, without acknowledging we'd also been aligning it to the state standards for years before the

Common Core. Each parent listened politely, furrowing brows or clearing throats or shrugging and shaking heads as if to suggest they had more pressing issues to deal with. What they really wanted to know was how their kid was doing and if he acted up in class. They didn't inquire, for example, whether he *writes narratives to develop real or imagined experiences or events, using effective technique, descriptive details, and well-structured event sequences.* Could I just please convey some anecdote which revealed a unique and special characteristic (*He hangs his coat up every day? Really? At home he dumps it on the floor!*) or even some oddball endearing personality trait (*Your daughter lets me know whenever I miss a spot shaving!*)? This was the same stuff I wanted to hear whenever I spoke with teachers about my own kids. I didn't give a damn about Beatrice's latest MCAS scores or Apphia's organization skills or whether Justina liked a particular class (she'd hated school since kindergarten). Neither did I want to hear a description of their beautiful smiles, which was code for *Which one is your kid again?* What I wanted, what every parent wanted, was to see a connection between my kid and the adult she spent her days with.

Friday, December 13

Today, the second afternoon of report card conferences, Daniella's mother filled me on her last few years. She'd left her husband after he'd broken her arm, pushed her down a flight of stairs, and punched her in the face. Then she'd taken him back, become an alcoholic at thirty-nine and ended up in a facility for abused, drug-dependent women. Sober for two years now, she was open about her problems, too open, because after a few minutes I realized she was on a mission, and that mission was to tell everyone what she'd been through, with all its graphic details, to get the story out regardless of whether her audience attended or tuned her out, to keep talking until the listener figured out a way to get her to stop (*Unfortunately our fifteen minutes are up now,* I said, glancing at the clock half an hour later. *There's another parent waiting.*). She had a narrow, drawn face, rings on all her fingers, long yellow nails she tapped on the table, a ski jacket zipped to her throat. She was a good decent person with many struggles trying to do what she considered best for her kid.

Daniella's always liked school, she told me.

She's an excellent student.

Any problems? I mean, she's lived through a lot. I pray every day she doesn't experience what I have.

You're doing a great job.

She worries about me all the time.

In class, Daniella sat in the front row by choice and completed her work before the other kids and charged up to my desk announcing she'd finished and so what should she do now? I'd hand her another worksheet and she'd finish that lickety-split and the cycle would repeat itself until I ran out and would tell her to go read, which she did. She was one of the few kids who could sit at her desk absorbed in a book without distracting everyone around her. She liked to talk and act like a know-it-all which drove the other kids nuts, though perhaps her behavior was a kind of survival mechanism to cover her insecurity and anxiety. Nonetheless I liked her. She was sweet, personable and well-behaved. Her mother and I shook hands and she thanked me for what I'd done for her daughter. I wished her luck and felt after she left the room that I had nothing in my life to complain about.

Monday, December 16

I took the day off to bring Justina to have a cast removed after she'd sprained her wrist six weeks ago. Later I got a haircut, redeemed some empty bottles and cans, bought booze, did some Christmas shopping and went to track practice at the high school where I was an assistant coach. With more than a hundred sick days, all of which would evaporate on the last day of school, I considered banging in sick every Monday and Friday or showing up one week and taking the next off. There was little incentive not to exercise these options as there once was when we were compensated for accrued sick time. That had its drawbacks too—for the district. Each year funds had to be set aside to dispense in a lump sum to retirees. The practice also encouraged teachers to drag themselves to work half dead and contagious with the flu. A dozen years ago during a contract negotiation the policy was changed. Instead of cashing in sick days at the end of her career, a teacher would now receive a matching sum of $400 per year toward a retirement fund. Overnight teachers near the end of their careers who'd stockpiled their sick days in anticipation of a windfall were out a tidy sum and rightly incensed about how their negotiating colleagues had screwed them. So while I hadn't planned on undergoing elective bunion surgery in February, I saw no reason why a teacher who'd saved hundreds of sick days shouldn't use a month's worth to have hers done if she felt like it.

Tuesday, December 17

A substitute named Fred left a note on my desk saying the kids were well behaved, which wasn't the type of message I was used to getting. Anton returned from his trip to Mexico with a small black and red ceramic skull he placed among the collection of wind-up toys and trinkets on my desk. Snow fell by the window while I read the travelogue I'd assigned him to write (the half dozen pages describing his zooming around the mountain town on the back of his cousin's mufflerless moped, throwing up after devouring a pile of French fries smothered in what he'd thought was ketchup, ignoring a *No Swimming* sign on the rocky beach of a swift moving river). I distributed busy work, hoping to keep 6D's minds off the upcoming holidays. From their own history they knew how the next couple of weeks would go with unstable relatives falling off the wagon, no money to buy presents, the false cheer and expectations messing up little routine in their lives. I took my walking/singing eighteen-inch snowman in top hat and tails from a shelf in the broom closet and hoped the batteries weren't dead.

He's adorable! exclaimed Cheyenne. *What's his name?*

Mr. Frost.

Is Mrs. Frost in there too?

We gathered around to watch him slide on his black plastic skis across the linoleum in rhythm to his internal recording of *Frosty the Snowman.* When he bumped into the leg of a desk or the baseboard he had enough sense to reverse himself and head off in another direction. To further test his self-preservation skills, the kids scooped him up and set him on a table. Would Mr. Frost know enough to sense danger when he approached the edge and not be victimized by his own impulsive actions? We were all eager to see how he would handle this challenge. Without hesitation he took off, skiing in a beeline toward the edge until, about to be undone by his own recklessness, he left us no choice but to scoop him out of midair.

We gave him a consoling hug. We all understood. Sometimes you couldn't but help doing what you knew was crazy to begin with. Sometimes a situation got the best of you. Life always seemed to happen when you weren't looking.

Everyone wanted a turn with Mr. Frost. First permission had to be granted for a chance to switch him on. Then he would have to be supervised so he didn't hurt himself.

It's because he can't think before he acts, Brielle told us.

Nothing much got done in these few days before vacation, it being understood that with the kids so amped up why not try something other than usual grind? Clearly at this time of year the usual grind was an even tougher sell. During the holiday concert in the cafeteria I sat in a folding chair in back, 6D spread out cross-legged on the floor in front of me, the indefatigable SES band plugging away on stage (6D members Daniella on flute, Nyla on trumpet, Derrick percussion) impressing us all with their talent, the kids preferring the performance of their peers to that of adults, much like adults, given the choice, preferred the performance of their peers to that of kids. Later I handed out a seasonal word search along with orange highlighters, 6D far from thrilled until I told them it was in lieu of a geography quiz (it wasn't) and promised Dum Dums to all who finished. Word had come down we weren't supposed to show movies (none of us did much anyway but our supervisors figured they ought to step in and save us from our own sloth and incompetence). Whose business was it but ours what we did to survive the week before Christmas vacation? Anyway, showing more than a movie or two made the kids act up even more as they'd seen every one a hundred times. If you decided to choose the movie, it being a favorite of yours, they'd invariably hate it and goof off. And since most of their choices weren't appropriate for school, that left only the lame stuff, narrowed to a handful of titles after a heated class debate, with me making the final decision (*Elf* my top choice).

Wednesday, December 18

With three days left before Christmas vacation, Carla and I shovelled the driveway at 6 a.m. Half a foot of wet snow had fallen overnight on the crusty old stuff, drifting onto the driver's side of the cars and burying the front steps. We were expecting a two-hour delay but when one did not come we pulled on rubber boots, wool hats, insulated gloves and got to work.

Where was the delay? We couldn't understand having to shovel frantically like the rest of our neighbors up and down the street. Though we loved snow days, a delay was preferable to a cancellation. Snow days seemed like a gift until June when the air in the building turned as sticky as a rainforest. Teachers, desperate for the year to be over, fought to engage kids feverish with summer's approach, converting every lesson into a dance routine, scavenger hunt or classroom cleaning exercise to preserve their sanity. No learning got done. With summer's arrival, who did work in all this heat?

Grades are not finalized! I would hear myself say more than once in a last ditch effort to hold 6D's attention (though I'd submitted report cards to the office as requested for Mr. B's perusal a week ago).

It's June! cried the kids. *The school year is over! We can't do no lessons in this stupid oven!*

May I please have your eyes up here! I would order. *Don't make me take away the first five minutes of recess again!*

One year this charade carried on until the thirtieth, the last day of the fiscal calendar, the dozen or more snow days tacked on not enough for Massachusetts school officials to show clemency and grant us a waiver. By the time vacation finally rolled around, all of us–kids, teachers, administrators, custodial staff–were hoping never to see one another again.

I thought about that now as the snow tapered to sleet. Sink or swim, we would do our one hundred and eighty-days, including this one, preferable in its wintry mix to one as hot as a kiln.

Thursday, December 19

We had a *Mancala* tournament today for no particular reason. I'd just learned the game from my own kids so I decided we ought to spend an afternoon playing it. Those who owned a game brought it from home. The rest I scrounged from colleagues around the building. When I told those colleagues what I was doing they regarded me dubiously.

Who would take a chance like that?

I reminded them I was retiring. I could do whatever I wanted.

That must be a special feeling!

Before the tournament I explained to the kids where the game originated and how it was one of the oldest in the world, pointing out North Africa on the map. No one cared. They just wanted to play, grabbing the boards and marbles and spreading out all over the room. Any kid who didn't know how picked it up from those who did. *Mancala* had it all: the soothing feel of marbles rolling around in your palm, the clack of them spinning in cups carved into the wooden game board, a frenetic pace necessitating quick thinking, and enough chance to give everyone a shot at winning. Kids got busy strategizing, shifting the marbles from cup to cup with blazing speed, much faster than I could, my brain no longer able to calibrate at the level required for competency in a game like this. While they were agile and planned ahead I was clumsy and dull-witted, spilling marbles on the floor, getting myself bounced out of each round not long after it began. Amidst the clatter of marbles and the cries of elation or defeat, I considered the risk any teacher other than myself would take engaging in this sort of activity with unannounced evaluations going on, administrators dropping in expecting to see The Initiative being taught, scanning for posters adhering to its SOP, an ear tuned to hear the babble of jargon, etc. Instead, they would find kids hunched over the game board, the teacher playing along, everyone desperate to stay alive into the next round, everyone sharp-eyed, incisive, ebullient. No matter how fervently a teacher tried to explain what the class getting out of it, this activity would be less than conducive to a positive evaluation.

Friday, December 20

On our trip to the North Shore Music Theater to see *A Christmas Carol*, I claimed the small seat in the back of the school bus next to the emergency door so I wouldn't have to share and could doze off on the way home and not be noticed. Other teachers sequestered themselves up front, as did the chaperones, the kids gravitating toward the rear, squishing three to a seat to be as far back as possible. From my seat I could also supervise without having to turn around. Plus no one could give me the finger behind my back. The drawback was that every time the bus hit a bump I was launched into the air and slammed back down, my head jerking forward, my pelvic bones walloping the springs, the shock eliciting a *Shit!* or *Holy Fuck!* The kids, intoxicated by those same bumps and equally excited to witness firsthand my unrestrained use of profanity, somehow anticipated them, shrieking with joy as if we were on a carnival ride.

A few years ago the bus company raised the backs of seats six inches to increase safety, or to keep the kids from climbing over them and having sex, or beating up one another, or whatever. Not being able to see straight ahead without having to grab the top of the seat and haul myself upright was disconcerting as hell. School buses were horrible vehicles anyway—epically uncomfortable, always too hot or too cold, roaring like taxiing jetliners and making my eyes water whenever the kids slid down the windows which for some reason they loved to do even in the dead of winter. My headache lingered, my ears rang, my spine went numb. If they were utilized as public transportation in this country, as they were in Third World countries where the broken-down wrecks got shipped, no sane person would ride them. And why no seat belts? A recent study claimed that if a school bus rolled over, there would be significant casualties. Seatbelts would also keep the kids secured so I wouldn't have to shout *Sit Down!* a hundred times a trip.

Before we left school for the play I received my last Christmas gift tie (this one featuring a button that played *Rudolph the Rednosed Reindeer*), a hot chocolate kit (mug, cocoa tin, tiny marshmallows), a box of green and red M&M homebaked cookies, a tube of hand cream, a can of mints, four ceramic Christmas mugs, half a dozen gift cards for coffee shops, and (perhaps because I was retiring) a large silver magnifying glass. At my desk I opened the gifts in front of the givers. For those looking on who didn't have anything the moment was an awkward one (*Mr. D, I wanted to get you such and such*, someone would say, *but my mother's car wouldn't start so I couldn't get to the store.* That was code for *We didn't have the money.*).

One year a kid presented to me his favorite toy. Without a word, he placed, unwrapped on my desk, a one-armed Max Steele action figure.

What happened to his arm?

My pitbull. His superhuman strength only works against humans.

Are you sure you want me to have it?

He'll be safer here. I can visit him every day.

Max Steele stayed with us until June, warding off evildoers, then returned home to meet his fate with the pitbull, my qualms about accepting him in the first place resolved. The holiday gift giving and all its perturbations were enough for me, back when I taught fourth grade in Woburn, to send a letter home requesting a donation to charity in lieu of a gift. The other teachers got wind of it and were pissed off. New to the school, I'd upset tradition. They liked those gifts because it made them feel appreciated. On my high horse, I was thinking only about those kids who had nothing to give, though I had no idea whether they were embarrassed by the sight of classmates bearing presents or didn't care one way or another. Gift giving has always been part of the teacher-student relationship and it was human nature to show gratitude, so long as the gift's value didn't exceed $50, thereby opening the possibility that as a public servant in Massachusetts I could be in violation of the state ethics code.

Wednesday, January 1, 2014

New Year's Day
This morning in the bitter cold I ran *The Hangover Classic*, a 10k road race along Salisbury Beach sponsored by *The Winner's*

Circle, my running club (and also the name of the bar who supported us and where in return we did our post race rehydrating). At the two-mile mark, Iris and Phoebe were sitting on the curb clapping and cheering without hats or gloves, their jackets unzipped and flapping in the breeze. A small wreck of dog between them restrained by a cord yipped at the runners. Seemingly immune to the weather, they screamed my name and ran a few steps with me, startled and delighted to see their teacher in public, in black Spandex tights, battling the headwind along North End Boulevard with a thousand other frozen souls. Equally excited to see them, I struggled to form a smile on my ice-encrusted face. Nearly inseparable, the two resided in a ramshackle duplex near the beach center, reared by grandmothers tied to oxygen tanks. To further cement their bond, they spoke a street language no one but they understood. Once in awhile I heard snippets in the hallway, classroom, or at recess, odd guttural vocalizations as if they were members of a lost tribe. I'd listened closely to try to translate a few words into English, to attempt to figure out just what they were saying to one another and, more essentially, what they might be saying about me. Similar to twins in height, weight (under what would be considered normal for their age), demeanor and temperament, they addressed one another endearingly as *Naa Naa,* their connection sustaining them through the lamentable circumstances of their lives. That they craved attention and that I was enamored by their personalities meant we spent a fair amount of time together. Their fathers, long absent from their lives, were never mentioned by either of them, which seemed as much a loss for those men as for the kids. Though their reading and writing skills were abysmal, they loved staying busy, rearranging the toys and trinkets I kept on my desk, putting straight the art supply drawers, emptying our blue recycle bin into the dumpster behind the school and taking half an hour to do it, reminding me whenever the paper towel dispenser needing refilling. Proficient at faking it academically, they cradled their binders and textbooks as they walked between classrooms with the erect posture and studious focus of college coeds. Armed with an ample supply of sharpened pencils capped with erasers they safeguarded in bright vinyl cases, they would nod enthusiastically whether or not they had any clue what I was talking about. As they were easily frustrated, I knew enough not to press the issue. Whenever I challenged them to read a paragraph aloud, or write out a few sentences on a topic, they would narrow their eyes and glare at me, crossing their arms and shaking their heads. They had some success with basic primers and learned to construct simple sentences by using word cards which they haltingly read aloud before asking if they could illustrate them. Keeping them engaged required nearly constant exertion but it was not without reward. I learned a lot from them, like how to survive and be happy and find an ally when everything else in the world was stacked against you.

Monday, January 6

Indoor recess on account of rain. A quartet of girls worked on a 750 piece jigsaw puzzle of the Swan Boats in Boston's Public Gardens, beginning at the corners and then holding hands to pray out loud that all the pieces were still in the box. A few boys sprawled on the floor racing Matchbox cars along the lines of the tiles. The rest of the kids shuffled between class-rooms, angling desks into tables and turning chairs around to play cards or dominoes or just sit and chat, trying to forget they were back in school being watched and listened to by us, their teachers, and that, with vacation over, their right of self-determination was again extinguished.

Other than supervised recess, free play was non-existent at SES. What would the role of a teacher when it no longer involved telling kids what to do and how to do it? Here, left alone, they were learning plenty– how to strategize and wait for a turn, how to offer and ask for assistance, to think for themselves and socialize in a civil manner. In fact, once engaged, they ignored me completely.

In my graduate school days, the open classroom was not an uncommon arrangement in public schools. The teacher supplied resources and left kids to learn on their own, alone or in groups, her role one of advisor and mediator. Many thrived in this environment, freed up to follow the path of their own inventiveness, while others sought guidance and desired less commotion. It went the same for teachers. Some thought the loosened format just what they and their students needed, while others chafed in this untraditional role, longing for visible structure and expectations, a library-like atmosphere, and their voice above everyone else's. Like any movement in education, its seams were picked apart by those seeking to find fault with it. What was best for kids, detractors claimed, were lots of rules, direct instruction, frequent assessments. After a decade-long run, the open classroom was roundly mocked for the liberties it bestowed. Once headed for the scrap heap, it was never heard from again. Now we were firmly entrenched on the other side–demanding kids stay in their seats and speak when spoken to, offering them little choice about their own education while force-feeding them a circumscribed curriculum they had no interest in. There was a little clamor to change this type of instruction, which made me think that the general public, thanks to the influence of drill-and-test crowd, had been thoroughly bamboozled.

Tuesday, January 7

Fourteen years ago today I dashed out of SES in the middle of an explanation on desertification, telling the kids my wife was in labor. *What? Right now? What do you mean?* Those kids were twenty-six now and off in the world but I bet they remember the day their teacher bolted from the classroom without his coat, without leaving instructions for whoever would take his place, flying down the stairs and out the front door, falling twice in the icy parking lot and not feeling a thing before speeding south down Route 1 toward Beverly Hospital, nearly forgetting to pick up his wife on the way.

When Apphia was born, Beatrice was one and a half, Justina arriving just nine and a half months later, giving Carla and me, through adoption and biology, three kids ages two and under. She took a leave from teaching and I found odd jobs after school and on weekends–tutoring, coaching, stringing for the local weekly, landscaping. Together we managed, the way couples do in these situations, too preoccupied to think, eat, sleep, or shower, keeping track of every nickel, up nights and sleepwalking through days, she at home with the kids and me at school feeling guilty I had it so easy.

Not long after we'd met I'd informed her I had no intention of having children. If that was the case, she countered, she had no intention of continuing our relationship. We compromised on one kid and ended up with three. To my surprise I found I enjoyed parenting, even suggesting the number might be too low. Carla, crazed and exhausted from its demands, suggested I see a psychiatrist. Late one night, while lobbing a tightly secured diaper across the bedroom toward a plastic bucket, I considered the surge of connection those new to parenthood rave about, even wondering if I was capable of extending that bond to my students. Could I honestly claim my three children deserved more of me because I was their father, the kids of 6D less, the affection I felt mutually exclusive, my students on the other side of that divide? Was something wrong with me for considering such a thing? But still, wasn't the first role of a teacher that of stand-in parent, at least legally? (In the event of nuclear meltdown from the power plant up the street in Seabrook, once I distributed the potassium iodide tablets the nurse stocked to shield young thyroids from radiation poisoning, I would be designated *en parentis loco*, in charge of leading the students of 6D to safety south on Route 1, the main exit out of town during an evacuation.).

Perhaps this bout of inflated reasoning was brought about by sleep deprivation. I was, as my colleague Fay bluntly put it, a walking zombie. Naturally I understood I was a father first, a teacher second, and yet catering to the needs of children ages zero to twelve twenty-four hours a day not only blurred that distinction but made me lose track of what I was saying and to whom. Too exhausted to care about formalities, I permitted whoever saw fit the chance to approach me in my stupefied state and say whatever was on his mind, like my own toddlers when they babbled away without fear of my interruption to correct syntax or to interpret what it was they were trying to spit out. This technique worked just as well with twelve-year-olds. By providing air time they were in no rush to speak, not having to fight to get their words out since in my torpor I was no longer swatting them back in a furious volley. In that sense weren't we all toddlers, yammering away to anyone who'd listen, desperate to be heard, appreciated, loved, hoping not to be contradicted or worse, dismissed and sent on our way? Being a father not only made this clearer, it also made me realize I talked too much as it was, acting like a toddler myself, desperate to get *my* words out there over *theirs*, and perhaps now was a good time to move beyond that particular age group.

Wednesday, January 8

I complained about the frigid conditions in my classroom to Tom, our head custodian, a stocky easy-going guy in his mid-forties who wore Bermuda shorts, cotton gym socks and Patriots tee shirts year round. I, on the other hand, was attired in flannel pants, a long and short sleeve tee shirt, a collared shirt, a sweater, wool socks and Timberlands. He pointed to the monitor in his office next to the boiler room which indicated the temperature in my classroom.

It's right here in black and white.

I put on my reading glasses. A grid displayed the climate in every classroom in the building, including 6D, where the temperature was, as he pointed out, a toasty and unassailable seventy-two.

It feels like fifty up there, I said, disputing the obvious. *I have four layers on.*

Maybe you need a fifth.

I liked Tom. He called up to my classroom whenever he needed a platoon of kids to set up rows of chairs in the cafeteria for any school or town-wide event happening that evening. I was always happy to provide a crew and the kids sprang at the chance for manual labor. For twenty minutes they spun iron dollies of stacked chairs willy-nilly around the lunch room floor, crashing into one another while ignoring all of his directions and hand signals. That was fine with him. He orchestrated their movements with a bemused smile, knowing it was late in the day and everyone was nuts. He was one of the few people in the building who understood the simple yet inscrutable fact that kids were kids and should be treated as such. Eventually he got them to align those chairs in precise rows two feet apart with a six-foot aisle up the middle and proclaimed what an outstanding job everyone had done. All they needed, all anyone needed, according to Tom's worldview, was a bit of fine tuning. Nothing wrong that some fine tuning wouldn't fix. Like a lot of the paraprofessional and custodial staff, he lived in town and knew all the kids and their families. Because of his unruffled style, every kid in the school loved spending time with him and would do anything to be selected to assist with a chore. He was always on me to reconsider retirement, as there were too few men at SES as it was, and we couldn't, according to his estimation, afford to lose another one.

Thursday, January 9

After handing out copies, I read aloud the short story *To Build a Fire* by Jack London, stopping to explain *degrees of frost obtained* and other phrases they didn't understand. I'd never read it to 6D before, suspecting the vocabulary too difficult, the syntax too thorny, the theme too existential. But I'd been wrong, and given the drafty conditions in the classroom, hearing London's description of the weather in the Yukon made us feel warm and grateful. Had I forced kids to take turns grinding through paragraphs or had them read the story to themselves, they would have grown frustrated and given up. By reading aloud I was able to quickly interpret vocabulary without slowing the pace. When we came to the passage where the desperate prospector attempts to strangle the Huskie with the intention of slicing open the dog's flanks and shoving his hands inside as a speedy way of thawing them so he could strike a match to light a fire, everyone looked at me with befuddled expressions. *Wait, was he really trying to kill the dog? Why? What was the reason for that?* He was, but couldn't, as his fingers were frozen into inflexible claws, the dog alert enough to the man's intentions to keep its distance, sensing something amiss, and now, out of chances, the prospector had come to the end of the trail in more ways than one. We debated what we would have done had we been dumb enough to venture out of a warm cabin into conditions as frigid as seventy-five degrees below zero. And we weren't surprised when the dog's instincts trumped the man's hubris.

I found the story on *Youtube*, a grainy black-and-white fifty minute video we watched at the end of the day. *Youtube* was a perfect teaching tool I'd only discovered last year. I could download videos on just about anything (not always having time to preview them, I occasionally showed iffy stuff, the kids consoling me saying they'd seen worse), I was able to reinforce the story we'd just heard.

Abandoning the literacy curriculum map, I decided to read exclusively short stories. It was my favorite genre both for reading and writing. The form was perfect for the kids' attenuated attention spans and after finishing one we ran next door to watch the Youtube version on the Smartboard screen. From there we wrote sequels, read them aloud, revised and illustrated our work for the bulletin board. The process was fairly effortless and the kids never tired of it.

I was still ruminating on my decision to remain until June, figuring I ought to be out in the real world getting the feel of things and not stuck in the classroom trying to come up with lessons which did not involve the hassle of planning. Frankly, I wanted to enjoy the kids and not think about the future. I wanted to spend time gazing out the window at the frozen milky surface of the vernal pond, to be lulled by the moan of those swaying pines. With a new phase in my life about to begin, I figured sooner rather than later I'd have to consider the mountain of buried feelings I had about my career. And yet I also realized that after nearly thirty-seven years these last six months were turning out to be my most enjoyable and stress-free. I was content to sit at my desk offering assistance and encouragement while at the same time not really caring what the kids did. They showed me their work and I told them it was great. They smiled, nodded in agreement and returned to their seats to keep plugging away, getting up when they thought they ought to check with me again. I would scan a paragraph, size up a drawing or a map, chat about a book, offer a suggestion, all while holding my criticism in check. Using this strategy I found that no one's work was turning out better or worse than anyone else's. It was all fine. Hearing me compliment everything they did, they began to compliment one another. It was a different mode of assessment, the antidote I'd been searching for which made for a place where everyone's work was as worthy as everyone else's. If a kid needed help, someone provided it. If someone wanted to provide help, well that was fine too. We worked together, dispensing ideas and helpful tips, everyone free to give or take, everyone saying what a great job his neighbor was doing.

Friday, January 10

Today I gave my annual (and final) *Growing Up* talk, a lecture and discussion scheduled once a year on hygiene and sexuality, usually conducted in the spring, though on occasion earlier in the year. It might take place in November or December, or even as early as October, depending on the number of windows we found ourselves opening after the kids returned from physical education class.

Now forty or so adrenalized boys from all four six grade classes shoved their chairs in front of the TV to watch the dated twenty-minute *Growing Up* video covering adolescent health and human reproduction. In another classroom down the hall the girls were doing the same. Earlier we'd handed out slips of paper for kids to write questions to be addressed by teachers. After the video, I read one aloud–the only one–submitted by the boys.

What is a kliterouse?
It took me a minute to decipher the inventive spelling.
It's a part of the female genitals.
What does it look like?
A dot.
A what?
A dot. A raised dot.
Huh?
It's tiny.
Where is it?
It's a part of the female genitals.
What does it do again?
When stimulated a woman can have an orgasm.
How do you know when you've found it?
They studied my face while I gazed out over their heads at the back wall of the classroom, feeling, given subject matter

and audience, as if I was having an outer body experience. Even though I'd done this numerous times, I had never received any training and was far from comfortable. As the only male teacher on the team, I saw this assignment as mine alone, affronted by any suggestion from colleagues the task might be better handled with some company. I was fine, I told them (not daring to disclose my awkwardness discussing sex with another adult male present). Now, with no choice but to wing it, I left my body and from somewhere above observed myself speaking, affording me the safety of distance as well as infusing me with an air of false confidence. I reviewed what I'd said as matter-of-factly as if I was teaching geography, which in a sense I was. Though I didn't exactly know where the clitoris was located, I acted as if I did, being a teacher and all. They, meanwhile, enraptured by the breadth and depth of my knowledge on this component of female anatomy and its function, stared at me in awe while absorbing everything I said.

From there I wrote *condom* on the whiteboard, asked who knew what it was–some hands went up–and explained its purpose, how to use it, where to purchase one and for how much. I added more vocabulary, steering clear of any unorthodox sexual practices as instructed by Mr. B. A few years ago I would list any word or phrase I could think of on the whiteboard and explain it, slang or otherwise, and then have them call out whatever they'd heard on the street. In the hour I was allotted to teach human sexuality, I tried to impart as much information as possible. As it turned out, one of those kids went home shell-shocked, having never heard any of the terminology we discussed. His father called the superintendent who called Mr. B. who subsequently summoned me to his office. Since every kid was required to return a signed permission slip in order to participate, I assumed the father had a hunch what I might cover.

Did you discuss gay sex, orgies, and gang bangs with the kids?
Mr. B. asked me.

I indicated I had, assuming that was the point of having
a teacher lead a discussion on human reproduction and the
various practices potentially resulting in that reproduction. He
said yes, he understood, relieved I hadn't asked him to assist,
but was it necessary to go into such elaboration? At SES, the
topic of human sexual behavior was restricted to a sanitized
version only, which didn't help the kids out much, since most
had some idea of the general stuff (i.e. sticking your penis in
a girl could get her pregnant). No administrator wanted to
deal with some parent threatening to go to *Fox News* because
his kid's teacher had expounded on blow jobs and threesomes
during a sex ed class. I called the father twice and left messages
about what I'd talked about, hoping by the end of our conversation he might thank me for getting him off the hook with
his son. He never returned my calls.

Having the fixed attention of forty boys on the edge
of their seats hanging on my every word, fearing their classmates might pick up vital facts they missed, was something I
wasn't used to. After handing out complimentary deodorant
sticks supplied by the nurse, I would end our discussion by
adding that we as men, while always needing to be respectful
of women (our mothers and sisters were female, right?) would
think about sex every day–and there was a good chance on
some of those days we would think about sex *all day*–for the
rest of our lives, and how that thinking was normal and okay
and something we couldn't do anything about but which was
nothing to be ashamed of. This eye-popping revelation, along
with everything else we'd talked about during our short time
together, earned me a certain cachet I couldn't duplicate with
any other lesson.

Wednesday, January 15

Rachel, a third-grade teacher, came to see me about her *Needs Improvement* evaluation. As her building representative, was there anything I could do to help? During the observation, rather than forge ahead with new material, she'd reviewed a previous vocabulary lesson to see if the kids remembered any of the words she introduced before Christmas break. As far as The Initiative's strategies went, she hadn't given them much thought, choosing instead to rely on exercises that had worked for her in the past.

Isn't the new evaluation system meant to foster collaboration with the goal of producing better teaching? she asked me.

In theory, I said.

She gave me a puzzled look.

In reality, she corrected, *it seems to have become a tool for targeting those whose teaching style doesn't fit what evaluators expect to see.*

This updated version would finally take care of all those bush league teachers mucking up the cogs of educational progress we'd been hearing so much about on the news. No longer would administrators have to compile detailed forms and sit through due process hearings to terminate someone from a tenured position (officially called *Professional Status*). What was now in place was meant to streamline matters. As a significant amount of time, money, and effort had gone into this new method, it was incumbent on supervisors to get heads rolling. Except, as it turned out, lousy teachers were few and far between. Already there was an outcry in the media over the high percentage of teachers in Boston Public Schools, for example, who'd received a rating of *Proficient* or *Exemplary* on their summative evaluations. What kind of bullshit was that?

The process must have been rigged, or how else could all those deadbeats receive such solid ratings? To further expose the process, the majority of those deemed subpar were minority and older teachers, thus revealing the unconscious bias of the evaluators. Here at SES there was no discussion on how an assessment tool by its nature was undermined by partiality. Where evaluator and teacher on friendly or adversarial terms (Had my role as building representative affected my own evaluation)? A teacher certainly could challenge the outcome, insist on fairness by enlisting help from her building representative, though her evaluator had the final say and the risk was considerable, as she found herself raising a stink against the very person who would evaluate her performance the next time.

Thursday, January 16

At the end of the day Carole, who'd taught fourth grade for over twenty years, came into my classroom to confess that teaching her students how to construct two-column notes hadn't won them over. Their notebooks were a mess, their attention far from undivided, their opinion of The Initiative unequivocally unfavorable. She spent less time reading stories aloud and more time behaving like an engineer with a blueprint. To her The Initiative's strategies felt better suited for high school or college students.

But I have no right to complain, she said. *We're supposed to do what they tell us to do.*

Whenever a teacher dropped by my classroom with a complaint, she would close the door before bringing up an issue regarding working conditions, perhaps suggesting there'd been a violation of the collective bargaining agreement. She would preface what she was about to say by making me promise not to mention her name when I brought the issue forward to either Mr. B. or Maggie, our association president. Maggie would then ask me what was wrong with someone who didn't want her name used by an organization whose sole purpose was to protect her rights as a teacher.

Perhaps elementary school teachers were reticent by nature, or suffered from a persecution complex, or were genuinely afraid to say what was on their minds for fear of reprisal. Many, like myself, having been in school since the age of six, had long ago been conditioned to fear authority, keep quiet, follow orders, and acquiesce to any and all requests from higher-ups. That our own opinions mattered never occurred to us as we'd been told all along that our voices were secondary to those in charge. The profession had always promoted this sort of constraint, having evolved from a time when teachers—predominantly women—were prohibited from marrying, smoking, drinking, keeping the company of men or even chaste socializing in the evening (unless it happened to be a school function). This long tradition of surrendering basic rights and privileges seemed nearly as strong today, at least at SES, and try as I might to convince complainants to forward their names, I was met with a vigorous shake of the head.

Friday, January 17

A neighbor dropped by last night and we ended up talking about her son who attended a private school in Maine. Every morning she drove him to Newburyport where he caught the shuttle van to Berwick. It seemed extreme to me but she'd made the sacrifice because he was always in trouble for refusing to sit at Pine Grove (the same elementary school my three kids had attended, which along with Newbury and SES comprised the three in our district). Five other boys in the neighborhood, according to her, were on medication for ADHD for also refusing to sit down, be quiet, follow directions and stay on task. The problem, as she saw it, was that elementary schools were full of matronly types who expected boys to follow a strict code of conduct, a big part of which demanded they stay put for hours, a compliance they were incapable of carrying out despite dire threats placed upon their heads (When Carla volunteered in Justina's kindergarten class, for example, the class was made to sit on a rug for an hour long ELA lesson. If a student failed to muster the monk-like self-discipline required, he was directed to a separate three by three-foot carpet square and ordered to stay there. And he did, Carla told me, spinning in circles like a bored chimpanzee on a saucer.).

Teachers, at wit's end by this steadfast refusal of young children to tow the line, would introduce the topic of ADHD to the parents, suggesting the kid get checked out by his pediatrician who in turn would send to school a behavioral checklist (number of times he interrupts, gets out of the seat, needs redirection, etc.) for the teacher to fill out. Nine times out of ten the kid ended up on medication, the time-released pill making him do what he was supposed to do, suppressing those fidgety impulses that drove the teacher nuts. But, of course, he wasn't the same kid, as he now had a diminished appetite, sleep issues and bouts of moodiness.

In defense of those exasperated matrons, I myself had undertaken similar action. A kid would show up in September I had no idea what to do with. He'd bug the other kids who in turn would bug me to get him to stop, roam around the classroom in spite of my exhortations to take a seat, fiddle with pencils, paper clips, erasers, water bottles, and whatever other items he felt the need to amass in his desk, interrupting me while I listed the major exports of Tunisia on the whiteboard. I'd finally get his attention only to lose it thirty seconds later. Repeated efforts got me nowhere. Despite producing little or no work he garnered more of my attention than anyone else. It wasn't long before I had all I could do not to strangle him. One solution was daily vigorous physical exercise, a half-hour session in the morning and afternoon, but that wasn't an option at SES. So I'd get to the point where I'd mention this conduct to his parents, outlining specifics in an unemotional tone like a trial lawyer leading a witness, asking questions about his behavior at home I knew the answers to, eventually getting them to come around so by the end of the meeting they were thanking me for my insight and concern. A few days later the kid would arrive at school clutching an envelope from his pediatrician containing a three-page checklist. I was well aware of what I was doing, encouraging parents to medicate their kid to make my life easier, and for a while I would feel guilty and tell myself I wouldn't take this easy out anymore, that he was the last one. By hook or by crook I'd devise a strategy that worked for the next kid. But once the drug kicked in and he was subdued, compliant, staying in his seat and using the bathroom twice a day instead of half a dozen, acting like *a normal kid*, doing what everyone else was supposed to be doing, I'd tell myself medication wasn't so bad after all. So what if his personality had changed. Maybe he wasn't as witty or quirky as he'd been a month ago, maybe he didn't want to eat his snack, or nodded off because he wasn't sleeping, but was that such a big deal now that he was *attending and learning* (that is, doing what I wanted him to do)?

Monday, January 20

No school–MLK Day.

On Friday I gave a talk about Martin Luther King, civil rights and segregation, describing separate water fountains, schools, restaurants, blacks sitting in the back of buses, etc.

What country is this again? Cheyenne interrupted.

America, dummy, replied Leo.

Salisbury?

Not here, in the South, I said.

How black was black? Tanner wanted to know.

What? I asked.

You know, was there like a test to see who had to go to those crappy schools depending on how dark you were? If you were Latino did you have to go?

I don't know, I said. *I never thought about that.*

Sierra called Tanner a racist. He said it was no crime to ask your teacher a question. That was why you went to school, to get answers to your questions. She didn't care. He was still a racist. Well, if he was a racist, then she was a slut. They refused to apologize until I threatened to call their parents. My effort to steer our conversation toward a discussion of nonviolence, to get them all to see what MLK had accomplished, with the goal that we might apply some of his tactics to ourselves in 6D, at least as far as tossing insults back and forth went, failed miserably, as they were now more intrigued by who would end up in those rotten schools, who would make the cut and who wouldn't.

Would Sierra have to go?

Sierra, fuming over Tanner's insult, had forgotten what we were talking about.

Me? What? Go where?

Nowhere, I said.

Yes she would, Leo corrected. *Anton too and probably Phoebe.*
Not me, said Phoebe. *I would never go to one of those places.*
They'd make you go, said Tanner.
Who?
Police with guns and tear gas. And their dogs would bite you in the butt. I watched a show once.
Okay, let's get back to MLK and what he stood for.
Who's MLK?

I soldiered on, both because of King's legacy and because it was my job to make them care about important topics. Countless times throughout the year I struggled to link some important social issue (the environment, civil liberties, climate change, immigration, etc.) and ourselves, hoping to glean and fortify a salient point or two that might make us better people, more perceptive and compassionate, and they in turn would take possession of whatever issue I was holding forth on and do whatever the hell they wanted with it. *Fine,* I would think, *they have every right to express what's on their minds.* And for a while, seeing them engaged, I would play along, doing my best to pilot the discussion back to where I thought it ought to go. Except, despite my best effort, there were times like this when it would spiral downward from its lofty height, ejecting any of its *teachable moments,* and explode into an outright argument. At that point the only workable solution to dissolve the tension was to issue the entire class a bathroom break.

Tuesday, January 21

Nyla was spinning in circles and tapping her head against the wall as we waited to go into technology class. I asked her what she was doing.

Trying to figure myself out.

I held shoulders to steady her.

I haven't been sleeping.

A week ago she'd moved into a fourth-floor apartment where a staircase ran along an exterior wall, the bedroom having a door opening onto the landing. Strangers trooped by all night and she worried one might take a wrong turn and stagger into her room, the flimsy door offering little protection against the marginal types residing in the building. How was she supposed to sleep with the possibility of being awoken to something like that?

Short, cute, freckled-faced and connected to an ever-running generator, she was skilled enough to zip through her work for the pleasure of announcing she'd finished, jumping from her seat and waving the assignment as if it were a winning bingo card. Thus I was forever hunting for something to keep her occupied. Our social worker Greta labelled her a *pot stirrer* which I thought was an apt description. But I liked her for-the-most-part pleasant personality.

Why don't you lock the door?

It is locked.

What about moving into a different bedroom?

My mother and her boyfriend have the other room. Mine's too small for them.

I nodded, out of ideas. She went back to spinning in circles, trying to figure herself out.

It was late in the day and we were waiting around for Sam to come out of the bathroom. Already two minutes into my planning period, I had the kids lined up against the wall in a half-assed attempt for order which they wanted no part of, preferring instead to make noise and chase one another around, using their *outdoor voices* and lurching into one another for the sheer pleasure of physical contact. They were on his watch now–*three minutes into my planning period already!*–and this teacher, this friend of mine, was in the bathroom, relieving himself *on my time*, an unforgivable offense, and although he had the worst job in the building, cooped up all day in a stuffy room full of computers, I did not feel the least bit sorry for him. Yet once I saw him walking toward me, I morphed back into someone with a modicum of understanding. Here was a person capable of an adult conversation!

How's work on the boat going? I asked (Sam hoped to run a deep sea fishing charter out of Newburyport over the summer.).

It's a boat, he reminded me as he directed the kids inside to their assigned stations. *A hole you shovel money into.*

A decade ago he'd left the soul-sucking world of high tech office work only to find himself stuck in an interior classroom with no windows. He loved to hunt and fish, had done some skydiving and enjoyed preaching the merits of the Great Outdoors to the kids which they in turn were able to view on their monitors. Both of us were close in age, had three kids, along with two sets of parents needing looking after.

So how many days? he asked. *I hate you, by the way.*

I won't take it personally.

Can you do me a favor? See if you can find me a window. That one's not cutting it.

He pointed to a poster of a window overlooking a meadow which he'd tacked to his bulletin board.

I'll see what I can do.

Wednesday, January 22

Two inches of snow fell overnight. Along with the usual midwinter bouts of the flu, the fluffy accumulation was enough to keep almost half the class home, leaving me with a dozen kids whose expectations, given the circumstances, was that I have no expectations.

There's only twelve of us! We can't have class with just twelve kids!

Since outdoor recess was cancelled (the office declaring a couple of inches of snow detrimental to student health) and having no outlet in which to release their bottled ardor, they were amped up and united in their resistance to doing anything other than what they wanted to do, that being to sit around and do nothing. I had no intention of indulging them, past days like this having taught me that however they chose to occupy themselves, the results within a few minutes were generally chaotic. Instead I promised something fun, but knowing their idea of fun and my idea of fun resided in different galaxies. I couldn't think of anything to do which might exist in their definition of the word and not dissolve into disorder ten minutes after it had commenced.

How can we start a lesson with so many kids absent? asked Thad.

He had a point. Anything I started I'd have to repeat whenever the rest of the class appeared. It came down to a judgment call based on percentages. If, for example, twenty-five percent of the kids were missing, should I start something new or wait for them to return? What if attendance continued to lag? How long could I remain in a holding pattern? Then again, if I forged ahead, a quarter of the class would have no idea what was going on once they turned up, necessitating a teach-over and boring the hell out of the other seventy-five percent.

Can we do jumping jacks instead? asked Raelynn.

We could. We did. A hundred jumping jacks, led by Raelynn, who through the course of her bumpy existence had somehow mastered this particular exercise. She positioned herself at the front of the room like a fitness instructor and yelled at anyone slacking off for not slapping their palms over their heads.

Hey no fake jumping jacks!

She counted, we all joined in–58!, 59!, 60!, 61!–while the floor trembled and the third-grade teacher below waited for us to come crashing through the ceiling. No one finished in the same place where they'd begun. Why was that? I started next to my desk and ended up in another corner of the room. Everyone was everywhere.

How did I get over here to this place here? Iris wondered, bewildered.

The exercise killed all of two minutes. Gasping, they plunked down into their seats and stared at me. *What now, Mr. D?* Out of breath myself, I had no idea. But as if I'd planned it all along, I strode over to a shelf behind my desk and did something I vowed I would never do: I stole from my substitute folder. It had sat on the same shelf for years, stocked with worksheets that would keep 6D from driving a substitute nuts – *fun* worksheets, which sounded like an oxymoron but which consisted of puzzles, word searches, and geometric coloring designs. A thick elastic band secured the folder and kept me from removing anything whenever I had the urge. Lots of times I wondered why I kept all the good stuff for the sub, but knowing what his or her day was like, how $75 hardly compensated for the exertion required to contain 6D (some subs wouldn't take my class), making the task a bit easier seemed like the moral and just thing to do. Now I removed a few sets of those worksheets, determined to replace each with twice the number to penalize myself and promised never to take from this folder again. The kids looked them over, graciously thanking me for distributing these exciting activities.

Hey, said Barrett. *This looks like the fun stuff the sub gives us!*

Thursday, January 23

Today as we left the cafeteria after lunch a kid from another sixth-grade class collapsed to the floor in front of me and grabbed his crotch. Lying in a fetal position, he blocked the hallway, howling and remonstrating and demanding I administer justice to the culprit who assaulted him. A couple of times a year a boy would pull this stunt, proclaiming that he was just walking along minding his own business when so-and-so belted him in the nuts. It was always in a packed hallway with a lot of girls around and I was never quite sure whether to believe the kid or ignore him so I ended up pulling aside the alleged perpetrator who then announced to all present that he had no idea what I was talking about. I confronted the victim who also proclaimed his innocence. I then proceeded to lecture about endangering hallway safety only to hear *I was kicked in the balls and I'm being punished!* or *You have to believe me, Mr. D, I had nothing to do with it!* If I took no action, the 'victim' would pull the same maneuver again with even more zeal. If I handed out a punishment (e.g. taking away a recess) and the accused had done nothing wrong (or convinced his parents thus), I'd hear it from the parents and likely my supervisors. So I warned the two and sent them off to class. Undertaking to sort out incidents when I hadn't seen what actually happened oftentimes created more problems than if I just sent those involved on their way with the simple command: *Go to class.*

Given the personalities in SES, we spent a good portion of our day sorting out squabbles and aiming to teach good behavior. But in a school with a sizeable population of nonconformists we discovered that the antics we did not want to reinforce were indeed being promoted by those who saw it as their duty to act as role models for poor deportment. Ironically, singling out and disciplining these types only heightened the status they enjoyed among their peers. During my intervention, while I attempted to figure out who had done what, a crowd gathered in support behind the alleged victim whose facial expression had gone from a mock wince to a wry smile. The longer I lectured about inappropriate behavior during transition times, the wider the grin became, unleashing a surge of fury that seemed to lift the scalp off the top of my head. Still, this physical reaction wasn't enough for me to end the matter then and there and walk away. In my perturbed state, even if no one cared to listen, even if I was being made fun of, I had to have the last word.

Friday, January 24

The kids were always hounding me for a chance to meditate. Once I put in the CD, they sat up straight and folded their hands on their desks. Before I turned off the lights I reminded them about maintaining correct posture, following the breath, letting thoughts go, etc. They knew the drill, as we'd been doing it since the start of the year. Whether they genuinely liked it or saw it as a legitimate reason to get out of work didn't matter. Practicing put them at ease, each session a bit less foreign than the one before so at this point the routine had grown safe and comfortable. Afterwards every kid proclaimed how much better he felt, relaxed and hopeful, some volunteering to share vivid images and sensations popping up in their minds, others sitting and saying nothing, some pushing to go longer. I would sit with them in that calm space, none of us in a hurry, the one time of the day we were able to access a quiet and reflective refuge, everything else on hold, this rare contemplative side startling me, so overpowered was it by the other side, the mania triggered by the overstimulated environment we found themselves in, and of course me a major part of that environment. Seeing the kids like this I would thereby resolve to provide more opportunities, but soon we would be swept back into the enterprise of getting through the day, executing chores and duties and responsibilities all because we felt compelled to, and it was easy to forget what moments like this did for us.

I'd begun practicing meditation myself in the spring of 1987. Thirty-two at the time, I lived alone in a street-level, drabby four-room apartment a hundred yards from a commuter rail line. I was also in the last few months of a two year teaching stint in an alternative high school which was completely unravelling me. I hated the job, I couldn't sleep, and, most pressingly, I was preoccupied that something was physically wrong with me. Convinced I was dying from *something* and *soon*, my suspicion was liver disease, as I'd contracted hepatitis in 1979 while working as an aide in a day program with developmentally delayed teenagers who resided at Fernald State School in Waltham. One of my students was a carrier (unbeknownst to me) and part of my job was to assist him with toileting (this before the era of latex gloves to clean up vomit, blood, and feces.). For two weeks after my diagnosis I collected workmen's compensation until the yellow faded from the whites of my eyes and I could return to work. Eight years later, morbid and depressed, my unshakeable faith in my own demise from my self-diagnosed chronic hepatitis making me unbearable to be around, I ignored my therapist's suggestion I submit to a blood test (which would only confirm what I already knew to be true). Instead I embarked on a macrobiotic diet as my one and only chance for survival. After doing some research, I eliminated fats and sugar, subsisting on sea vegetables, brown rice, miso soup and an occasional tin of sardines as a treat. Starving myself in an effort to return to health, I dropped twenty pounds from my already thin frame, my pants hanging from the ridges of my hips, my ribcage protuberant, my clavicles and cheekbones appropriated from a cadaver, my libido extinguished, and my self-esteem nonexistent (especially after I caught sight of myself in a storefront window). The outcome of my health regimen scared the hell out of everyone I knew.

At the end of my rope, I found my way to a free Tuesday night meditation class for beginners at the Cambridge Insight Meditation Center. What startled me was the number of people in the carpeted basement unlike me–guys carrying hardhats and metal lunch boxes, grandmothers too arthritic to sit on floor cushions, two teenage girls who giggled through much of the session, all of us anxious basketcases. Though the benefits didn't come without a struggle (was everyone sitting cross-legged in as much pain as I was?), I came away with a glimpse of clear mindedness, a touch of respite, and enough of a dividend to return the next week. Determined to get the hang of it, I started meditating on my own, pushing to breathe for five straight minutes, managing two or three, then restarting until I reached my goal. Bit by bit I edged forward in small steps, gaining some distance from the cloud of dread riding my shoulder. If I could meditate, I figured, anyone could, so I taught the practice to my students, asking them to sit quietly and breathe for a minute, a long time for twelve-year-olds. They loved the challenge and begged for more, not only to prove they could do it but because it offered them what they couldn't get anywhere else. After numerous attempts we worked up to five full minutes though what we'd achieved wasn't without resistance. Every year a few kids were uneasy with the silence, the act of sitting and breathing with their eyes closed (or focused on a spot on their desk tops) or else outright refused to do it, or were from religious families where meditation conflicted with their beliefs. So I would tell those kids to just sit or pray or go hang out in the hallway until we were finished.

When the taped ended, I asked 6D about their worrying habits–what they worried about, whether worrying occupied much of their time, etc. Yes, yes, they all agreed, it did. They worried about what people thought or posted about them, about their performance in school and in sports, their looks and personalities, whether they would get cancer or go blind or end up paralyzed, whether that would happen to someone they loved; they worried they were failures, they couldn't sleep, had done something for which they would never be forgiven; they worried that they would end up alone and abandoned. They were always worrying, which was why they chewed their fingernails and got migraines and bellyaches and had no appetite or else couldn't stop eating junk food, why they weren't able to pay attention and remember to do what they were supposed to do even when they got yelled at for it. For sure they worried more than anybody else on the face of the earth. It was as much a part of them as their own names. I listened and had no idea what to say except to tell them they were normal. We all worried, and worried a lot, and the way they felt right now, composed and confident and maybe not worrying so much, was a state they could return to anytime, just by breathing in and out for a few minutes. What could be easier than that? They looked at me and nodded, allowing the idea to sink in. Yeah, okay, that sounds like something we could all do.

Monday, January 27

During our weekly team meeting we debated the topic of prompts for our next writing assessment. From a list generated from sixth-grade teachers district-wide we were supposed to come to a consensus. Complaints abounded about each suggestion (too confusing, requiring background information, necessitating a skill such a map reading, etc.) with us eager to promote our own choices and point out the weaknesses in our colleagues'. Martha, our reading/writing/data specialist, jotted down and scratched out our feedback because we kept changing our minds. She arrived at these meetings armed with a stack of loose leaf binders and a stout resolve to remain unflustered. I finally cracked that resolve by asking whether we needed prompts in the first place.

Why are you saying no prompts? my colleagues demanded to know.

What if we told kids to write on whatever subject they chose? Then they wouldn't have to interpret a prompt.

But what will they write about if we don't tell them what to write about? they asked. *What about the time and energy all of us have put into the brainstorming and discussion of these prompts? Are you proposing we trash everything in favor of no prompts at all? That we hand kids a piece of blank paper? Are you being serious?*

Well that was the silliest idea they'd heard in a long time. What were kids supposed to do with a piece of blank paper in front of them? How could they possibly come up with a topic to write about on their own?

My idea to dismiss prompts was promptly dismissed. In a way I understood. Again, how would kids know what to do if we didn't tell them what to do and how to do it? Life at

SES had always been this way and here I was turning tradition on its ear. What was wrong with me? By now I'd come to the conclusion that what I had to say was being ignored with even more dispatch than usual, as I was retiring in five months and what did it matter anyway?

Tuesday, January 28

A trio of boys–Leland, Thad, Ivan– stood over the wastebasket sharpening their pencils. One would get out of his seat and the other two would stop whatever they were doing and pop up to join him. Shavings drifted inside the wastebasket, or were caught on the plastic liner or ended up on the floor. It didn't matter to them one way or the other. The three would glance out the door to take in any hallway activity while shooting the breeze, their fingers twirling those pencils shoved into hand-held sharpeners. The fact that I was standing six feet away introducing a lesson on Thailand's monsoon season didn't matter to them in the slightest. They were sharpening their pencils was all, and how could they do their work if the tips were broken?

Every year I ordered boxes of inexpensive sharpeners which I distributed whenever a kid asked for one. But because they were cheap, the blades didn't hold an edge and it took forever to get a serviceable point, and with the pencils I also handed out being cheap too, this combination necessitated endless trips to the waste paper basket (the point falling out once it had been honed). Because I couldn't prevent kids from sharpening their pencils (there was a school policy forbidding the use of pens as kids couldn't erase, the inky mess making their writing even more illegible), the trio, having discovered a loophole which allowed them to socialize under the auspices of acceptable class-room behavior, made regular trips to the front of the room. Though I admired their ingenuity, particularly since they knew I was powerless to do anything about it, this interruption irritated the hell out of me, for I longed for control and order and they longed to push this undefined limit, getting up three or four times, nodding to me, gesturing toward their destination and clutching their second-rate sharpeners and pencils, letting me know it was all good, this ritual of theirs required for the increased work production I was forever preaching about. The old manual sharpener screwed into a bookcase devoured pencils down to nubs and was hard to manipulate, and thus ignored, while the electric one (I'd purchased a few over the years) roared like a blender and so the kids loved it, grinding their pencils so the blades dulled after two weeks, rendering these machines useless too. So I had to permit endless daily wastebasket-gatherings, and as I was not good at letting things go, I was forever telling them to hurry up and finish.

We're almost done, Mr. D. See? said Ivan, holding up his pencil.

You've been standing there a full two minutes already.

We're going as fast as we can.

Not fast enough.

We're trying.

Try harder.

We are trying harder.

Do you know what it's like to have to teach with three people sharpening pencils and talking beside me?

We're almost done. Look, see?

Hurry up and hurry then.

I could have allotted a designated time for pencil sharpening, but pencil tips broke/were broken all the time. And honestly, I needed a chance to verbalize all the injustices heaped upon me, to let them know what it was like to haul us through the school day when faced with one indignity after another, to push a maddening curriculum in spite of obstacles thrust up in front of me. And fair or not, they had to listen, trapped in the room and knowing what would happen if they told me off. Their only defense was to tune me out, which they had perfected, having had years of practice with others just like me.

Wednesday, January 29

I left before lunch and drove to the middle school to sign Apphia out for a periodontist's appointment. Both middle school and high school shared the same campus, cinder block structures connected by a long low hallway with little natural light and not much artificial light either. How did kids read their combinations or find anything inside their lockers? Rows of those lockers were divided by solid steel classroom doors with wire-enforced vertical glass, more arrow slits than windows, like you'd see on a cell door. In fact, the whole place had the bleak feel of a penitentiary. The dismal picture of my three children spending their days there was counterbalanced by the comfort I felt imaging an intruder attempting to breach those fortified doors and portals. The glass panel doors of SES classrooms, on the other hand, seemed especially designed to be smashed by a brick, bat, or boot heel. Even the exterior doors of SES consisted of large glass panels. In an era when incidents of school violence had lost their shock value, our school, only fourteen years old, presented little challenge to anyone wishing to gain entry. Whenever we had a lockdown I bolted the classroom door and clicked off the lights as instructed and hurried the kids into a far corner where we would crouch down by the sink and out of the line of fire hoping that a drawn breath wouldn't be audible enough to give us away. Silent and perspiring, ears perked for the slightest of sounds from the hallway, we knew all an intruder had to do was to kick in the bottom panel, step over shards of glass and find twenty-two sitting ducks squatting under the paper towel dispenser. None of the kids ever brought up this obvious shortcoming and I, not wanting to terrify them any more than sitting through lockdowns wondering if this was the real deal already did, didn't remind them. And if all this wasn't enough to fuel our sense of paranoia, right next door to SES stood *Original Bob's Gun Shop and Shooting Range*, voted the most popular public shooting range in Massachusetts.

Thursday, January 30

Martha dropped by my classroom while I was eating lunch to give me a spreadsheet of data she'd collected from assessments I'd done. A large part of her job as reading/writing/data specialist was to conduct meetings, whether here or at Central Office, where she labored until six or seven in the evening checking and rechecking all those numbers, trying to keep straight what statistics went with what assessments and which meeting. She and I complained about the current state of affairs, the tasks we were ordered to carry out which made little sense but which we had to do anyway. Her two young boys were forever breaking one bone or another playing football and ice hockey, causing her to drop everything and rush off to the ER after getting word on her cellphone. When they were healthy she was guilt-ridden about leaving school to watch their games, as if she ought to go on analyzing data until midnight. Her job description was anything but static, always changing for the worse, with additional duties handed down to be piled on top of the ones she already didn't have time to finish.

Last year, at the behest of Ms.G., she'd come to help me straighten out those geography groups and demonstrate the proper manner in which The Initiative should be taught. Arriving late in the afternoon when the kids were sliding out of their chairs and at the mercy of every impulse, she displayed such an easy-going manner that I worried for a moment that all hell might break loose. How, at this hour, could she possibly get them to align those tricky two-column notes? Would they even listen to a word she said? But right off they took to her, sensing she was the type of teacher unafraid to tell them about herself. She confessed she loved to shop, had two sons around their age who played hockey and had the broken bones to prove it, and that before she had kids she'd scuba dived for lobsters off the coast of Gloucester.

Where do you get your hair cut? asked Sierra. *I love it! Your shoes too. Did you used to be a model?*

What bones specifically? asked Karter. *I have a bone collection.*

That's so creepy, said Desiree. *Yuck!*

Did you ever run out of air? asked Barrett. *Were you ever with someone who did and tried to grab your regulator away from you? Did you carry a Bowie knife strapped to your leg?*

After just a few minutes everyone sensed Martha was a genuine caring person they could trust and who was fun to be around. She clearly understood how kids operated and enjoyed being with them. I thought she'd be happier and less frazzled as a classroom teacher, as her role as reading data specialist seemed more about burdening staff through mandated directives than assisting us with comprehension strategies. The mounting fiats had her apologizing every time she told us what we were supposed to do next. When she came around looking for the results of my latest reading assessment I would pretend to hide in the supply closet before begging for more time, to which she would always smile and acquiesce.

Friday, January 31

By luck I'd unearthed a stack of dusty reading texts in a storage closet in the staff lunch room. Published in 1972, they'd belonged to a fifth grade teacher who retired three years ago but were still in halfway decent shape, the pages dog-eared, the illustrations faded but the print large and in clearly readable format. Even so, some kids couldn't get through a paragraph without help. Others, behind grade level themselves, didn't fare much better. And of course adding to our woes was the usual lack of focus. No sooner had I handed out the books and had a chance to rave about my discovery than I was throwing Leland out of class for grunting like a buffalo. After reinstating him I ejected Cheyenne for telling him he made more sense when he grunted than when he spoke. Apropos of nothing she put her head between her knees and began to brush out her long tresses in brisk strokes, ignoring my requests to style her hair at home. I removed Ivan from the room for calling Leland and Cheyenne losers. In the hallway he brought his hands together in supplication, a last-ditch plea for a second chance before I called his mother. What seemed like seconds after his return to class he was off task again.

Dealing with abysmal reading skills and erratic behavior drained me by mid-afternoon. Even the special education services a third of the class received couldn't keep pace with the demands of whatever grade they happened to be slogging through. And with me as their teacher they were falling even further behind. I'd hoped these lower grade texts would give them a shot to read with more proficiency, to advance with minimum effort from paragraph to paragraph without getting snagged on every third word. Despite the immature and dated content (e.g. a young girl pushing a doll carriage through a city park comes upon a bluebird nest) or maybe because of it, they enjoyed the stories, though at times I would take over, frustrated by the pace dictated by a reader using his finger to keep track of those two and three syllable words (whenever someone hesitated, his peers would pounce on the word for him, ignoring my pleas to give him a second or two, my own patience nearly as thin as theirs). Though they all professed a desire to become better readers, understanding this would make their lives easier, their impulsiveness overrode any motivation and there was little I could do about it. Thus our afternoons became pitched battles, me fighting to maintain my waning cool while encouraging them along, and they hunched over texts nodding away as if they were real honest-to-goodness readers.

Monday, February 3

Time magazine ran a cover story about the benefits of mindfulness with instructions on how to meditate. Were you able to sit in a chair? Could you breathe on your own? Then you were the perfect candidate! I handed out copies of the article, thrilled that what we'd been doing had legitimacy in the outside world. I even promising to play the fifteen-minute tape if the kids continued to show me they could handle the five minute one. All you had to do, I reminded them, was sit up straight and take long slow breaths. Who couldn't manage that for fifteen minutes?

Meditation, I added, could help them in their regular lives too, regardless of the jam they found themselves in. If someone got on their nerves, all they had to do was breathe. If they couldn't sleep or had a dentist appointment or lost their phone or forgot their homework, a few minutes of breathing would set things right again.

Some years ago, after reading about movie director David Lynch's effort to introduce meditation into public schools, I contacted his foundation to ask for assistance. The foundation sent a couple in their fifties, veteran instructors in Transcendental Meditation, both dressed in white linen from head to toe, she in a long dress and he in a suit and tie. Soft-spoken, willowy, and oozing the type of calm and focused awareness that made me think I was the most antsy and mindless person on the face of the earth, they presented a folder of information to Mr. B., myself, and my friend Kate (my colleague who'd donated the boombox, read to us every morning from her book of affirmations, and like to inspire the kids by playing a CD of Barbra Streisand's greatest hits). Research articles and teacher testimonials inside the folder outlined how meditation had helped thousands of kids no matter what their issues by reducing stress, increasing concentration and enhancing self esteem. Mr. B. and I both knew that even with this reassurance, a formal meditation practice would be a hard sell to both district and parents (I wasn't entirely sold on his position either). The T.M. instructors asked for a two-year commitment to follow progress from one grade to the next. But because our sixth graders would be moving onto the middle school in June and we had no control over what happened there, that wasn't possible. So the program didn't get off the ground, though since then I'd tried to boost meditation time, to elaborate on ways it could help kids negotiate the struggles of their daily lives. Some told me they practiced on their own, sitting alone in their bedrooms, or brazenly right out in the open where everyone could see them, enduring quizzical looks from parents and taunts from siblings.

Tuesday, February 4

During recess, having no protection from solar glare bouncing off the snow, I squinted through my balled fists as if holding a pair of binoculars, eyeing a scrum of boys wrestling for a football out on the ballfield. From where I stood on the basketball court I could see bodies flying, kid pile driving one another into the frozen white surface. A girl next to me mentioned something about a fistfight so I tromped across the crusty snow in my loafers and thin socks, bits of icy crystals tumbling inside. Everyone I interrogated denied knowing anything about said fight despite snow clinging to eyelashes, packed into ears, up nostrils and under collars, patches of it chapping faces and watering eyes. I stood there, numb and snowblind, glad to have them running around and not marooned on the pavement the way some teachers restricted their classes. A chilly northeast wind swept over the open field with no effect on the kids in unzipped jackets and untied sneakers. In that moment the wind eased and the sun high in a radiant sky delivered a touch of warmth to my cheeks. Unexpectedly I found that I was happy. Why here? Why now? Where had this bliss come from all of a sudden? How might I get it to last? Fearing even a twitch might shake off this pixie dust, I remained absolutely still, holding onto this unexpected measure of contentment. Now used to my presence and concluding no disciplinary action was forthcoming, the boys resumed chasing and tackling one another. I barked without conviction *Hey No Tackling* into the wind but no one heard me and so nothing changed and that was fine too. I closed my eyes to the sounds of cavorting, voices carrying and bodies flying. In the middle of the tundra with the wind at my back, I listened to this gleeful tumult until the tweet of the whistle from my colleague Adelle back on the pavement signalled the end of recess. Straightaway the boys stopped what they were doing and rushed past me toward the cafeteria doors, mad with hunger and desperate to get to the front of the chow line. A green jacket left behind spread itself over a patch of unbroken snow. I moved toward it and picked it up. Would its owner remember it was his? How did a person forget what he had worn to school a few hours earlier, or wore every day, like this jacket, especially in the dead of winter? Not recognizing their own clothing was a particular problem with twelve-year-olds. Whenever I held up a sweatshirt or coat which had resided at the bottom of the cubbies for a month I was met with blank stares and shrugs, either because nobody remembered it was his or was too embarrassed to say so because of its condition, and so off it went to Lost and Found and from there to resupply the nurse's closet.

Wednesday, February 5

No school because of a nor'easter. Living in New England, I had another job every winter, one that beat the hell out of me and for which I received no compensation. That job was snow removal. I shovelled the driveway, the walk, the stairs, the roof of the back porch where snow drifted over the bedroom windows, and then went back and cleaned off the cars. Then did it two or three times over the duration of a storm. Rigorous mindless work offered balance to the cerebral ordeal of instructing sixth graders. I'd swing the wide blade of the shovel into the snow, steady a wobbly tower before tossing it with a *whump* off to the side. I cut a path and doubled back, lifting each load just high enough over what I'd already piled, stripping off layers until I was down to shirtsleeves, not stopping until I hit bare ground. Later, by the woodstove, I fell onto a soft armchair and pulled off two pair of wet wool socks and drank a couple of cups of strong tea, my head clear and body relaxed as only exhausting physical labor can provide.

During my graduate school days I worked as an aide in a day program for developmentally delayed adolescents. One of my students, a manic sixteen-year-old, refused to stay put atop his shop stool. His task consisted of assembling ball point pen components in a mock workshop setting for an hour a day, earning a penny for each completed set, a minimum of ten cents required to purchase a treat at the classroom gift shop, the goal that one day he would be disciplined and proficient enough to engage in a similar line of work for forty hours a week. For my behavioral analysis class I performed a baseline assessment and found that over the course of one minute he left his stool eight times. To decrease this behavior, I wrote up an action plan to get him to sit for ten seconds, then twenty, etc., providing reinforcement (M&Ms) at those intervals to entice him to remain at his post and stay on task. In the end, however, I didn't get the results I'd hoped for, as the behavior I intended to decrease actually *increased*, such was his loathing for monotonous sedentary work. His steadfast refusal to sit, along with his distaste for piecemeal labor, doomed my project from the start. But he'd taught me a valuable lesson which unfortunately didn't stay with me at the time: how to think for yourself in the face of demeaning bribes and the pressure to bend to conformity, both so much a part of every school setting.

He did, however, love shovelling snow. The driveway, steps and walk weren't enough for him so, according to his mother, he took on the backyard, removing a cubic foot of snow at a time, first clearing a path, doubling back and widening it again and again until he'd exposed the frozen grass and was up against the chain link fence on the property line. Where did he put all that snow? In the neighbors' yards, of course. What did they care? No doubt they wanted him exhausted also. From the kitchen window his mother supervised the work while a pot of cocoa simmered on the stove and a stack of peanut butter and pickle sandwiches (his favorite) waited on the counter.

Shoveling snow is the best thing in the world for him, she told me. *It puts that overactive mind of his at ease for the rest of the day.*

Thursday, February 6

Marcia couldn't sleep. She was worried about her job. Her asthma had worsened since September. And all because, she told me, she'd tried to be straight with her students. She'd gotten in trouble for making the kind of comments kids misconstrued and reported to their parents, who in turn went to Mr. B. and insisted they be removed from her class (for example, she'd addressed their ADHD and poor study habits, telling them they shouldn't be ashamed of their disability and could help themselves by working harder. This they interpreted as her implying they were dumb and lazy.).

Why is he believing kids all of a sudden? she asked me.

I shrugged. I had no idea. Believing kids could lead you down a road.

As her building representative, I was the one she came to for advice. She felt she'd never be the teacher Mr. B. expected her to be. And Mr. B., having spoken to Marcia on other occasions, concluded a zebra wasn't capable of changing its stripes. In his attempt to show he was playing fair, he sent Ms. G. to evaluate her, though of course since he was Ms. G.'s boss too (and she being aware of his feelings), he wasn't fooling anybody. I threw out some suggestions I didn't think did much good (*Try not to worry. Tomorrow's another day. Everyone's paranoid. Have you tried taking something?*). She thanked me for listening. I said it was my job was. She said she appreciated being heard.

For what it's worth, she said.

Friday, February 7

Dismissal was 11:40 because of an afternoon of professional development. Our instructions were to bring student work demonstrating how we'd incorporated components of The Initiative into various academic subjects. In previous sessions we'd done the same and thus were torqued off about having to do it again. To us the assignment amounted to busywork, the same sort of thing we gave the kids when we'd run out of ideas. But since we were told to do it we would do as we were told. If we complained, it was only to one another. What we really wanted was to tackle all that organizing, planning and paperwork that gnawed at us and kept us up nights wondering when we would ever have time to finish it. Would we ever be at peace about being where we wanted to be in the classroom?

Initially I'd headed for the parking lot but for some reason decided to turn around. Maybe it was out of a sense of guilt or worry about what might happen to me for neglecting my duty. Or maybe I was just plain lonely. As I was supposed to attend then why was I heading in the opposite direction, going home, even if I found the session a waste of time and would likely suffer no penalty other than losing a half-day absence if anyone cared to dock me at this point? In the classroom doorway I hesitated, looking for the right place to sit, meaning with a group of people who would be the most likely to screw around with me, to mock what we were doing as a way to get revenge, passing comments out of earshot of the presenters, and not with the serious types who took everything seriously. As soon as I sat down, I scolded myself for returning, knowing I was now trapped for two and a half hours. I couldn't just get up and parade out in front of everyone after I'd found the perfect bunch of screw-offs to sit with. What would they think if I left, that I was too good for them? Yet how could I remain here and not lose my mind? With four months to go in my career I was still afraid to make a decision in favor of improving my mental well-being.

Once the session got underway, Mr. B. and Ms. G. wandered in, armed with IPADs and taking notes as usual. My colleagues, aware of this, infused their commentary with success stories which could only have been brought about by The Initiative. Whenever anyone spoke everyone nodded along approvingly and concurred how effective The Initiative was and how lucky we were to have such a mighty tool at our disposal (*My kids can practically teach it themselves now!*). Mr. B. and Ms. G. typed away, recording what was said, our words reaffirming what they believed to be true. We all loved The Initiative! Thank you for bringing it to SES! With nothing to lose I should have dissented, stood up and ranted like a madman that it was nothing more than a device inducing somnolence among the kids, but with Mr. B. and Ms. G. looking on I knew my colleagues would set upon me and rip me to pieces.

Though many of us had twenty or even thirty years of teaching experience, our evaluators, on the other hand, had taught a fraction of that time before moving out of the class-room. In Massachusetts it was possible to become a public school administrator without having had so much as a minute of classroom experience (you could, for example, procure a job as an administrator in a private school and subsequently take courses for certification in public school administration). Once certified you obtained a position as assistant principal, stayed a few years before moving on to principal, assistant superinten-dent, etc., each step up the ladder moving you further away from the classroom, earning you a larger salary, and allowing you to evaluate teachers who spent their days doing what you hadn't done in years, if ever. Would anyone be allowed to eval-uate surgeons or lawyers, auto mechanics or cosmetologists without having been one himself? In public schools, this sort of thing was not uncommon, the apparent rationale being that anyone could do what we did.

So as the shadows lengthened across the basketball court below our window, we sat together and did what we'd already done. We looked at student work we didn't care about while we waited for our colleagues to shut up about their classes so we could go on about ours. We took a break midway, taking our sweet time coming back from the bathroom, lingering in the hallway to chit chat. At the end of the session, as a reward for our diligence, Mr. B. allowed us to leave ten minutes early, after we'd filled out the district evaluation forms on which we emphasized how valuable we'd found this particular session, circling 5's all the way down the page.

Monday, February 10

I hurt my knee running a road race yesterday and this morning hauled myself up the stairs using the bannister. With my leg stretched under my desk, I hoped for an easy day. It didn't happen. The kids refused to listen, even the few regulars. As happened every year around this time, they'd become obsessed with classmates of the opposite sex. Over the past forty-eight hours a seismic hormonal shift had sorted them by gender to gossip and ogle one another. During breaks they collected in the back of the room or by the coat cubbies or went into the bathroom (boys wrestling and swinging from stall doors; girls applying makeup while fighting for a position in front of the two mirrors) and refused to leave until I hauled them out (or found a female colleague to empty the girls' room). Back in the classroom they reformed their groups, both clusters chatting in low voices and glancing over their shoulders to see if I was eavesdropping. Any status I'd held with them had eroded over a single weekend with this sudden outbreak of puberty. Without warning I had been reduced to nothing other than someone whose role was to keep them apart when they needed desperately to be together, who ordered them around even during what they reminded me was *our free time,* who made demands of them when just being with their peers demanded everything they had. As I'd allotted a five-minute break because they'd been working so hard (their words), who was I to tell them to exit the bathroom or to maintain an appropriate distance from one another in the classroom? What was *free* about that? Every now and then a boy would get hauled into the girls' group and vice versa, all for the purpose of being interrogated about what he or she knew about what had happened between so-and-so and so-and-so on the bus that morning or during lunch yesterday, or, more crucially, who might like whom and was the passion being returned? Eventually I made my way over and ordered them to disperse. Perhaps, rather than point and command, I should have reminded them I'd been in sixth grade once and had such a paralyzing crush on Janet O'Malley I was terrified to go within twenty feet of her. Instead I appointed an emissary, Vic Sucheki, to gauge my chances, handing him an unsigned note, then waved it off (she would recognize my penmanship), then called it back on, then off again, etc. until he, fed up, asked her out himself.

I knew the risk of any discussion of puberty, hormones, etc. entailed. Inevitably whatever I said to recognize what they were experiencing would get misconstrued and reported to parents who would then make calls to the office, inquiring was it any of business of mine what was going on with their children's personal lives? And why was I so interested in their physical development all of a sudden?

And sometimes there were accusations even when I said or did nothing. Back when I'd taught fourth grade in Woburn, a student ended up in my classroom who'd moved to a new foster home in the city. Thin, pallid, obsessed with twirling a patch of hair above her forehead, she didn't interact with any of us, electing to spend her day studying me in an unsettling manner. Even with my back turned I could feel the intensity of her stare. While I struggled to get everyone's attention, here was a kid who looked nowhere else but at me. But what could I do about it? She wasn't breaking any rules, not disturbing the class or making anyone (other than me) uncomfortable. After a while I couldn't think straight, preoccupied as I was about what was going on in that head of hers. Was I that intriguing she felt compelled to study me hour after hour? At the end of the week, when her caseworker arrived to see how she was doing, the kid reported that while standing in front of the class instructing I was also *playing pocket pool*, an accusation the caseworker then reported to the office, apparently having been convinced by her charge that all sorts of deviants were allowed to teach in public schools. My principal, a level-headed woman who stood up for her teachers, immediately transferred the girl to another classroom for my safety (I was the only male teacher in the school) and confronted the case worker in my defense. Events could have transpired differently, of course, had there been someone else running things, and I was grateful that what could have been a career-threatening allegation was quickly quashed.

Now, unable to get anyone's attention, I was determined to keep my chin up. I still mattered, I told myself. I watched them, passionate in their gossip, as I adjusted to my new role, having gone from a semi-respected teacher to *that guy behind the desk whose job it is to hassle us when we have way more pressing issues to deal with.* As this transformation happened every year I couldn't really say I'd been caught by surprise.

Tuesday, February 11

To mark the hundredth day of school, a kindergarten class marched in twos through the lobby outfitted in capes and oaktag eyeglasses in the shape of the number 100. I happened to be down by the mailroom late in the day watching the parade go by. One kid trailed behind, a crooked pair of glasses taped to his nose, a sneaker flopping off his foot. A paraprofessional encouraged him to keep up, guiding him by the shoulder, making sure he didn't wander away from the herd, imploring him to *pay attention* and *stay in line*. He looked at me in the fleeting, slightly frightened way small children regard male teachers. I gave him a little wave. He returned it. I told him *Good job* and reached out to pat his shoulder. The paraprofessional stopped to wait for him while the rest filed in for viewing by the office staff.

You're lucky you won't be around to get this little guy.

She hadn't meant anything by it. You could tell by the way he reached for her hand what he thought of her. I'd had his kind over the years, many of them who, according to past teachers, needed *a male-role model.* I passed the test because I was a man and I did not have a rap sheet. Because a good number of fathers had a nose for trouble (I kept track of their activities in *The Daily News* police logs), all I had to do was act like a law-abiding citizen to have a salubrious effect on their kids' lives. Conversely, it wasn't fair to female teachers who worked so hard to reach these kids but often saw their efforts spurned because they reminded them of their limit-setting, stressed-out, abandoned and pissed off mothers (while they idolized and feared their absentee and unreliable fathers and, by extension, me).

Wednesday, February 12

I ran out of nurse's slips (each requiring the kid's name, time of day, and what you suspected the malady was) and asked Sheila if she could get some. Whenever I needed something she was happy to comply. She'd be in the middle of task, organizing someone's desk or confronting someone else for mouthing off, and would do it right after she finished. She had a straight-forward way about her, patient and understanding when kids were cooperative, strict and unbending when they weren't. Having resided in town for twenty-five years and having her own two children go through SES (one had been in 6D), she knew the population, where everybody lived, what they did outside of school, the goings-on of siblings, aunts, uncles, grandparents, all of which conferred on her a status I envied. Yet despite her worth both to me and the school–she was regularly pulled from my class to sub for other teachers who had to attend a meeting or go home sick– she didn't earn enough to live on. Her husband's health kept him from steady work, her car was always breaking down, the mortgage and her kids' college loans piling up, etc. She baked delicious oatmeal raisin cookies and brought them in still warm from the oven and I would devour every one of them as soon as she handed them to me while listening to her wonder how she'd survive until her next paycheck. Like other paraprofessionals in our building (all women) she'd taken the position not only for the salary but for the health insurance benefits, as her husband's employment didn't provide adequate coverage. Paraprofessionals occupied the bottom rung of the ladder in terms of money and status, were paid by the hour (so vacations and summer meant no income) and took orders from teachers on up, yet SES couldn't function without them. Their union didn't carry the weight of ours and whenever they negotiated a contract the result was a negligible increase in salary, benefits and working conditions. Yet because they weren't under the stress of having to push a curriculum, didn't have to manage a class (unless the teacher wasn't around), and because most lived in Salisbury and ran into the kids outside of school, they were on more informal terms and could often get them to do what we teachers couldn't. Whenever kids approached Sheila for help with their work or just to hang out by her desk to catch up on neighborhood gossip I felt a tinge of jealousy over the ease of these relationships.

Thursday, February 13

No school because of another nor'easter. At 8 o'clock I forced open the back door to let the dogs out, downed a cup of black coffee, bundled up and went out to shovel the walk, the driveway, the roof of the back porch. I broomed off the cars and removed for a second time cinder block-size chunks thrown across the driveway by sleep-deprived, over-caffeinated snow-plow drivers who relished this brand of torment. I was the only person outside and in this sculpted landscape felt as if I owned the world. Out back a stand of birch bent under their wet load and would stay that way until temperatures warmed enough for them to slip their burden and spring upright. The storm muffled everything but birdsong which in the dead silence was sharper than usual. How did anyone not the recipient of a snow day summon the will to rise an hour or two earlier than usual to excavate their cars and suffer through a miserable long commute? When I was a kid my mother would call *No school* up the attic stairs where my brothers and I slept. Throughout my career I loved those two words, the hoped-for and still surprising day off when everyone not connected to schools had their day ruined by the weather. Certainly they longed for the day when they were young and did not have to stir from their warm cocoon during a blizzard which seemed like the natural and normal thing to do. For all schools were guilty of and the criticism they endured, the creation of the snow day was a remarkable achievement which for some curious reason had not caught on in any other segment of the American workforce.

Friday, February 14

As it was Valentine's Day, for a treat I agreed to play the longer meditation tape after promising to do so all year. Fifteen minutes was a considerable time for anyone to sit and breathe; for twenty-one antsy twelve years olds it was a challenge I wasn't sure they could handle. But they were game so after giving the usual instructions– *feet flat on the floor, shoulders relaxed, back straight, hands folded, eyes closed*– I pressed the start button. With the lights off, we listened to a soothing female voice encouraging us to relax. Starting at the top of our heads she would bring us all the way down to the tip of our toes. During our journey, I closed my eyes just enough to peek through my eyelashes. I wanted to make sure– what did I want to make sure? I wasn't sure. The kids were doing exactly what they'd been asked to do. They were following her instructions, inhaling and exhaling, sitting quietly with good posture. And yet, though they were just a few feet away from me, it was far from business as usual. Not far in, a deep calm settled over us, one we'd only brushed up against during the shorter sessions. Along with this came a subtle vibrancy which agreed with them but which unnerved me. It was clear they'd gone off somewhere, not caring whether I joined them. On their own they'd become a cohesive unit, quietly breathing as if I wasn't there. Through my barely fluttering eyelids I peeked out as random thoughts flew through my head. *Was this even okay? What if the superintendent should mosey on by? What about a fire drill or a lockdown? What would their parents say when they went home with this latest bit of news?* There wasn't a sound but for that female voice telling us to loosen our knees and relax our ankles. I sat facing them as someone who, like them, was tapping into a stillness that had been there all along. What came over me dissolved my role as a teacher and their roles as people taught by me. Though they weren't looking at me–their eyes were closed–I sensed their awareness sharper than ever. Simply sitting silently and breathing together, we had moved beyond the sum of our parts, becoming everything and nothing at the same time. I kept on with my breathing, releasing those crazy thoughts along with the idea of my role as someone who needed to have things a certain way, who'd spent his life judging his own actions and the actions of everyone around him, and who by doing so was not-so-slowly driving himself insane. All of it, I realized, was completely unnecessary.

After our fifteen minutes were up, they came to in their own time, some continuing to meditate while others blinked or stretched and or glanced around, eventually recognizing and tuning into their surroundings. After our five minute sessions some kids volunteered to describe what they'd experienced, trying to make sense of thoughts racing through their minds, or saying how relaxed they felt, or how a rich memory or dream they'd forgotten sprang into consciousness. But there was none of that now, everyone content to sit and in no hurry to do anything. A few more minutes passed without a sound. The silence was both awkward and refreshing and so foreign to the running of a classroom I felt as if I wasn't doing my job. Whereas during the school day they clamored to be heard (and so their pleas lost in the din) while I struggled to get their attention (my pleas lost in the same din), now, finally, we had what we wanted from one another. We sat together saying nothing for a bit longer before I got up from my chair and turn the lights back on.

Friday, February 21

On the last day of a snowy school vacation week, the weather turned mild and sunny. With a view of the bird feeder, I sat with my computer and a cup of coffee, filling out the second trimester report cards. Beginning with the behavior and conduct section, I inserted numbers from 1-4 (a '1' meaning lousy). Plucking away, I found it easy to be generous since I hadn't seen the kids in a week. Assigning numbers to indicate whether a kid behaved or not generally went like this: if you kept quiet and did what you were supposed to do, you got a 4; if you spoke up and did things your way you got a 1. The mild-mannered kids made my job easier so I felt obliged to reward them. Those who forced me to strategize to manage their personalities I felt ought to pay for my effort. It wasn't fair but I did it anyway. The report card format with its tiny little boxes encouraged this, allowing just enough room to insert a number but providing no place to elaborate with actual words. Though numbers had replaced traditional letters they fooled nobody, especially when teachers amended them with +/- signs. You could give a kid a 1 but feel less guilty by inserting a + after it. Conversely, in your crusade to combat grade inflation, you could insert a - after a 3, or, if you were all in for grade inflation, you could place a + after a 4 as a gift to those eager-to-please types who sprayed and wiped down your whiteboard and always noticed when you got a haircut.

Since no lines were provided for commentary, to indicate the document had been filled by a real live human being and not a robot, I jotted some prosaic comments along the bottom of the third page.

Solid effort this term! or *Showing improvement!* or *Attendance improving!* or *Achieving to your potential!*

Sometimes when I handed out a report card, a kid, thinking he'd flunked for sure, would scan it in disbelief, relieved to have been granted a stay of execution. He'd figured his indifference and lack of effort would cost him. But after much cajoling he'd produced enough to squeeze by. I was never comfortable giving F's anyway, as it seemed the grade meant more than simply flunking. It implied you were worthless with no redeeming characteristics. Maybe in high school, where you had the option of skipping class, it implied something else but I didn't believe a twelve-year-old was capable of such turpitude.

Monday, February 24

On the first day back after vacation, the kids, stunned by this interruption in their nocturnal cycle, dreaded the return to routine as much as I did, except I had less than eighty days to go. After more than half a century on the school calendar, I'd left it only once for a span of six weeks. In June of 1987, having taught for nearly a decade, I completed my second year as the only male teacher in a public alternative high school and vowed never to return to teaching. The school was part of a collaborative enrolling twenty-four adolescents from half a dozen towns. The kids—entitled, obnoxious, unmotivated, nearly all from well-to-do homes—had been thrown out of their own high schools for acting like jackasses. To nurture their troubled psyches, the director bestowed on them the freedom to curse, mouth off, smoke cigarettes, devour jelly donuts and blast heavy metal from a gigantic boombox during their many breaks from the rigors of academics, of which they showed little interest. The job was a recipe for burnout and it was only through the willful suppression of any self-preservation instinct that I was able to survive my two year tour of duty.

The following September I searched for employment as far from the profession as I could get and found a job as a UPS driver. The one requirement was that I lift a fifty pound box of roofing nails in the presence of a company doctor to demonstrate I possessed adequate back strength. Delivering packages all day, though physically demanding and not without its share of stress, didn't require much thought. Maneuvering a big brown box truck through the congested neighborhoods of Watertown, I was supposed to finish my route within a specific time frame. As I sped up and down side streets narrowed by parked cars, I prayed a pedestrian wouldn't be dumb enough to step off the sidewalk. If no one answered the door, I followed company policy and left the packages with a neighbor. Loading and unloading boxes eight or ten hours a day was the type of mindless work I thought I needed but the exertion failed to distract me from the career I'd left behind. After ten years in the classroom I couldn't go an hour without imaging how schools were managing to function without me. They were, of course, and I figured sooner or later I'd get over the urge to return.

It wasn't until one afternoon as I stacked a dozen large boxes of Tupperware in the cramped apartment of a frail and confused ninety year old (she'd simply stared at me when I asked to leave the lot for an upstairs resident) that I began to wonder what the hell was wrong with me. Taking to the safety of the couch, she clutched a throw pillow as I shifted an armchair and a coffee table out of the way to make more room. The boxes, tightly arranged from floor to ceiling, not only blocked the soap opera she'd been watching but left her almost no room to leave the couch. As soon as she scrawled her signature on my clipboard, I thanked her and fled out the door, my truck empty, my time card ready to be punched, my soul barren.

Disgusted with who I'd become, depleted from the daily grind of couriering goods consisting of purchases mainly from the Shopping Channel, I found I missed school–the kids, the teachers, the bells, the four walls of the classroom whose confines I was always inveighing against to anyone who'd listen. Out on the street as a member of the private sector, I'd become rudderless and unglued. Like an ex-con itching to return to prison after survival in the real world became untenable, I longed for the only life I'd known.

A week later, while making a delivery to the office of a junior high school, I overheard the principal on the telephone.

It's mid October for God's sake. Don't ask me where you can find a certified special education teacher this time of year. They're like hen's teeth.

I'm certified in special education, I interrupted as I slid the parcel onto his desk and offered my clipboard for a signature. He sized up my earnest expression, chocolate brown uniform, regular boy's haircut, and vinyl pocket protector accommodating three extra pens, not sure if my admission was some kind of put-on.

Hold on a minute, he said into the receiver. *This UPS guy standing right here in front of me claims he's certified.*

He held out the phone with a limp wrist, not sure of my interest. I lunged for it, startling him and bumping the package into a coffee mug he managed to catch just before it flew off the desk.

On the other end was the director of special education for the Woburn Public Schools who invited me for an interview.

Would tomorrow work? he asked.

What a coincidence! That happens to be my day off!

The day after Columbus Day, my six-week stint with UPS finished, I reignited my teaching career, this time as an eighth-grade resource room teacher. For the next dozen years I taught in Woburn.

Tuesday, February 25

We read an adaptation about Beowulf slaying Grendel and yanking off his arm in the process.

How about we sketch Grendel, Ryder suggested, *using the drawings in the magazine to look at?*

I was all for it so I handed out sheets of heavy white art paper and gave a simplistic lesson on drawing anatomy–something I knew nothing about–and then went further by announcing I would also draw Grendel, that we all would learn by doing, though I immediately regretted saying it, anxious my work would be inferior to theirs. We sketched quietly for an hour during which I found myself erasing and then erasing again, exasperated that my sketch wasn't coming out the way I'd drawn it in my head. Working alongside a bunch of twelve year olds was intimidating as hell which was why whenever I assigned an art or writing exercise I didn't do it with them. Nevertheless they were happy for me, generous with their comments, encouraging one another to come look at Mr. D.'s Grendel–*Isn't it awesome?*– as if I was some accomplished artist taking a break from his studio to demonstrate the basics of craft. I thanked them, though my Grendel's head was tiny, his pectorals over inflated, his legs sawed-off stumps. In the end, we were all satisfied with our effort enough to tape our drawings on the whiteboard, to have a gallery viewing and vote for the top three, the winners being awarded coveted Dum Dum pops. I didn't enter mine so one would feel compelled to vote for me. Realistically I wouldn't have made the top dozen. But I'd taken a risk, survived, and felt fine. The difference was I'd elected to take that risk. That wasn't the case whenever I ordered 6D to do something. Like it or lump they had to. My job was to put kids on the spot all day long, thereby increasing their anxiety, the very thing I was attempting to lessen.

Wednesday, February 26

The principal of the middle school visited this afternoon to talk about the opportunities awaiting our sixth graders next year. We sat in the commons room, eighty-five or so of us squeezed together on carpeted tiers, eagerly anticipating his PowerPoint presentation on classes, lockers, after school activities, food options, etc. The slides weren't of the best quality and didn't provide much of a window into the place but it didn't matter. There was no need for a sales pitch as nearly all assembled would be spending the next two years of their lives there. Despite their conscription, the kids were enthralled by what was in store, impatient as they were to depart SES and move on with their lives. They had lots of questions (*Can we chew gum, use our phones, drink coffee, wear baseball hats, dress in spaghetti straps and crop tops and flipflops? What about dogs sniffing our lockers?*) most of which he'd answered as in their fervor they were even less attentive than usual. One prospect that hadn't occurred to them was that life at Triton Regional Middle School would be more of the same – lots of rules and lack of choices and high stakes testing and two-column notes and graphic organizers and having to sit and listen to teachers all day. But at least there they'd get to move around between classes, stow their belongings in a locker provided they could remember the combination (a fear shared by all), purchase fruit smoothies during lunch (reportedly as good as a McDonald's shake), and go home an hour earlier (that they would start an hour earlier had for some reason not registered).

Whenever a kid came back to visit me in September he claimed to like it, either because the limited freedoms bestowed topped those of elementary school, or because he had a bunch of different teachers, or else he thought I'd be offended if he said otherwise. But after a month or so middle school life lost its luster. At least for my own three kids this was the case, as they soon found out that though the packaging might be different, what was inside was pretty much what they'd left behind.

Thursday, February 27

I distributed the latest district-wide writing assessment prompt: *You have one hundred dollars. How would you make your community a better place by helping people?* The kids ignored the graphic organizer stapled to the first page and commenced writing without a second thought, as if this was the most natural activity a human being could engage in. All of them knew right off what they would do with the cash and were hellbent on detailing their proposals. *Can we write about helping animals, too?* For once they understood the prompt without me having to go into particulars. Thus they embarked on a wealth of topics: *cancer, Africa, the homeless, Haiti, hungry people, St Jude's Hospital, Afghanistan, Wounded Warriors, cats, dogs, my family, that guy in my neighborhood with the shopping cart.* Allotted two forty-five minute periods over two days, everyone finished in twenty minutes, having addressed the topic as instructed and wanting to be done with it. *Fine,* I told them, though I'd heard later of teachers who'd brainstormed ideas with their classes, required the use of webs, provided lists of transition words, threw out suggestions of what they themselves would do with the money, etc. It wasn't enough that 6D had done all that had been asked of them. The implication, given the time frame, was that they would embark on some kind of dissertation on altruism, cranking out page after page which we teachers would then have to read and assess. All of us knew what kind of writers we had in our classrooms and did our best to improve their skills, yet our administration, rabid in its love of assessment and data collection, concluded this support wasn't enough.

That we had to compare our students' efforts with every other sixth grade in the district might have made some sense if any of us could come to an agreement on what constituted good writing. During one of our team meetings while we attempted to judge samples I mentioned I thought voice was important and wondered how we might assess it. Everyone looked at me.

'Voice'? What do you mean 'voice'?

'Voice', I repeated. *Like when you say, Oh my God! You won't believe the story so-and-so just told me! 'Voice' sucks you in immediately. You forget time and place you're so taken by what you're hearing or reading. You drop everything. It's like a drug. It overtakes you. Nothing else matters.*

'Citing from the text', you mean? 'Brainstorming'? 'Topic sentences'? 'Claim and evidence'? What are you talking about? What do you mean 'voice'?'

No one seemed to understand voice, never mind how to teach it. Though I was no expert myself, my colleagues seemed to be doing their darndest to eliminate any hint of it, giving low grades to pieces with heart in which you heard personality coming through. They tended to dismiss this sort of prose as lazy writing, preferring instead construction strictly adhering to the rules of English syntax. It made me nuts, all this back-and-forth about what to look for and how to improve it, as it struck me that the craft ought to be taught by people who partook of it themselves on some regular basis, who struggled to find their own voice and might recognize one when they heard it. Most SES teachers didn't write themselves, yet saw no contradiction in insisting that there was a right way and a wrong way to teach it.

Friday, February 28

This morning before I left the house I tried to find my birth certificate to attach to my retirement application, gave up and sent for a copy for a fee of $14. While I monitored a chaotic indoor recess, a second-grader whose mother had been a student of mine stopped by with a paraprofessional in tow. As stipulated on her IEP the kid was entitled to regular breaks from the drudgery of classroom routine, a luxury unavailable to those not on IEPs.

Unlike some of my colleagues, I wouldn't be at SES long enough to have the *children* of former students. Like this second grader, they were in the lower grades winding their way toward me but wouldn't make it in time, though occasionally I did run into their parents. Ten years ago, for example, I had a student named Eddie who happened to be a few years older than the typical SES sixth grader. The odd thing was he wasn't officially in my class. His teacher was new to the school, young, female, attractive, all of which were too much for him. His endless attention in a class where nobody paid attention intimidated her and she asked if I minded if he spent his afternoons with me. Planting himself at the kidney table, he idled away his time flipping through car magazines, sketching superheroes, combing his hair and declining my tepid requests to do the work he was supposed to do. Already six feet tall and a hundred-eighty pounds, he wore starched white collared shirts, a heavy gold chain, stonewashed blue jeans and unlaced work boots. As he intended to quit school in a year to enter the family paving and septic business, his contention was that he didn't need to do anything he didn't feel like doing, which of course rang a bell with rest of the class. As it was, he was logging twenty hours a week driving a dump truck around town, despite being too young to have a license. All that driving tired him out, and couldn't he just sit back so long as he minded his own business?

On the last day of school, once the kids had departed for the summer, an elderly woman appeared at my door dressed in a pleated peasant skirt, purple headscarf, and pendulous silver earrings. She asked if I was Mr. D. and when I said I was she handed me an envelope with a fifty dollar gift card to a local restaurant in appreciation for what I'd done for her grandson, which was basically nothing. We chatted a few minutes, and to my relief she didn't ask for specifics about Eddie's academic progress, the work he'd produced in my class, why she'd never seen a single assignment, test or anything with my comments on it. For three months, because of me, he hadn't learned a thing. Because I wanted to stay on his good side, to be more *friend* than *a teacher*, to be seen as cool by a kid I found intimidating, I'd made no demands and had no expectations. All of us were aware of Eddie's hijinks in and out of school, his first name basis with the cops, his keeping the neighbors up all night with that backfiring dump truck, his swindling classmates, etc., but because he possessed a certain pizzazz and persuasiveness, because he was my height and outweighed me, it was easy to forget all that. Over the years I'd seen plenty of teachers fawn over kids for one reason or another (good looking, bright, popular, scary, influential parents, etc.), the double standard apparent to everyone, the classroom environment as a result one of mistrust and inconsistency. Not only had I also become one of those obsequious types, I'd sunk even lower by accepting compensation for it.

Anyway, I ran into Eddie one morning while he was standing with a group of parents at the entrance to the preschool. Twenty-five now, with three kids and a fourth on the way, he was trying to corral the two oldest as they careened into one another and stomped on his snakeskin boots. I wondered if he'd been listening during my sex education talk, or perhaps he'd listened too well. Maybe he just wanted a lot of kids and figured he might as well start early. He congratulated me on my impending retirement and said I was lucky I wouldn't be around to have his kids in my class.

I can't get them to sit still and pay attention, he admitted. *They're not the kind of student I was.*

Monday, March 3

The Daily News police log mentioned Tanner's father having been busted for possession. A decent guy who loved his kid, he got himself arrested in a motel room on Salisbury Beach. Maybe he had the same issues with ADHD as his son and turned to illicit drugs to manage his symptoms and hold down a job. Maybe he didn't have time to refill the prescription. Whatever the reason, I hoped for Tanner's sake the rest of the sixth grade didn't find out. Even when Tanner told me he'd taken his pill before he'd left the house (I was always asking, in hopeful anticipation of the medication kicking in), I didn't notice much difference in his ability to concentrate. He still went on not paying attention, fiddling with the contents of his desk, getting up and searching for that woodpecker as it hunted for insects in the tall dead pine outside the window behind my desk, not leaving until he spotted it, grabbing my arm to get me to turn around and look. Together we would follow the muted *thunk-thunk-thunk* through the glass until we found it, marvelling at its black and white plumage with a dab of scarlet on its crown. Did I know woodpeckers had built-in shock absorbers which prevented their getting headaches?

Tanner wished humans did too as he got plenty of headaches himself.

Doing its own school work, he would add as we observed, and I thought had it not been for his ADHD it was unlikely either of us would have had that blissful moment together studying this magnificent creature not thirty feet away. Later he found a photograph online and learned this particular species saved our forests by devouring wood boring beetles. It also summoned mates by hammering out love songs on dead tree limbs. And most amazing of all, it was called a *hairy woodpecker*, a named that made us both laugh.

Who thought up that? he asked me. *That's the type of job I'd be good at. Giving birds crazy names.*

Tuesday, March 4

While purchasing a Macbook Air at the North Shore Mall, I also signed up for a year's worth of unlimited classes for ninety-nine dollars. My intention was to pick up a marketable skill as opposed to what I had now, which was the suspect ability to manage a group of twelve-year-olds. Over the summer I intended to drive to the mall every day and learn how to operate my new laptop. The salesman informed me I was getting a deal no one in his right mind would pass up. I could come morning, noon, and night, weekends included. Any questions, no matter how dumb, would be answered with politeness and understanding. No one would make fun of my lack of technical merit or sluggish retention when taught basic skills. I would be treated as if I was just another techie (who just happened to have the computer grasp of a three-year-old). But the fact was I hated malls and wasn't very fond of PCs either. Though taking classes didn't appeal to me in the slightest, if all else failed I could find a word processing job five nights a week in a windowless data-storage facility the size of a blimp hangar where I would be surrounded by fellow oddballs who guzzled Diet Coke by the liter and reminded me every ten minutes how long it had been since their last cigarette, or inquired why I'd quit teaching only to end up doing this line of work, or obsessed over whether they'd done right by booting their thirty-seven year old out of the basement after he'd maxed out their credit cards and totalled the Camry. Still, it was income, and having been in school for over five decades I was certainly skilled at following directions, keeping my hands to myself, getting along well with others and using the bathroom only during designated break times.

Wednesday, March 5

I took a day off to take my mother to the gastroenterologist. She had blood in her stool and was worried about a recurrence of colon cancer she'd had seven years ago. Doctor Bennett reminded me of the wizard in *The Wizard of Oz* –wiry white halo of hair, round open face and kind eyes, disheveled look (Was that really a piece of electrical tape holding his stethoscope together?), scuffed brown leather shoes, argyle socks, easy smile and reassuring manner. When he told my mother she did not have cancer, a healthy pink glow instantly returned to her face. She then invited him to tea. Twice. Her colon, he explained, was a vascular organ and occasional bleeding was not uncommon for someone her age. His calm voice, warm touch (*I wish my own hands felt like yours,* she told him.) and bright optimism (*So now that you know it isn't cancer go out there and enjoy life!*) gave me the sense patients left his office with high hopes and positive thoughts no matter what the diagnosis.

Afterwards I held her arm as we crossed the coated parking lot, our jackets collecting flakes of blowing snow. A chronic chionophobic, she'd been terrified on the ride over, gripping the armrest and telling me to slow down. Now she didn't notice those downy flakes clinging to the shoulders of her overcoat. All she talked about was how hungry she was. When was the last time she'd had a bite to eat? She couldn't remember. What about that restaurant right over there across the street? Was that okay with me? She pulled her wool scarf up to her eyes and tightened her grip on my elbow. *It's on me. I'm famished. How about we start with a cocktail to celebrate?*

I vowed then and there that I would try to be more like Dr. Bennett over the next four months. The best models for teachers weren't necessarily other teachers, as it was always tough to tell whether what they were selling was real or a put-on, reminding me of those demonstration videos of classroom instruction where you knew both the teacher and students were actors even though you were informed at the start they were real genuine people. The best models were those who demonstrated unaffected human decency–who had little desire to be someone other than who they were, who weren't in it for money or status or some perceived ego-boost, who because they had no desire to impress gave you their full attention. Just being in their presence you felt an immediate calm and afterward were left with a warmth that stayed with you.

Thursday, March 6

Today I began *The Outsiders* by S.E. Hinton. From my many years of reading the novel, I could nearly recite it from memory. With plenty of scenes of violence, drinking, parental neglect and tension between social classes, it drew the kids in immediately from its opening line which also happened to be the last sentence of the book: *When I walked into the bright sunlight from the darkness of the movie house, I had only two things on my mind: Paul Newman and a ride home.* With backgrounds parallelling those of the characters, 6D not only loved the writing but used the theme to validate their own lives.

While other teachers played a taped recording, reading the story aloud infused it with authenticity and immediacy, as if I myself had been an eyewitness to the rivalry between the greasers and the Socs. Even kids with ADHD sat unmoving, hushing everyone and threatening to kill the first person who coughed, raised his hand, or shifted in his seat. The class hunched over their worn paperback copies, following every line, even the worst readers, as the words put them in the midst of the gang members by the fountain in the park on that cold autumn night when Johnny killed Bob, one of the Socs, with his switchblade to save Ponyboy from the Socs drowning him. There was, as always when any story held them, a sanctuary of quiet focus where sentences, immediately ingested, brought to life action scenes, transporting us out of the classroom without having to leave our seats. No one stirred, resisting the urge to use the bathroom, get a snack, or scratch an itch. And none dared to lift the finger tracing those words.

That's the way it's always been, I thought, even before literacy was called *literacy*, before there even *was* literary. For eons tribe members had sat listening around a campfire, and not once during that time–I'll go out on a limb here–had anyone suggested the use of two-column notes as a way to better comprehend the story they were hearing.

Friday, March 7

I left school today with copies of my retirement application, intending to mail the original at the post office. Colleagues I passed in the hallway had the same question: *Counting the days?*, implying I couldn't wait, or that they would be counting had they been me, longing as they were for their own retirement, even if it was decades away. The month of March, dreary and endless, minus holidays and vacations, was like swimming under a sheet of lake ice with no holes chopped in the surface. Survival was your only concern. If it helped to sob at your desk after school, everyone understood. If you mule-kicked the copy machine, so be it. If you spent your planning period smoking a butt down by the beach (you'd quit on New Year's Day), fair play to you. March made you wonder whether could you hack it another year. The answer was always no, never, forget about it. Except you were good at what you did. You had a reputation. Everyone wanted their kid in your class. You just needed a few good habits to see you through. You'd walk, sign up for yoga, take a watercolor class. But how could you do that when you collapsed on the couch as soon as you got home? When you woke up and binge-watched? For supper you shoved something in the microwave and forgot it was there. You snapped at your spouse and kids because they had the nerve to walk into the room. They thought you nuts until you explained yourself.

It's March, goddam it! That's why! What is it you don't understand?

Monday, March 10

A memo came from Ms.G. regarding behavior at recess. Yesterday a kid tossed a snowball and as punishment the sixth grade was restricted to a patch of blacktop under the basketball hoop, eighty students pressed against the high brick wall of the gym on one side and a chain link border fence on the other with little room to do much other than stare at one another. Later I learned a teacher had witnessed the snowball toss from her window and reported the infraction to the office. I told Ms. G. I would be extra watchful if she would allow the kids to decamp from the pavement and run free over the baseball field. There was snow on that field, however, and thus existed the possibility another snowball might be tossed. I begged for her indulgence nonetheless, feeling ridiculous, a pleading fifty-eight year old teacher promising an assistant principal fifteen years my junior I'd do a better job being vigilant. Well, I couldn't guarantee kids wouldn't throw the snow lying under their feet or else make believe it wasn't there. All of it was nonsense anyway, some buttinsky squealing about the behavior of students on my watch (and so implicating me) and me interrogated on what I'd seen (nothing) and who were the lawbreakers (I had no idea). I shrugged and apologized and promised it wouldn't happen again. *Could we please have our recess back?* And she said okay this one time and I thanked her, then dragged my drooping spine out the door behind me.

Tuesday, March 11

I read aloud an adapted version of Poe's *The Tell Tale Heart* while 6D sat stone-still with their mouths agape. Brynn, a sweet little thing who lived with her grandmother, at one point plugged her ears. Maybe I'd overdone it but my thinking was they'd hear the story eventually as it was an American classic and I'd assumed–perhaps incorrectly–that every kid loved horror. The visceral reaction a good story brought out in them had me sneaking peeks at their faces as I read, scanning for a crinkled forehead, pursed lips or unbroken stare telling me that vivid scenes of terror were indeed playing out in their young minds.

I've always loved stories myself, written or spoken, as they infused me with contentment and happiness or, deeper than that, something more elemental like air or water. They delivered me out of my funk, deflated my anxiety, filled me with hope. Telling or listening to a good story I could feel my batteries recharge, allowing me to lift off and drift away from the morose state I'd been stewing in to a better, more enlightened place. And so I was regularly telling stories to the kids, sometimes planned and sometimes impromptu, sometimes embellished into allegory, other times leaving the interpretation up to them. And they, feeling as I did, stopped to listen regardless of the hectic state in which we found ourselves. As I started in, they would sense it coming, stilling themselves and adjusting their antennas accordingly. There was an essential essence in the air they had no intention of missing. Stories, we all concluded, were what made our lives worth living.

Later we watched a twenty-six minute black and white Youtube video (which of course I hadn't previewed) as graphic as Poe's prose. The narrator took a handsaw to the body in the tub, cutting off one limb at a time, blood spattering his face and neck as he worked, the kids quiet and taking it all in, me sitting there sweating and wondering what the hell was wrong with me, hoping to God they wouldn't tell their parents, or download the video when they got home for everyone in the family to sit around and watch. When the video ended there was an awkward silence. We were in shock. Or at least I was. What had I expected, a Disney version on Youtube? I was about ask how everyone was doing when Iris turned around.

Don't worry, Mr. D. We've all seen worse. I have every one of the 'Friday the 13th' movies. If you really want to see something scary, watch 'The Chernobyl Diaries'.

That made me feel a little better.

Wednesday, March 12

I was required to sacrifice my planning period listening to Mr. B. elaborate on the proctoring rules for the upcoming MCAS, our annual statewide assessment. The training session was mandated by the state despite the fact that my colleagues and I had given the test every year since its inception. So we sat around a table in the conference room and reviewed the instructions we knew by heart, and knew better than Mr. B. would ever know, as he did not administer it. Some kids, he reminded us, would take the test in small groups in various settings around the building, with staff implementing accommodations as detailed on IEPs or 504s. A few of those staff members would also act as scribes. According to the rules, a kid who received the services of a scribe didn't have to say *capital letter* or *period*. The scribe could assume as much.

What about semicolon? I blurted out. I was losing my mind, peeved that I'd been compelled to attend this silly meeting in lieu of my free period where I could do sit around and do whatever I wanted to do. Anyway, the use of scribes was ridiculous. A kid ought to be able to write a response to a reading passage in his own words using an adaptive device if necessary. Having a paraprofessional transcribe rambling speech was no way to judge comprehension. Would these kids have scribes following them around for the rest of their lives, like the kings of Mesopotamia? What were they supposed to do once they left school?

No one was in the mood to answer my question. In fact, no one even bothered to look at me. This was serious business and there was to be no monkeying around. More than anything I wanted to go back to my empty classroom, close the door, turn my chair around and gaze out the window at the towering pines not thirty feet away. On windy days like today they swayed over the vernal pool in a stately majestic dance, somehow keeping perfect time, a mesmerizing recital that left me spellbound.

Thursday, March 13

Every year the kids asked me why they had to take the MCAS. Their performance anxiety had kept them up nights, as they were always reminded of what was expected of them, which was not only to pass but to carry the SES battle flag against all those other six grade classes state-wide. They'd been drilled since third grade, inculcated with formulaic devices like the *Hamburger Paragraph Method* (*Make sure the patty is your juiciest detail!*) to answer any and all questions in the exact same manner. Talk of the gravity of the MCAS, hinted at by both teachers and administrators early in the year and becoming more urgent as the months rolled by, had by March become a runaway locomotive hurtling down the tracks. Tied to the rails, the members of 6D had by then abandoned all hope. *Why us?* they cried. *And if we don't pass we won't get our high school diplomas, right?* As they needed to score a *Needs Improvement* to graduate from high school (more than a few of them had never achieved that, having earned a *Warning* since they'd begun taking it), they were understandably scared stiff.

Then go to a private school then, announced Derrick. *At them places you don't need to take no stupid test.*

He sat back in his chair to allow this astounding fact to sink in.

What? Where are them schools? There's no such thing! Corbin cried, though Derrick was ready with an answer, as a well-heeled friend of his cousin attended a private school not far from SES.

It's where those rich kids go, over the river at The Governor's Academy!

He waved an arm in the general direction, five miles south of us, just off Route 1 in Byfield and close to our high school. Some of them knew the place, a bucolic boarding school of ivy-covered brick and sweeping groomed lawns on four hundred and fifty acres established in 1763 along the banks of the Parker River. Occasionally SES kids visited there on weekends to ice skate in one of the indoor rinks or shoot baskets in the expansive fieldhouse. Construction equipment dotted the campus, new dorms and science centers and indoor pavilions rising from the rolling landscape. The student-teacher ratio was five to one, with classes regularly travelling to the theater in Boston, visiting assorted museums, historical sights, etc. The dining hall was supposedly overseen by a French chef. And, most crucial of all, their school year was a month shorter than ours.

It ain't fair rich people who make the rules force us take the MCAS when their own kids do fun stuff and don't have to take no dumb test! Brynne proclaimed in disbelief.

That's just the way it is, consoled Derrick. *And it's not going to change on account of us.*

Friday, March 14

I asked for an illustrated horror story. There were no other requests or instructions. They nodded that they understood. No one uttered a word. They got up and collected what they needed. They were writers and artists whose only desire was for time, space and material. Did a person exist on this earth who did not enjoy writing and illustrating a horror story?

At this point I was assigning lessons which met with no opposition. In a sense I'd given up, abandoning the district curriculum map while falling back on my own choices (those involving as little planning as possible, as chances were better than not that the activity I'd spent my precious time designing would be meet with hostility). Hence 6D got busy writing, drawing and getting feedback on the outrageousness of their prose and the ghoulish mien of their drawings. I hadn't bothered to preface the assignment by requiring the use of webs and other graphic organizers or by having them brainstorm topics, etc., techniques that I was supposed to employ which sucked the joy out of whatever we were doing. Instead they flipped open their notebooks and scrambled to write as fast as possible lest the words evaporate into thin air, never to be retrieved again.

No problem, Mr. D. promised Tanner. *But now that I've started I can't stop writing after just one page.*

Once immersed, they left me in peace at my desk where I taught by not teaching which was my favorite part of instruction–watching them do what excited them while having enough sense to keep quiet and stay out of the way.

Monday, March 17

Kyle, a former student of mine and a college junior (his sister was presently in my class) visited to collect writing samples from the kids about their favorite comic book characters (*Spiderman, Wonder Woman*, etc.) for a research project in his media analysis class. This was the same kid who ten years ago during my lesson on Congo River transportation was uncharacteristically focused, taking notes and oblivious to his classmates shenanigans. On the pulldown map I pointed out rivers which spread like fine hairs across the African country, thinking I'd finally turned a corner with him. A few minutes later I walked up behind his desk to find that he'd been drawing a porcelain toilet with a sizeable stool in the bowl. Without a word I slipped the sheet of paper out from under his hand. With his pencil in midair, he looked up at me.

May I have my drawing back?

Had it been poorly rendered I might have simply torn it up and thrown it away. But clearly he'd put considerable effort into it so I placed the work in my desk drawer under some folders.

A week later when his mother arrived for report card conferences I showed her the drawing. She inspected it before turning the sheet over, searching for the artist's signature. Confused, she said nothing at first. Then she cleared her throat.

This wasn't some kind of assignment, was it?

I assured her it wasn't. She reached for a tissue in her purse.

Is there any chance you could be mistaken about the artist?

Unfortunately there isn't, I said, *I caught him in the act.*

Sorry for asking. I never thought he was capable of such a thing.

Sliding the drawing under his report card, she promised to speak with him and asked how he was doing otherwise.

Now here was Kyle again, twenty-two years old, six feet tall, dressed in a button down shirt and a down vest, wearing a five o'clock shadow and frameless eyeglasses, looking very much the graduate student he intended to be in two year's time. The class listened and followed his directions as he patiently answered their questions and thanked them for their help. Afterwards he passed out chocolate and vanilla cupcakes he'd baked and fruit he'd sliced up and pierced with multi-colored toothpicks. I didn't mention the drawing but I wondered how the exchange had gone with his mother that day, whether the humiliation she felt had changed him. Whatever the outcome, from then on he and I never had another issue. Looking at him now, I wondered if he'd drawn what he'd drawn *to get caught.* There were times when kids, through some subconscious desire to vent their anger or frustration, used the teacher as a conduit to get the response and attention they were unable to procure another way. By putting something out there they knew we wouldn't ignore, they didn't have to struggle to find a way of framing their confusion verbally.

Or maybe I was just boring the hell out of him and he'd decided to try his hand at drawing a toilet.

Tuesday, March 18

The kids constructed crossword puzzles on half-inch graph paper, the goal being to squeeze all twenty vocabulary words inside the squares, then to arrange a second sheet with blank vertical and horizontal boxes and corresponding numbers, including a list of clues. The reward for completion? A Dum Dum pop. This regular class exercise by now didn't require much involvement from me until the end when, desperate for sugar, they surrounded my desk and begged for help plugging in the last word or two, thus earning the cheapest candy I could purchase which they wouldn't have touched had they been anywhere but in school. Everything tasted better when a teacher handed it out, even a Dum Dum pop. (Though they preferred Jolly Ranchers, those had been banned as they did not come affixed to a stick and could potentially lodge in a windpipe. I was fine with that, Dum Dums being cheaper anyway.).

Preaching good nutrition while offering rewards of refined sugar for the attainment of goals made me not only a hypocrite but a drug pusher. That I was not above dispensing sugar to motivate them and they in turn having the good judgment not to make an issue of my sanctimoniousness created and maintained a system that worked for both of us. Like any hypocrite I rationalized my behavior by telling myself it was only a spoonful of sugar in comparison to the mountains they consumed every day. Dum Dums were prime motivators and had no expiration date which meant I could purchase them in bulk and keep them in my bottom drawer for the entire year. Had I offered carrot sticks or cucumber slices few if any of them would have responded by meeting the demands of getting those twenty words on the grid.

Wednesday, March 19

Today we had Mexican Food Day. Though we weren't studying Mexico per se, a couple of other sixth grade classes had recently celebrated African Food Day (apparently deciding to take on the cuisine of an entire continent) so 6D demanded they be allowed to bring in food they knew something about. I pulled down the map to see if anyone could locate Mexico (Anton, who had given me the green and white skull after his trip there, bounded up and slapped a palm on the country). *Yes,* I said, *our neighbor to the south.* What followed were predictable comments about drugs and illegal immigrants pouring over the border I did my best to counter by mentioning the rich history and cultural contributions of the country. For home-work I assigned dishes, leaving it up to them, and thus we ended up with a buffet consisting of Betty Crocker brownies, rice and beans and Jose Ole beef tacos. Having eaten lunch ninety minutes earlier did nothing to diminish their appetites. They charged back for seconds and thirds and finished most of the selections, even those with shreds of lettuce hanging out of them. A group of mothers (and grandmothers) bearing young children, casserole dishes and jugs of fruit juice stayed to eat with us, perhaps wondering why there was nothing about Mexico adorning the walls or bulletin boards. It was a flash mob in that respect, except it was a flash food day. Everyone enjoyed themselves and was in no hurry to leave, the classroom bustling with people of all ages, eating, conversing, relaxing. In my enthusiasm over how well things had gone with so little planning, I promised more food days. The kids cheered and thanked me but I knew it wouldn't happen. The idea of everyone moving freely about helping themselves to the dishes they'd made troubled me, what with the structure of the day on its ear, my voice one among many, the desks arranged into a single large table, trays, plates, cups and utensils everywhere, the atmosphere festive and loose and utterly unschool-like. Though I had no say over what kids learned and how they should be taught, I was still the teacher and could *pretend* I did. So once the food was gone and with half an hour left in the school day I stood up and thanked everyone, proclaiming we had classwork still to be done (though I had nothing planned). The surprised adults regarded me curiously, put their empty casserole dishes into their tote bags, corralled the young children and moved toward the door.

Thursday, March 20

The kids were dismissed at 11:40 because of parent conferences where I would distribute and discuss the second trimester report cards. Tate's father, who I'd spoken to a couple times and who loved the idea that his son got to run before school, arrived with his new wife who taught at a science and math public high school somewhere in Boston. She started in on me right away, asking for data on Tate's reading and writing progress, a description of the program I used to teach writing, etc. As he'd gotten a point above Warning on last year's Reading MCAS, how did I plan to rectify that problem in five days' time when he took the MCAS again? The couple sat on the other side of the table, she directly across from me jotting notes on a pad of paper she'd pulled from her handbag and he sitting sideways, deferring to her. I had no specifics in front of me and planned only to hand over the report card, say a few words, and be done with it. Caught off guard, I proceeded to launch into my own version of the writing process which sounded crazy, even to me, but which I believed to be true, how you ought to crank out as many pages as it took until you had something resembling what you wanted to say, have someone read it to get feedback, keep writing until you had a closer version of what you wanted, read it aloud to find the rhythm, keep writing, revising, etc. Plus (and just as importantly) you had to give a damn about the subject you were writing about. I mentioned how Phillip Roth wrote two hundred pages to get a single paragraph he could live with. Or so I'd heard. She regarded me with knitted brow. Was there a name for this method of mine? From what sources had I drawn my ideas? What about templates and graphic organizers? I got up and pulled a couple of samples out of Tate's desk which failed to impress her. He was, in my opinion, doing just fine. As his handwriting was nearly illegible maybe that was the issue—no one could read what he wrote—and I would speak to him, assuring her his score would improve, which was easy to promise since I was out the door in June.

From time to time you had those parents hellbent on exposing you as incompetent, their minds made up before they came through the door. All you could do was stay calm, let them have their say, toss out a few comments in your defense until the fifteen minutes were up and you indicated that another parent was waiting in the hallway, apologize how you didn't have more time to discuss what a jackass you were, then forget about it.

Friday, March 21

Raelynn rushed up to my desk to inform me she couldn't breathe, flapping her hands in front of her face to summon airflow into her lungs in case I wasn't getting the message.

Where did all the air go? she stammered. *What just happened to me?*

Earlier in the year her mobile home had burned to the ground and now her aunt was back in rehab.

Put your arms up over your head like this, I told her. *Breathe nice and slow and easy. Like this.*

I modelled how to breath as if she'd suddenly forgotten.

Okay, yeah, okay, I see. Yeah, that's right. In and out.

I filled out a pass for the nurse as she raised her arms halfway, a tepid surrender, and drew audible breaths through her teeth. I opened the window hoping for a fresh breeze. Her eyelids fluttered and she swayed a bit, going another shade of white. I pulled a chair over and had her sit down. She clasped her hands on her knees to steady herself while I encouraged her to keep breathing, promising it would work, this tried-and-true method that had been around for ages, reminding her I knew a thing or two about panic attacks.

Isn't it crazy how they come out of nowhere when a person is just minding her own business? I said. *One minute you're fine and then the next there's trouble.*

Yeah. And not fair too. I always get them. It feels like I'm gonna die every time.

And couldn't we also get them to leave us alone if we kept taking those slow deep breaths just you're doing right now?

Yeah, maybe. But where did all the air go? Just keep breathing, right?

Right. Just keep breathing.

When Raelynn did attend school these days she spent considerable time on a cot in the nurse's office. She was sweet and respectful regardless of the misery she was in which made me want to hug her and tell her she'd be okay, that she wasn't dying, that this rotten time would pass and she had a long life ahead of her, but as a male teacher physical contact was out of the question. She was two feet away from me, the same age as one of my own daughters, her big brown eyes imploring me to save her. She shook herself and pressed those brown eyes shut, squeezing out a few tears, while I forced our conversation to distract her from herself, telling her to hang in there, she was amazing, everyone thought so, we all loved her, etc. Then I assigned Sierra to accompany her to the nurse's office, telling her to hold her arm tight in case she collapsed on the way.

Having no physical contact made sense on one level; on another it turned me into a robot. I hugged my own children all the time, whether to comfort, congratulate, or for no good reason at all. That's what fathers did. And I wanted to hug my students because I felt close to them. I wasn't a hugger in the general sense—chronic huggers made me uncomfortable—but what was wrong with a quick embrace when someone needed one? It was painful to see a kid in distress and not be able to put my arm around him or her for a moment, hold a hand or rub a shoulder. Not linger there, just offer a brief physical connection. But no male teacher in his right mind would take that chance, and not doing so made you less human. People, at least the ones I knew, clutched, clasped, patted and squeezed one another for support when the going got tough. It was a normal and healthy response, making both the recipient and giver feel better, and one I had done my damnedest to suppress my entire career.

Monday, March 23

By one o'clock, having been encased by four walls since 8 a.m. and with another two hours to go, their blood sugar spiking after carbohydrate-heavy lunches, all twenty-one of them, restive and indifferent, simply wanted to hang out and do nothing. Okay, fine. But I had to be here too. On this dreary afternoon cold air seeped into the room despite the work of the space heater ratcheted to its highest setting. Any day now I expected to see wisps of black smoke rising from the back of it. Out of ideas, I struggled to come up with something that might grab them. Whatever I devised had to appeal not to normal people but to twelve-year-olds whose attention spans had flagged beyond resuscitation. I'd also eaten carbohydrates for lunch (cold spaghetti from last night's dinner) and was battling my own fogged brain. Okay, so I would read to them. They liked that idea. *Yeah, read to us then!*

Exactly thirteen minutes later my voice was gone. I closed the book and told them I could no longer continue without risking my health and that they should take out their vocabulary workbooks and open to such-and-such a page. They groaned and regarded me with contempt. *Why do we have to do any work then? Could we take a bathroom break first?* Yeah, fine, sure, take a bathroom break. The entire class rose as one and fled the room. In the ensuing silence I listened to the thrum of the air duct fan above the suspended ceiling tiles. I looked out the window at the vernal pool where a turtle's head poked above the calm black surface, or maybe it was just a stick. And what was that being pushed by the breeze? A curled oak leaf in the shape of a trireme perhaps. Haunting this serene moment were images of boys hanging from stall doors, practicing chokeholds, jamming rolls of toilet paper into toilets. Someone could die in there and here I was studying a stick I thought might be a turtle's head. And yet I couldn't move, lost as I was in the pool's rippling surface. I continued to stare, irritated by the fact that I was always in the boys' bathroom anyway, summoned by female staff who'd heard the racket from their own classes across the hall when other boys were going apeshit, me saying yeah sure and holding the bathroom door open with my foot, arms crossed, barking at them to finish their business and wash their hands, leaning in but not actually going in so the door would not close behind me, trapping me in that forbidden space. Occasionally the door did close behind me, as when I was called inside to inspect a clogged toilet or overflowing sink or was asked to take a closer look at that brown object by the floor drain. Was it really what everyone thought it was? In those moments I panicked about my own safety, never wanting to be alone with them like that, the simple act of my being in there incriminating me from the start. It was similar to being stuck in an elevator or sealed in a mine shaft where, once realizing you were trapped, your survival instinct kicked in and you were ready to claw at the walls. So this time I decided to latch onto that trireme as it made its way unhurriedly to the western shore of the vernal pool. In a week's time the mating calls of peeper frogs would fill the air day and night. That was absolutely my favorite sound in the world. And in less than three months I would be retired.

Tuesday, March 24

Today was Day 1 of the ELA /Reading Comprehension MCAS, the first part of our state mandated assessment. After I distributed the #2 pencils the office had sent up, the kids picked them up and studied these unexpected gifts. *Are these for us?* They sat straight and attentive despite not having slept or eaten. I knew because I'd asked. Their performance would influence how they were perceived by us, their teachers, as well as by their parents and members of the Salisbury community. This was serious business (the large plate glass window of the conference room by the office where the MCAS tests were stored overnight in neat stacks had been crisscrossed with yellow caution tape by Mr. B.). Talk of a rules enforcement squadron dispensing punishment for any security breach had been around since the test's inception. Nasty rumors about what could become of you if you screwed around while either taking or administering the test left us in a heightened state of anxiety.

The instructions in the administrator's handbook, including the warning about cheating, were printed in boldface paragraphs, meaning I was required to read each and every word aloud. The kids pretended to listen, having heard these same instructions since they'd first encountered the MCAS in third grade. As the test was untimed, once we started I had a couple of hours to myself during which I planned to sit at my desk and read, getting up once or twice to wander around the room and dispense Jolly Ranchers from a plastic tub and hoping no one choked to death (candy unattached to a stick against school rules but we all loved Jolly Ranchers).

Throughout the session they worked tirelessly, closing their eyes in desperation or mumbling to themselves or opening their fists to relieve hand cramps as they toiled to decipher and analyze prose and poetry years beyond their ability level (a passage from Steinbeck's *Grapes of Wrath* featured vocabulary such as *fetlock, anlage, oat beards, thresh*), trying to make heads or tails of it all, scribbling responses then erasing, writing over what they'd written, grinding their pencils down to nubs with the little sharpeners I'd given them, writing some more to get as much down as they could because they loved me and wanted to make me happy and knew the key to my heart was to write down as much crap as possible, scribbling to the bottom of the page with the hope that the poor sap whose job it was to read through all this detritus would detect something within a mile of the mark and be kind enough to award a point or two.

Though I was forbidden to say anything once the test was underway, as I moved around the room I'd come upon a kid who'd jotted a couple of anemic sentences addressing the open response for each passage and left the rest of the page blank, his uninspired effort at odds with my edict about *filling the entire page* with anything remotely approximating an answer. His test booklet closed, his pencil at rest, a graphic novel in his hands (kids were required to have a book on the rack below their seats to keep them quiet while the rest of the class finished), he assumed he was done for the day. In response to his indifference regarding my instructions, I broke protocol by tapping the answer booklet and whispering in his ear *Please write more!*, to which he would whisper back *But I can't think of anything else to write!* To which I would lean closer and repeat with more urgency, *I don't care! Just write anything!* and he would shrug and dig his pencil out of the channel and recommence with the laborious task of writing about a topic he had zero interest in while I, elated to see his pencil being dragged across the paper once more, to see words nearly legible enough to be deciphered, would nod in satisfaction, offer a Jolly Rancher as a reward, then scan the room for anyone else rash enough to think he'd said all he had to say.

Wednesday, March 26

Today was Day 2 of the English/Language Arts MCAS and for the second time I recited aloud the same boldfaced instructions from the test administrator's handbook. And again 6D sat still and mute, pretending their ears were meant for listening. Their scores, I read to them, would be reported to their school and their parents and used to help made them better students (and, thought it wasn't stated in the test administrator's handbook, affect property values in Salisbury). When the results arrived at SES in the fall a label with both math and ELA scores would be affixed to their cumulative folders which followed them from grade to grade. Any teacher who picked up the folder had a snapshot of a kid's MCAS performance and from that was free to judge for himself before he'd even had him in class. I'd done it myself, until I stopped caring about the MCAS or any other assessment scores, until I realized a kid was an actual person and not a number on a score sheet. Now, my reading of the instructions complete, their anxiety at its apogee, they did the best they could, plugging away, making a go of it for my sake, determined to demonstrate that we were just as good as all those other towns across the state of Massachusetts (like the ones with no motels, campgrounds, or boardwalk junkies, like the ones with tight zoning bylaws and landscaping trucks zipping through neighborhoods) whose scores would be compared to ours. We'd come this far over all these months together and even if we didn't succeed, even if some of us could never succeed, at least we could look good trying.

Thursday, March 27

Today after dinner my daughter Beatrice, a high school sophomore, asked for help with her geometry homework. On the table lay her textbook, dense and menacing, all nine hundred and sixty glossy pages of it, transported, along with her other textbooks, in a backpack she hauled to and from school every day. The stitching securing the straps to the top were frayed and ready to give. The ponderous weight of my children's textbooks required my replacing their backpacks midway through each school year, at a cost of eighty bucks per, while my own backpack purchased from L.L. Bean thirty years ago for twenty dollars was still in decent condition.

I reviewed some pages in the chapter to see if I could figure out what she was struggling with. No dice. I ventured into the glossary, hoping to decrypt terms which would help me figure out the problem. No luck there either. I flipped back and forth, babbling and nodding away to indicate the haze might be lifting, which wasn't the same as thinking out loud, which she in any case correctly discerned as me bullshitting my way through and being of no assistance whatsoever. Like those sixth-grade geography texts I was no longer using, this one seemed to have been designed by a committee with a sadistic streak, or else one with the misguided notion that the kids using it were Advanced Placement types who could go to their Advanced Placement parents for help. Had there been a section where the process of solving a problem was broken down into small coherent steps for the average math phobic student, Beatrice wouldn't have had to waste her time asking her math phobic father for help. After ten minutes, her patience worn thin (she had other homework to get through), she consoled me by saying it was okay, thanks anyway, she still loved me, I wasn't a failure (at least in other ways) and besides, who used any of this dumb stuff in real life anyway? She would ask her teacher to clarify the problem before class. I volunteered to write a note explaining my incompetence but she politely declined.

Friday, March 28

I took the day off to take my eighty-nine year old father home from the hospital after he'd had a pacemaker installed. He'd retired over twenty years ago from the Boston Gas Company after decades of digging up streets in search of ruptured gas lines. Many nights at 3 a.m. after getting an emergency call he'd stand in the kitchen laying himself in wool while my mother made a thermos of strong tea with milk and sugar and enough ham and cheese sandwiches to maintain body heat. He loved the satisfaction of searching for the source of those leaks and sealing them, jackhammering pavement in the dead of winter or the furnace of summer. The camaraderie of his crew (the Irish and Jamaicans, having left their beloved islands for work in America, shared a love of storytelling, a sense of humor, and a weakness for a nightcap or two at the end of their shifts) along with overtime calls that doubled his paycheck were perks he didn't want to give up, despite replacement knees and frozen shoulders. Now that he had his pacemaker, he hinted he might go back to tearing up those streets again. I, on the other hand, was happy to retire at fifty-eight and never go back. My shoulders and knees were fine but I had no desire to teach in a public school classroom. Unlike my father, though I could identify the source of problems, I couldn't fix them. And if I couldn't fix them then what exactly was I doing there? None of my colleagues who struggled day in and day out could patch up these problems either. Many kids couldn't read and write at grade level, struggled with depression and a miserable home life or were simply bored and hated school and were upfront about admitting it, like my own daughter Justina. The intractable routine was such that no change was coming for those kids, for any kids, or for us teachers either. There were leaks all over the place and so long as schools kept doing things the same way none of them stood a chance of getting fixed.

Monday, March 31

Mirabelle, a second-grade teacher, was upset about not being included in a meeting with a parent and Mr. B. about a kid in her class who'd been suspended six times. She'd thought, given her investment, she ought to be in on that meeting though Mr. B. was under no obligation to invite her. In response to this perceived oversight, she'd exchanged words in his office, walked out and promptly packed up and left for the day. Attempting to bring her back to resolve the issue, he'd gone searching, hunting up and down the halls and inquiring did anyone see Mirabelle and wondering where the hell she'd gone to until he was informed by her paraprofessional she'd departed the premises.

So the following day, Hannah, my fellow building representative (since September no person of sound mind had expressed interest in the position until Hannah gallantly stepped forward a month ago) and I met with Mirabelle at the behest of Mr. B., doing our best to save her from herself only to have her refuse to budge on our suggestion she apologize.

Mr. B. doesn't respect me!

Why, she asked us, couldn't he understand how much she loved this child and acknowledge the effort she'd put into saving him, how he'd achieved academic progress in spite of those six suspensions? And why didn't Mr. B. have enough sense to invite her to the damn meeting in the first place? How else was she supposed to be heard?

Both Hannah and I exclaimed we would be happy *not* to be invited to a meeting, *any* meeting, and reminded her that he was her supervisor, she'd ticked him off, then left school without notifying anyone.

He could write you up for insubordination, for Chrissakes!

We advised her to set up a meeting—*We'll even do it for you!*—and admit she'd had a bad day and leave it at that. She didn't have to apologize. Just meet with him and that would be enough.

There's no way I'm apologizing either way! she informed us. *In fact, I don't care to meet with him at all! I won't eat crow!*

Okay, fine, though we reminded her that Mr. B., being a human being, was not above holding a grudge. As with any boss it served to stay on his good side, or at least maintain a professional relationship.

Nothing doing, she continued. *How dare he not include me!*

In the end, she refused our advice. We couldn't make her take it, and perhaps she was right, gambling her stance would prove a good move in the end, showing him she wouldn't be played, she was her own person, etc. It took me a while to get over my indignation at having my worthy counsel rejected after spending over an hour imploring her to see things my way, but being ignored was part of the job of a building representative too.

Tuesday, April 1

During recess (fifty-five degrees and sunny) a group of kids started screaming and gesticulating at the vernal pool, telling me so-and-so had gone through the chain link gate without permission and waded in after a spotted salamander and now couldn't get out, was drowning in fact, sucked into the stinking muck and quickly taken under the deceptively tranquil surface, that it had happened so fast no one could believe their eyes, and now I had to get over there fast for him to have half a chance.

Please hurry Mr. D! Run! Before it's too late! Run!

I took off in a sprint, my heart thumping out of my chest, praying I'd make it in time, wondering should I shuck off my shoes and jacket, considering the depth, stunned by it, figuring all along it couldn't be more than a foot or so, and how stupid I'd been to think that after a week of steady rain and where the hell was the kid anyway? I circumnavigated the pool searching for ripples and found nothing but a placid unbroken surface and the group of kids who had caught up to me waving and laughing and shouting *April Fool's! Ha Ha Ha! Ha Ha Ha! April Fool's! We got you!* and me standing there gasping for air with a dopey grin on my face, making as if all along I knew I'd been had.

Of course I know what today is! I wheezed. *I knew you were all just kidding!*

Then why'd you run so fast then? Ha Ha! And why were you pulling off your shoes when you got to the gate? Ha Ha Ha! We got you! We got you good!

On this one day of the year you could make any claim, no matter how outrageous, and if your teacher was dumb enough to fall for it– as I was every year– you could scare the hell out of him and receive no punishment in return, not even a scolding.

Wednesday April 2

We read a magazine article about book burning in Germany during the Nazi regime. I defined *propaganda* as lies used by political parties to persuade the masses to act in a manner they wouldn't otherwise.

Are you victims of propaganda?

They had no idea, all except for Karter, a bright, lazy kid who had a lot to say about political issues, having formed his opinions watching *Fox News* with his grandfather.

Schools are controlled by the Left, he informed us. *The left says you don't even have to say The Pledge of Allegiance if you don't want.*

The rest of them spun around and regarded him.

What? No Pledge if we don't want to? said Anton. *Is that even true?*

Yes, I informed him, *it is.*

That's not right making us do something we don't have to do!

Once this revelation sank in, they resolved to no longer recite The Pledge of Allegiance. If they didn't have to do something, then why in heck were they doing it?

How come you lied to us, Mr. D.? Tanner wanted to know.

I shrugged.

I didn't lie to you. You never asked.

I'd been ambivalent about the Pledge of Allegiance since I'd begun teaching. While I understood it might be perceived as a propaganda tool and dangerous in its own right, the kids, having recited it every day since preschool, mumbled the words without thought or emotion. All along they'd been told to do it and complied, as they did with every request made of them or else. We never discussed what we were agreeing to when we stood in unison before the flag every morning at 8:30. Though the exercise meant nothing to them, had I provided the option to opt out when every other class in the building was doing it, I'd hear about it from parents and administrators. So what? I was an adult living in a republic. If free speech was protected by the First Amendment, so too was not having to say what you didn't feel like saying. But in SES, life was easier if you went along, even if that made you a hypocrite. Besides, given the wave of patriotism sweeping the country, not saying it might imply I didn't love the country, I was unAmerican, an Islamic terrorist sympathizer, etc. Who knew where that would lead? Nationalistic fervor had risen to such a pitch that we were pledging not only in our classrooms but at assemblies, concerts, district-wide professional development sessions and whenever the school community gathered for an evening event. On those days when we had an assembly followed by a school-wide parent meeting in the cafeteria, I found myself standing up and reciting the Pledge of Allegiance with a different group on three separate occasions. Any administrator knew the way to start off with a crowd was to step to the microphone and preface his speech by asking everyone to join him in reciting it.

Will we be arrested if we don't say The Pledge of Allegiance? asked Sierra.

No, I said. *Not yet, anyway.*

Some people burn the flag, Karter informed us.

What? said Mia. *That can't be true.*

So long as it's your own flag, I said.

My grandfather thinks those people should go to prison, he added, *along with anyone who wears the flag as a bathing suit.*

That's a lot of people! exclaimed Brielle. *Go to Salisbury Beach on the Fourth of July!*

He's so patriotic, Karter went on, *he had the flag tattooed on his back after 9/11.*

Then maybe he should go to jail! cried Brielle.

Thursday, April 3

Ray Bradbury's *All Summer in a Day* was another in my thrown-together collection of short stories. I'd been ignoring the district's curriculum map which directed every sixth-grade teacher to teach the same genre at the same time, pacing ourselves accordingly while keeping track of what everybody else was doing, no one nosing ahead or drifting behind, all of us arriving at the finish line in a dead heat come June.

One summer I'd spent a week with a group of colleagues creating a similar map. What genres were important to teach early in the year, the middle, the end? How much time should we allot to each? Trying to come to a consensus, we discussed whether fables or folklore should be taught in November or after February vacation. What about fairy tales and mythology? Legends and fantasy? Science fiction and essays? Narrative nonfiction, poetry, novels and short stories? Since it had already been established that a teacher could not be trusted to teach a genre whenever she felt the need to teach it, the decision was entrusted to us. So we got busy plugging away, filling up those weeks and months, somehow squeezing every genre in. Our finished product, ready to explode, still had us shaking our heads. Should science fiction get as much air time as folklore? What about mythology versus poetry? As the debate raged on, so did our exasperation. How was it possible to ask every six-grade class to know the particulars of one genre within a fixed time frame before charging on to the next? In the end, what we had was a map that was impossible to implement and seemed to work just as well held upside down.

Anyway, this close to retirement I could do what I wanted so I stuck with literature I enjoyed and thought would appeal to the kids. Hunting around on *Youtube*, I found a twenty-six minute video (How did I survive without *Youtube* to reinforce everything I'd ever taught?), a dated and gloomy version which did justice to the mood of Bradbury's story and spooked the hell out of them. After the video we rewrote the ending, giving

Margot a chance for some fun in the sun, or else deciding to keep her locked up even longer. We read our versions aloud and debated whether she deserved her fate for bragging about life on Earth until the kids on whatever planet it was—the children of colonists who'd never been to The Blue Planet—couldn't take it anymore and shoved her in that closet to shut her up. Everyone listened, not wanting to miss any gruesome details we'd visited upon poor old Margot. For homework I told them to come up with their own sci-fi story set on another planet (other than Mars). One page minimum, but it was okay if you wanted to keep on writing.

Friday, April 4

I took half a personal day to avoid an afternoon of professional development featuring more exercises on The Initiative. The memo outlining the agenda asked us to *Please share ideas and lessons you have used in your classrooms this year from various areas of The Initiative.* Well, we all had been teaching The Initiative long enough to be sick of it. The administration, sensing our ennui, had designated peer coaches, chosen from volunteers, to arm twist the rest of us into believing The Initiative was still an effective teaching tool which did not anesthetize both us and the kids. The session ran from 12:30 until 3:00 and I was glad I was missing it and equally happy for the kids who were out the door at 11:40, free to roam around town and wreak havoc all afternoon. This type of abbreviated school day brought out in them a certain frenzy so that getting through the morning required my expending as much energy as teaching a full day. With one scheduled per month, half days for professional development never failed to vex the parents, as arrangements had to be made for child care or taking time off from work. Schools justified the inconvenience as necessary for teacher training, even if professional development sessions were roundly bemoaned by us as more-of-the-same handed down by administrators. So, while my colleagues, resigning themselves to the task before them, collected water bottles, highlighters, notebooks, laptops and Tic Tacs and wandered off to their assigned classrooms, I headed in the other direction, not breaking my stride even when someone called my name.

Where do you think you're going? Come back here! You have no right not to suffer along the rest of us!

Monday, April 7, 2104

Over the weekend both Blaine and Leland moved to Haverhill. We'd had a little send-off on Friday, Nyla making chocolate cupcakes with green frosting, and we wished them well. When I heard they were leaving–together in the same week!–I was thrilled. Except today they were right back in 6D as if they hadn't gone anywhere, *school-choiced* by their parents who drove them from Haverhill to Salisbury. Though they were nice enough kids, not belligerent or disrespectful, their lack of focus on whatever I happened to be doing was another story. Blaine never shut up and Leland spent his day rooting through his desk for bits of wire and string and pen components he could fashion into shanks to wave around or little flexible men he could line up and issue commands to. As these two annoyed everybody around them, they brought out the worst in me. Try as I might, I had little success managing them. Whenever one or both were absent I felt a rush of lightheadedness as if I'd downed a couple of gin and tonics. Now they'd moved away but hadn't moved away, relocated to another town but not to another school, their parents deciding to hold it together long enough to haul them to and from SES every day, a thirty mile round trip. Somewhere in Haverhill sat a teacher blissfully ignorant of his good fortune. He didn't have them in *his class* thanks to their parents' determination to keep them in *my class*. He'd hit the lottery without realizing it.

Tuesday, April 8

We had our class picture taken this afternoon. Over the years I'd kept complimentary teacher copies in my desk drawer, taking them out from time to time to see how young I once was, not believing I'd worn a particular shirt or sweater or tie, flipping through the pile watching the hair recede from my forehead. Whatever happened to the free plastic combs we used to get, the ones with two different gauges of teeth you slipped into your back pocket and could play like a harmonica?

The photographer, a local guy with an easy, humorous style who was familiar with the kids and by means of pointing and facial gestures got them to follow every one of his many directions, arranged us in two rows against the back wall, the shorter kids seated on chairs in front, the bigger ones squeezed shoulder to shoulder behind them. If they all stood still and didn't fool around, he promised, they could pose for a silly photo once he'd taken the serious one. That got their attention though not once in my career had I—or anyone else—ever seen this so-called silly picture. Still, every year the kids fell for the same line. I pushed in on the right side in the back, freezing my smile through the whole ordeal and hoping my droopy right eyelid wasn't noticeable. For this, my last class photograph, I looked out over the heads of kids I'd taught all year and rather than feel sentimental, a groggy listlessness settled over me where all I wanted to do was lie down on a couch. In this stupified state I was forced to pose with a bunch of twelve-year-olds while endeavoring to maintain order as they fought for a spot beside their friends or planted donkey ears on the heads of the unaware or crossed their eyes or stuck middle fingers out where they thought they wouldn't be noticed until it was too late.

Smile, Mr. D, the photographer said, though I *was* smiling. I tried harder, and the effort triggered a mood change as the lens clicked, bringing me back to all those class photographs over the years with all those kids, many of whom I would run into and forget their names. And because kids changed physically so damn much from year to year, I'd have to search for the younger kid inside the older one, hoping to recognize the face but, too embarrassed to ask for a name, recite some anecdote to indicate I did indeed remember who he was. But I always felt terrible after these exchanges, convinced the kid had figured me out, that he wasn't worthy of my remembering (though, to be fair, those who stuck in my head were usually the uncooperative types who never gave me a moment's peace.). After one such after school visit, I rifled through a stack of SES sixth grade yearbooks hoping to get lucky. I found the photo with the kid's name under it and on the way home that day I spotted him walking alone by the town common. Jumping on the chance, I slowed down, lowered the window, beeped and shouted. *Justin, hey Justin! It was great seeing you today! Thanks for stopping by!*

After the photographer took what seemed like a hundred shots of us in our serious poses, he allowed us our one silly shot during which all hell broke loose. Wasting no time, he gathered his equipment and dashed off to the next class.

Wednesday, April 9

Since I was retiring in two months, four girls volunteered to clean and organize my classroom. I'd be in serious trouble unless I started now, as I hadn't lived up to my vow to deposit items on the free stuff table every day. Still surrounded by all the possessions I had to dispose of this late in the game, I admonished myself for my indolence, then dismissed it as part of my ongoing conflict. So long as the classroom was full of stuff, so long as everything stayed exactly where it was, reminding me of the person I'd been for the last almost thirty-seven years, I could go on pretending I was just another ordinary teacher who wasn't about to be catapulted onto the street in two and a half months.

The girls yanked plastic bins of paperbacks off shelves and set to battling dirt, dust motes and cobwebs along with sweeping up dead flies, gum wrappers and broken pencils. They alphabetized books I'd inherited from colleagues which no one had touched in years (*Do you go by the first name or the last?*), culling anything over two hundred pages (*No one's going to read these, Mr. D.*). The quartet pleasantly collaborated with a meticulous sense of duty, finding solace in the physical act of cleaning and organizing, excited to be released from the drudgery of seatwork. Their attention spans were not an issue despite the late hour, as they had initiated the job themselves, having identified the worthy purpose behind it, and thus intended to carry it out with a precision and attention missing from their academic pursuits. This was no longer school to them, at least in the usual sense, invigorated as they were by the goal of helping a teacher unable to help himself. The rest of the class, meanwhile, lukewarm to housekeeping, drew or read or dealt with the business of completing previous work. I wondered whether these girls behaved with similar diligence at home, if their rooms were kept neat and organized, or if when faced with the odious task of school work they found this a more desirable option. Upon finishing, they stood back to let me admire the fresh and well-ordered look of things, tugging my sleeve to get me out of my chair to come see what they'd done.

See, Mr. D! Check out what we did! Don't you feel better now with everything in its place? And this big pile of junk right here you can just get rid of! Just say the word and we'll be happy to drop everything and help you again! You still have a ways to go!

I thanked them and handed each a Dum Dum to which everyone else said *What about us? We do class work and they don't and they get a Dum Dum and not us!* I answered that if they tidied their desks they too would get a Dum Dum and the cleaners then lobbied that they should get a second DumDum for tidying their desks too although their desks were already pristine. The way out of this quandary was to dispense Dum Dums to everyone– the cleaners getting two–and thus all were satisfied and told me I was the best teacher they'd ever had and they meant it, really meant it, and swore they didn't go around saying that to every teacher they'd ever had who had given them something. And because of their kind words I didn't feel much like someone in the role of a teacher, more like a guy with a nice group of kids on an April afternoon, all of us happy to be around one another.

Thursday, April 10

The kids brought in the last project I'd ever assign, one I'd given them ten days to complete– creating books about books they'd read, their responses typed up and accompanied by hand drawn illustrations pasted inside those books. We propped the finished products up around the classroom, everyone checking to see who had the best and who had the crappiest. The day I handed out the instruction sheet I also distributed sheets of copy paper, five to a kid, which they folded in half. I then passed out sewing needles, spools of thread and thimbles, reviving a lost art which 6D thought was fantastic. I told them my mother had shown me how to sew when I was six years old so I could mend my socks. They didn't believe me, struck by the odd sight of their teacher moistening one end of a length of thread, squinting through his reading glasses, slipping the end through the needle's eye, pulling the thread halfway through and knotting the ends.

Why is it called that? asked Brynn. *It doesn't even look like an eye!*

We quickly learned that needles are sharp.

Why does the stupid thread keep bending back on itself right before you put it through the eye? asked a fed-up Blaine, who, desperate to figure out how to unlock the puzzle, sought help from Raelynn who'd been taught the craft by her grandmother.

Close one eye first, she gently instructing him, *then it's easy. Like this.*

He did close his eye, and it was easy. He smiled at his accomplishment of such an amazing feat. He thanked her. She smiled back and knotted the thread for him. If he needed any more help well he could just ask her.

We spent the next hour merrily sewing away, pushing the needle through the pencil dots we'd drawn on the paper to guide us, some kids picking it up fast, others needing numerous tries assisted by classmates but soon enough we had a classroom of tailors and seamstresses. From there, they carried the stitched paper home to bind it with two pieces of cardboard to be covered with fabric. I kept the cost low for the materials, available at Walmart, a five minute drive from school, though 6D was dependent on transportation and having to come up with a few bucks. As such I was never sure how to grade the final product, not wanting to penalize kids for their parents' lack of resources or plain old lassitude. Thus I awarded A's to the halfway decent ones (most) and gave the crappy editions C's. The reward for an A was to have your book displayed in the school library. To demonstrate that 6D was an egalitarian community both in belief and practice, I offered to assist the C's in redoing theirs during recess or after school.

Then you can have yours displayed in the library too! I told them.

Not a single kid took me up on the offer. They were fine, thank you, the grade of C as good or better than what they'd been getting since they'd entered school. Further exertion served no purpose in their minds, as they'd been told all along they were C students, which meant, officially, average/satisfactory/acceptable (though nowadays, with everybody awarded A's, C's meant you were dumb and didn't give a shit). Or more likely they smelled a rat, seeing my help as a setup. How could it be a real honest-to-goodness legitimate A if the teacher provided material and individual instruction, maybe even actually doing the hard parts himself like cutting the fabric and gluing the binding? Word would get out, everyone realizing it for what it was, not a real A but a bogus one. Better to save face, take the authentic C and be done with it, rather than allow the entire school see you for the phony you were.

Friday, April 11

I started reading aloud S.E. Hinton's *Tex,* a coming of age drama which in my opinion rivals *Catcher in the Rye* for both its voice and impact on this particular age group. Though written in 1979, the novel explores issues pertinent today–drugs, dating, teenage pregnancy, trouble with the law, sibling rivalry, parental neglect. The narrator in his convincing voice won the kids over fast. Some of the topics, especially the sex and drug dealing, had me thinking I should have sent a permission slip home. After we'd finished *The Outsiders*, the kids clamored for more S.E. Hinton. Not willing to wait for me to come up with something, Tanner, one of 6D's poorest readers, went out and borrowed *Tex* from the town library. He then proceeded to read it on his own, describing to me characters and setting, summarizing the plot and predicting that no matter what books eventually came into his life, *Tex* would always remain his favorite. A few days later he tracked down the movie and watched it with his dad who loved the book too. In Tanner's opinion it would make a solid choice to follow *The Outsiders*.

It's even better, he claimed. *It goes into more stuff.*

And he was right. I marvelled over how someone with his reading issues, who struggled with decoding and comprehension and refused to read aloud during class and at best slogged away at a third-grade level, could through sheer grit override those impediments, adamant to find a way to unlock a story which had so enthralled him from page one, lousy reading skills (at least according to our assessments) be damned. Was it possible, then, that the assessments he'd been taking since he'd entered school weren't doing what they purported to do? Were his scores, in fact, misleading? Had he figured out those tests, seeing them as nothing other than chunks of dull writing having no connection to the joy he derived from puzzling out a novel like *Tex*? Had he learned to distinguish between *reading* and *story*, deciding that the former was fake and boring and of no use to him and thus unworthy of his attention, the latter real and necessary and eliciting a passion which drove him to stay up all night to get something he couldn't live without? It seemed to me he had, as all year long he been describing books to me I was sure he couldn't read. He'd finally convinced me with *Tex.*

Monday, April 14

During recess kids exploded over the ballfield–running, shrieking, cartwheeling, throwing themselves onto the new grass, propelled by pure ebullience, then getting up and running again, sprinting so fast their legs went out from under them. They got right back up and kept at it, running and tumbling, rolling on the ground and popping up as if made of rubber. In the brilliant seventy degree weather their bliss was uncontained and contagious. Before long twenty or so boys organized themselves into a wiffle ball game, coming together like a flock of starlings on the pitching mound before dispersing over the diamond and outfield, clustering in twos and threes at each position, chattering away, hopping in place, flinging small stones and twigs and whatever else happened to be lying at their feet. When they had enough of that they spun in circles, fell over, got up, grabbed and punched whoever happened to be next to them because they happened to be next to them. At home plate a tidy line waited patiently for a chance to swing the plastic yellow bat, all of this orchestration done without adult intervention. Along the foul line a row of girls executed a series of perfect backflips until a teacher spotted them from her classroom window and reported this behavior to the office, whereby a message was relayed via walkie-talkie to my colleague Adelle standing next to me on the blacktop who blew her whistle and shouted, *Hey no backflips!* The girls turned, nodded and waved to us, then resumed their routine. Both Adelle and I were miffed about being spied upon, word going around that we were shirking our duty because of those backflippers, which got us on the topic of being treated like children ourselves by our supervisors despite the fact we were a good deal older and more experienced. Adelle had a couple of years left though she talked about retirement more than I did. A single mother with a couple of middle school age kids, she'd long ago run out of patience with dutiful co-workers who refused to mind their own business and went tattling to administrators about normal adolescent behavior. It was this kind of thing, she confessed, that made a rational woman like herself want to go into the building, hunt down the big mouth and beat the hell out of her.

Can she please find something else to do other than spy on us? Like teach?

Tuesday, April 15

This afternoon I attempted to show a *YouTube* video in the Smartboard room of Kipling's *Rikki Tikki Tavi* after I'd read an adapted version aloud. The kids goofed off even before it began and thus, smarted by their noncompliance, I ushered them all back into the classroom. To indicate my annoyance came at a cost, I scrawled a dozen comprehension questions on the board, writing until my hand cramped. I then ranted about their conduct and announced no more videos, fun, etc., all because a kid had used his ruler as a flute to mimic the sound track while another got on all fours pretending to be a mongoose after I'd been good enough to show this video in place of seatwork. Earlier I'd spent a good twenty minutes lecturing on etiquette after they'd acted like buffoons returning from lunch. My temples throbbed, my feet ached, and I couldn't find my reading glasses, all of which put me in the mood for retribution. Before me swam twenty-one fish in a barrel, easy targets I was free to punish in any way I saw fit. I demanded they all sit down and commence with the dreaded seatwork without uttering a sound. Having shown them who was boss, I continued to scowl at anyone with the nerve to look up from his desk. At this point in the year they knew me well enough to know guilt would eat away my insides, leading me to reflect on my behavior (to myself) and after a few minutes offer a second chance. It wasn't their fault they couldn't control themselves. They were out of their minds, or perhaps well within their minds, reacting to the plight of being twelve years old and stuck in a room with a man who may or may not be in full possession of his marbles. All around the school at this late hour teachers were demanding kids stay in their seats (*Please be seated! Thank you!*) and all around the school kids were popping out of them, refusing to sit or doing so only under dire threats. Because of this teachers blamed the kids for their headaches and vice versa, and so while each party had had it with the other, each understood neither was intrinsically evil.

Wednesday, April 16

Marcia showed me another *Needs Improvement* rating on her latest observation. She wrote a rebuttal to assistant principal Ms. G.'s summary of her performance and asked for my opinion. I read it over. It was clear she'd made valid points.

A teacher was free to write whatever she wanted as a rebuttal, going on for a page or two, but in the end it didn't mean much as her evaluator had the final say.

Knowledgeable, personable and dedicated to her work, Marcia's refusal to adjust her schedule to accommodate classroom teachers back in September hadn't won her many allies. Classroom teachers expected her to pull IEP kids out for math when the rest of the class had math, for example, and not when the rest of the class had science. Fair enough, she countered, but an impossibility, given the needs of her students who happened to be spread over four classes. As such she was viewed as less than a team player. Next year would be a probationary period, with more frequent evaluations done by the same people who'd written the subpar ones this year.

In my role as building representative there wasn't much I could do except listen. I tried to imagine what it might be like to feel your job at risk after having been committed to it for so long, to wake up one day without salary and benefits, to have to start all over again as a provisional teacher with a much lower salary–if Marcia in her mid-forties could even find work.

Thursday, April 17

My colleague Bernard, who taught fifth-grade next door, reminded me again how lucky I was not to be getting his class next year. He was thirty years old, had taught at SES for seven years, loved tattoos and recently had *R-E-A-D M-O-R-E* inked across the tops of his fingers. At the rate he was going, he doubted he'd survive until the end of the year. His crazy class loved him and he loved them back–he'd grown up in town and had gone to SES–yet on occasion his voice penetrated the cinder block wall between our class-rooms (he'd say the same about mine). The two of us joked about being designated *male role models*, our lot having been cast by previous teachers who'd identified that such-and-such a kid, with no adult male in his life, needed to observe how a normal one behaved (he and I having been decreed exam-ples of normal). By and large these kids had issues (anger, resentment, trust, motivation) and with so few male teachers in the building (three) and so many of them, we ended up with a sizeable contingent and would gripe to one another about our classrooms being dumping grounds. He and I coached track at the high school where six days a week we sold kids on the idea that running until they were nauseous built character. His dream was to become a personal fitness trainer, to run his own health club and work one-on-one with eager clients who listened patiently, were gracious and appreciative, followed his advice and paid him good money, except he didn't have the resources to start his own business. He put a lot of time and effort into his work and liked to show me ideas he'd come up with. Student projects hung on clotheslines stretched across his classroom, forcing me to duck whenever I walked around inspecting them. Kid work also adorned the walls and hung from string and paper clips from the ceiling.

Exasperated by the demands of the job, we wished for a time and place to decompress, to vent about the kids, the length of the school day, the many hassles visited upon us. It would be a good idea, we thought, to learn some techniques for dealing with stress too, even just a chance to shoot the breeze in a relaxed atmosphere where we could hear ourselves think. Though we had plenty of professional development sessions around The Initiative, nothing was provided which might save a young guy like Bernard from burnout, the thinking being, I guess, that if the administration didn't acknowledge teacher burnout it didn't exist.

Friday, April 18

On the Friday before April vacation, 6D created a large greeting card out of oak tag with a smiling running stick figure on the cover and lots of smiling moon faces cheering him on. Everyone signed it and wished me luck in The Boston Marathon on Monday. I'd done it for a number of years now and still was touched by the kids' support. *Good luck, Mr. D.! Hope you make it to the finish!* I read each little note and nodded thank yous as they surrounded my desk, studying my expression, adding that they would watch me on television or follow my progress on their computers. I said I would think about each of them on my trip from Hopkinton to Boston and they all agreed there was no way on earth they could or would run twenty-six miles, that doing so was a completely crazy thing to do, although one or two confessed they might give it a try someday and the rest thought them nuts.

My aunt did that one time, ran a marathon, though are all marathons twenty-six miles? Thad asked me.

Yeah, I said.

Then she did something else then, another race I think in Florida when she lived down there. That was before she died.

Obviously, Nyla said. *So how long will it take you?*

Hopefully under three and a half hours, I told her.

Is that running the whole time?

Yeah.

Why would you want to do that?

257

I guess I like to run.

I like chocolate donuts but I wouldn't eat a whole box of them.

I nodded.

Remember how you said you couldn't climb a curbstone afterwards without your wife helping you?

Yeah.

In fact, Nyla had me recalling that now, which wasn't something I wanted to recount three days before the race.

It's supposed to be hot, mentioned Lucy.

I know.

For the past week I'd become obsessed, googling *Weather Underground* half a dozen times a day.

People die in marathons, right?

I shooed them back to their seats.

People younger than you. A lot younger.

They were fixated on that possibility, especially since I'd stupidly told them I was required to list my next of kin on the back of my bib number.

Aren't you afraid?

In fact, despite my previous experience, I was terrified of running Boston—the four miles of hills starting at mile eighteen, each tougher than the one before it, the afternoon heat rising in shimmery waves off the pavement as the Prudential Tower came into view at the top of Heartbreak Hill, the searing pain in my quadriceps over the home stretch every time my foot struck the ground. In the days before the race my anxiety over what I was about to undertake made me miserable to be around.

It's fun actually.

They looked at me, unconvinced.

It's okay, Mr. D., Cheyenne said. *You have to tell yourself that, right?*

Monday, April 28

Veronica, who'd been in the district a dozen years, approached me about the *Needs Improvement* rating on her evaluation after an observation. As her building representative, what could I do to help? Ms. G. had expected to see components of The Initiative being taught but Veronica, who'd recently been trained in RETELL, the state mandated English Language Learner Program (of which her evaluator, she claimed, was unfamiliar) had instead taught an element of that program to her class of bilingual kids. The lesson had gone well, the kids showing their understanding of concepts by reciting them back to her, and it wasn't until she'd been sent a copy of the evaluation that she understood something else was expected of her entirely. Whose fault was it then? It occurred to me that our evaluators were just as hamstrung by The Initiative as we were. Since we'd been forced to teach it, they were forced to evaluate our teaching of it, thus eliminating any need to see the teacher as something other than a parrot of The Initiative's way of doing things. In turn teachers had begun to doubt themselves, gauging their level of competence only as it was reflected through their grasp of The Initiative. Veronica, though comfortable enough with it, had opted to pursue a more pressing need and in doing so had paid for her foresight.

She could fight it, I reminded her, as there was a place on the evaluation to counter what had been written about her performance, though the effort would likely be futile, as Mr. B. and Ms. G. were judge and jury, with Ms. G. already having outlined during her planning period exactly what she'd (Veronica) needed to correct. She would end up losing another planning period if she continued (in vain) to challenge the outcome. Better simply to place her chips on the next observation. That was hardly useful advice and her teary reaction was enough for me to apologize twice as I squeezed out of one of her students' desks and backed out of the room.

Tuesday, April 29

Struggling to cope with this long stretch until June, with kids even more restive as white buds blossomed on the magnolias and dogwoods and the temperature crept into the mid-seventies, teachers bore the onslaught by hiding out in their rooms, emerging only to dash to the copy machine or to the bathroom, not stopping to chat because who had the time and who wanted to hear about burnout from everyone else when you were burnt out yourself?

Leland came over to my desk to ask if he could have the pocket watch which had hung from a chain above the whiteboard for probably a decade. I couldn't remember how I'd come to own it, maybe I'd found it at a flea market or received it as a gift. At one time it worked before succumbing to overhandling by kids fascinated by a timepiece with a fob and an ornate gold cover that snapped open, its delicate slender hands ticking in a gentle whisper. Anyway, the watch had mesmerized him all year long. He loved to take it down and lay it across his palm as if it were a baby bird, stroking its star-embossed cover and wondering how to get it going again, desperate to disassemble it at his desk and realign those cogs and springs. He pointed to it in case I didn't know what he was talking about, which in many cases I didn't, as he mumbled and never made eye contact, towing me by the arm up to where it hung from the top of the whiteboard, saying *Please may I have it?* and me saying *Yeah sure,* touched by his sincerity and fondness for the watch and me wanting to get rid of it anyway. After the rest of the class departed for music class, he took it down, wrapped it carefully in a piece of paper towel and tucked it safely into his backpack.

Wednesday, April 30

At 1:30 the entire sixth grade gathered in the commons room to hear about our new service dog. There'd been a grant written and Nicole, who ran our behaviorally disordered class, had volunteered to care for the dog and spent a week at a training facility mastering how to handle it. Now we had our own black Lab to comfort kids having a bad day (and teachers too, we hoped). Enraptured by the sight of this gentle creature sprawled on the floor in front of us, we stared at him as if we'd never seen a dog before. The kids leaned forward with their hands out, burning to come forward and pet him, roll on the floor and squeeze him, scratch his soft belly and maybe get him a tennis ball to chase around but this being school there were loads of rules they were required to learn first, so many in fact that they'd forgotten most by the time they were done hearing them.

Just approaching Warren required many steps—requesting permission of the teacher/handler, walking toward him in a specific way, touching only his ears or a small spot on his back behind the red pack he wore—so that half the kids didn't want to bother when given the chance. In addition to all that, we weren't supposed to call him by his name as only his handler could do that so as not to confuse him. What were we supposed to call him then? There didn't seem to be an answer to this simple question. I liked the idea of having a dog in school, remembering when I was young how one would follow us inside in the morning, scrambling classroom to classroom in a frantic search for its owner, getting sidetracked on its mission by all our attention, sniffing our legs and licking our hands and bringing out whoops of joy before the owner could be located. But Warren was a different story, and given the parameters surrounding access, and the fact that he wouldn't be available to the average student, nearly all the kids in the room would never develop a relationship with him and would come to ignore his presence as he ambled around the building (he seemed equally unaware of us). His job was to assist the very needy, the small number of extremely troubled kids who from time to time found themselves in one of our two small *time out* rooms (more like closets), blockaded from view by a folding wall on wheels and guarded by two staff until the kids' tantrums subsided. Throughout the year we could hear them screaming and kicking the reinforced walls and eventually grew used to that too.

Thursday, May 1

With less than two months to go I spent more time getting rid of stuff–a teacher in the primary school requested one of my paper cutting boards (the one she could lift by herself, not the car battery). Another teacher would take the dozen 12x18 reams of multi-colored construction paper I'd stockpiled. Karter had his eye on my U.S. Marine Corps coffee mug and miniature American flag, both of which I planned to keep as I'd gotten them as gifts from a former student who'd visited between tours in Iraq and Afghanistan. At my request, he'd talked to the kids about military life, standing tall in his dress blues while the class ogled him as if he'd arrived from another planet. In the Marines, he told them, he'd learned manners and discipline and had come to believe in himself. Due to his training, he had the confidence needed for any of life's challenges. Nobody, he acknowledged, meant more to him than his fellow Marines. And no, he informed them, answering 6D's most pressing question, he'd never shot anyone and no one had shot him, an arrangement he hoped to keep permanent. As a student in my class he'd been a timid scrawny kid whose eyeglasses slid down his nose, who struggled to write a legible sentence and didn't come within two years of reading at grade level. I once asked a recruiter, a guy in my running club, how the Marines accomplished that, took kids lacking conviction and self-esteem no one seemed to be able to do anything with and turn them into skilled, fit, courteous and focused adults. All he would tell me was *We have our ways.* I didn't talk much to the kids about military life, certainly had my issues with it, having grown up in The Sixties and been assigned a draft number, though once I saw this transformation I began to see it as an option that might save a certain type of kid from a directionless life.

Friday, May 2

The annual Peace Poetry Awards was held at Northern Essex Community College tonight. The topic was, of course, peace, and the kids had plenty to say about it, and just as much to say about the dark forces of war and violence. Back in March we'd written poems and read them aloud so we could all listen and clap and tell one another what great poets we were. Convinced our submissions were the best, we'd stuffed them into a manilla envelope and mailed them off. This year we ended up with eight winners, the authors getting dressed up for the big night and bringing their folks along. Reciting their poems from the podium to a full auditorium, they seemed as relaxed as they had been reciting them in 6D. Whether for a crowd of twenty or three hundred, it was all the same to them. For their effort they were awarded certificates, chapbooks containing their poems, and key chains. I submitted a poem for the first time and when my name was called near the end of the ceremony, the kids turned to notify me that my name had been called and was I paying attention? I nodded and strolled to the front, past rows and rows of people, terrified and concentrating on every step so I wouldn't stumble because sometimes I did stumble for no particular reason whatsoever which always made Carla and the kids laugh thinking I'd done it as a gag. I wanted everyone to notice this purposeful gentleman, so at ease with himself, who'd spent the previous twenty minutes pretending to listen but instead engaged in deep breathing and positive thinking to keep his crushing anxiety at bay. If I stayed calm long enough I might be able to get the words out as the poem was a short one. With clammy hands dampening the page and a shaky voice helped along with the aid of the microphone, I recited a poem in public for the first time, the subject of the piece the futility of someone trying to meditate. Here and there I heard laughter. That was good, laughter. Afterwards applause. That was good too. As I left the podium I imagined a twelve-year-old up here, head just above the lectern, speaking *up* into the mic.

The professor who organized the evening, a guy around my age with a ponytail and corduroy jacket with elbow patches, greeted us when the ceremony concluded, thanking us for coming as he did every year. Always gracious, he understood the importance of this type of event for kids and their writing. When I mentioned I was retiring, he wished me good luck and told me to submit again next year. I said I would, but it wouldn't be the same coming here alone.

Monday, May 5

I took the day off to take Apphia to be examined by an oral surgeon. Before she could have braces installed she'd have to undergo a procedure whereby her gum would be slit open to expose a canine tooth, a bracket attached to its wall, a chain running from bracket to braces. Over time, if all went well, the tooth would be ratcheted from horizontal to vertical, joining the rest of the set.

The braces would cost one million dollars. At least that was what I heard the receptionist say. But how could you deny your kid braces when every other kid had them? Her sisters' teeth, fortunately, were judged straight enough, so in the end I'd saved two million dollars. Except now I had to break the news to the other two that, unlike everybody else, their teeth would not be adorned with stainless steel and rubber bands, they would never get to sleep with expensive retainers, the ones they would lose half a dozen times after swearing they never let them out of their sight.

Apphia wasn't so pleased with the prospect of having a chain installed in her mouth so I offered to take her to lunch. She insisted on a sandwich from a fast food drive-thru, wanting to make it quick, telling me to hurry up, wondering if she had time to eat at all, preoccupied as she was with getting back to class, terrified she'd miss something and not be able to get the notes. Once we had our food she insisted I drive while she ate.

Are you going this slow on purpose? Do you really hate me that much?

I thought I might be responsible for those jitters, her having inherited a healthy dose of my chronic anxiety, so I asked whether the high school did anything to help freshmen cope with stress. Before she took a bit of the chicken salad wrap laying on her lap, she rolled her eyes.

Is that a serious question?

Tuesday, May 6

At recess the boys organized themselves into a wiffle ball game, ten or twelve or so on a side, playing inning after inning without adult interference. They'd included everyone who wanted to play, even kids who missed the ball by a mile. There wasn't much talking, except to debate who was up next. From shallow left field I watched the white perforated ball float through the air or skip over the grass, get fielded and returned to the mound. When a less dexterous kid picked up the bat, the pitcher moved in a few steps and lobbed the ball underhand. Everyone cheered when contact was made and the ball dribbled down the third base line. Many of these same kids were targeted for their impulsive behaviors during class, lunch, assemblies, etc., and subsequently sent to the office, kicked off the school bus, or told to expect a call home. And yet here they were, away from their teachers (except for me who watched from a healthy distance), taking turns and doing just fine. Why did we badger them to walk in lines, to shut up, to follow this or that nonsensical request which we made of them a hundred times a day? I was pondering that when the whistle blew and their twenty-minute recess ended just like that, everyone abandoning the diamond and fleeing toward the cafeteria doors. Lunch for the sixth grade began promptly at 11:00

(by 11:05 most kids were still waiting to get their chow) and ended promptly at 11:20, setting off a cafeteria-wide clatter of tray dumping, piles of unfinished/untouched food tumbling into big rubber trash barrels, followed by orders from teachers to form eight single lines at the entrance doors (boys and girls separately). Methodical eaters crammed what they could grab into their mouths like chipmunks or stashed away something for later. Unhurried eaters (those lacking the ability to swallow food whole Joey Chestnut-style) had time for a bite or two before directed toward those lines, the fifth grade flowing in from their recess ready for their turn at speed-eating, the fourth grade beginning recess and so on. A half-hour from now I would be sitting at my desk filling out nurse's slips for upset stomachs.

Wednesday, May 7

During Ivan's IEP evaluation meeting, I watched his mother gamely attempt to follow the proceedings. The liaison sat at the head of the conference table, directing the flow of conversation from the team (classroom teacher, SPED teacher, psychologist, speech therapist, guidance counselor) regarding assessments, goals, objectives, and any other details pertinent to the IEP while his mother, bewildered, tried to decipher the jargon we threw around on a daily basis. Odd terms like *executive function,* for example, made me think of a branch of government and did nothing to enlighten her regarding her son's ability to access the curriculum. I knew how she felt because I'd been in that seat some years before, tense and perspiring, as Carla and I faced a phalanx of teachers and specialists who began by telling us how much they loved our daughter Beatrice, how sweet and kind and quiet she was, what a joy to behold (*We would all kill for those dimples!*) before getting to the heart of the matter, a line by line interpretation of her academic and psychological tests scores, some good, some average, some not-so-good. We sat there, crushed and in a daze, hearing only the not-so-good (which was all we talked about), half listening and without hope, scribbling notes, as a plan was presented to address her expressive language deficits brought about by selective mutism exacerbated by, of all things, the pressure of having to perform in school. Her scores, the team acknowledged, may not even be accurate, given her reluctance to speak to her tester. Even so, it was determined she should receive services, both in the classroom and out, provided by a special education teacher, a speech therapist, and a guidance counselor. I regretted right then granting permission to test her. It was the perfect Catch 22– the problem we were hoping to rectify made worse by the very institution everyone in the room was a part of! And now, it seemed to me, removing her from class in front of the other kids would only increase that anxiety. And as if that wasn't enough, how many others (administrators, teachers, paraprofessionals, substitutes) would be privy to this information, accurate or not, about my kid?

That afternoon we broke the news to Beatrice whom we'd neglected to consult beforehand.

No way, she said. *Forget it. I'm not doing that.*

We signed the IEP anyway, making it a legal document. She came home upset every day. Why had we done this to her? Whenever someone arrived at the classroom door to collect her, she told us, the other kids wondered where she was going. She shrugged, as if she had no idea, as if it was a big surprise to her too. Humiliated, she one-worded (or said nothing) to the persons whose job it was to strengthen those expressive language skills and help her deal with her anxiety, and who, she wished (though she liked them all well enough) would one day very soon vanish from the face of the earth.

Why do I have to do this? she asked us at the dinner table. *You didn't ask me!*

It will help you.

No it won't.

Give it a try.

I did. I hate it.

Just for now.

It's embarrassing! Everyone knows where I'm going!

Eventually we came around, signing off on services against the team's advice after Beatrice implored us to let her swim for herself. She was thrilled to be emancipated, back where she belonged, in the regular classroom again. She hugged us. We were the best. Seeing her happy made us happy, though we worried. What now? Would she make it? Yes, she would, through sheer doggedness and as much help as she would allow us to give her (and likely sensing the threat of our re-opening the IEP), she overcame her symptoms and figure out a way to achieve on her own.

Thursday, May 8

After school I was feted at a cocktail party held at a Newbury-port restaurant sponsored by the Triton Regional Teachers' Association. Along with my fellow retirees from across the district, I was presented with an eight-by-twelve framed watercolor of an estuary along with an engraved pen and pencil set. When my turn came to speak I followed a science teacher from the high school who had everyone in stitches using various props from her classroom in suggestive ways. Once the audience stopped laughing I was introduced and went to the front of the room with no props to wave around or jokes to tell which made me feel as if I'd left my clothes in the trunk of my car. I'd never been good at improv and had prepared only a few words of thanks, so I mentioned how fortunate I was to have taught in the district for fifteen years. Then I went on to thank Maggie, our union president, who was acting as the master of ceremonies and was a hero of mine for the tenacity and consistency with which she defended teachers and the collective bargaining agreement. Scanning the room, I wondered if I looked as exhausted as my fellow retirees.

Later, as we posed for a group photo, we asked one another how we'd survive the rest of our lives without professional development sessions, conducting assessments and attending all those meetings to analyze and interpret data. What would we do with ourselves? To a person we were ready to leave, smiling and happy and hugging all who came within arms' reach, surprised and happy we'd lived to see this day as we'd certainly had our doubts along the way. There was unbridled joy all around. What had the profession done to us if after all these years none of us had mixed feelings about leaving it?

Friday, May 9

I wanted to kill a kid this afternoon, three actually–Tanner, Corbin, Thad–all with ADHD, all pains in the neck who wouldn't leave me alone, and all possessing remarkable imaginations evident in their storytelling which enchanted me. Every day after lunch the trio would surround my desk demanding to be heard, leaning close to get and hold my attention, exclaiming altogether *Wait*

wait Mr. D. just listen to this just this thing and then we'll do our work promise we just have to tell you this you'll love this one please then we'll stop and do our work okay? Okay? Please? Not one of the three understood or cared what my role as a teacher involved, the duties I was required to dispense in this classroom of ours, my intention to cover this or that lesson be damned.

To a one they were courteous and respectful and thought I was a really good teacher and a great guy. Given how they felt about me, *their friend,* they approached me at will, sometimes one or two at a time, sometimes all three together. The problem for me was they were interesting to listen to, and because of this I would drop my role and become a normal person, allow myself to be fascinated by their love of words, their delight in hearing their own voices and seeing my reaction, mesmerized as I was by their abiding passion for stories. And yet they were three of the most learning disabled kids I'd ever worked with. What they lacked in their ability to read and write they made up for in their proficiency for conversation. Stories about what they'd witnessed or what had befallen them burst forth unbidden. They simply could not go on another second unless I agreed to hear what they couldn't contain. But what good did that do them in school other than to eventually tick teachers off, people like me so stuck in his role that even with a month to go before retirement he couldn't say yeah let's just tell one another stories for the rest of the afternoon, okay?

Monday, May 12

The last day of school was officially June 19. With five weeks to go, I was thinking about that during recess duty while kids played a wiffle ball game without a bat. Where was their bat?

A line of hitters snaked from home plate, each one stepping up for a turn to swat the ball with an open palm, handball style, and everyone thrown out at first for the effort. Either they'd misplaced the bat, or else its owner had lost the privilege of using it, or the bat was not allowed on the school bus as a result of a previous transgression. Now, having no bat, they'd managed just fine, thank you, a single carrying the weight of a homerun. As I admired their ingenuity, Greta, our social worker, wandered over with a two way radio attached to her belt (We were supposed to carry these in the event of an emergency though I never had, preferring to send a kid running inside for the nurse rather than trying to communicate over the static to someone in the office who might or might not understand what I was saying before relaying my semi-coherent message to the nurse's office). She pointed out a couple of kids she had her eye on who'd shoved one another a few days ago. Now the culprits were plucking needles off a defenseless thirty-foot cedar along the border fence, apparently having brokered a truce.

Look at what they're doing to that tree! She grabbed my arm to direct my attention to the far end of the outfield, though it wasn't worth the effort of squinting. *Something has to be done about that!*

Hey leave that tree alone! I shouted feebly, feeling like an idiot.

The two couldn't hear me, or else choose to ignore my silly request. My voice gone, I wasn't going to shout again. They continued to tug at the tips of those branches, waving them up and down in a ropy dance, as she charged off in their direction. I couldn't imagine what she would say and thought if she made an issue out of it she might really have a crisis on her hands. But like me, she'd been driven batty from years of fruitless struggle sorting out the antics of troubled twelve-year-olds. The line distinguishing a harmless behavior from one that necessitated intervention had long since blurred beyond all recognition. It wasn't her fault. I'd been at it a lot longer and depending on my mood either found myself ranting about something I'd have been better off ignoring (kids attempting to clear a mud puddle) while disregarding a potential problem (a pig pile out on the playing field).

I turned my attention back to the baseball/handball game. Somehow a kid had made it to second base. Was a runner on third too? Would someone cross home plate before recess ended? Who needed a bat to play whiffle ball anyway?

Tuesday, May 13

I administered my final MCAS this morning, session 1 in mathematics (session 2 would be tomorrow). The kids plugged away for a couple of hours after which I collected the test booklets, answers sheets, six inch plastic rulers and green oak tag formula sheets. As soon as they left for lunch I hurried the materials downstairs to deposit the lot in the locked conference room, its interior windows strung with yellow caution tape in case anyone was unaware of the seriousness of this endeavor. Under the watchful eye of Barbara, the head office secretary, I signed my name on an official form to verify that I was indeed myself and she initialled next to my signature to further sub-stantiate I was indeed myself and not some imposter though we had known one another fifteen years. Stacks of testing ma-terial were arranged in squared off piles by grade, ready to be picked up by teachers in the morning. If anything was out of place there would be hell to pay and so long as the room was free of human beings and their propensity for touching and moving items around everything would remain exactly where it had been left. Both Barbara and I were glad to be out of there so as not to be blamed for so much as a missing ruler.

Anytime I administered the MCAS I wanted to get the damn thing out of my hands as soon as the kids finished. A few years ago Effie, a fifth grade colleague, lost a blank test booklet somewhere in her classroom. She was an excellent teacher, organized, efficient and highly regarded, and because of these qualities losing the booklet left her distraught and desperate. She couldn't forgive herself and figured this lapse would be all she would be remembered for. After turning the room inside out, enlisting help from other teachers, all of us on our hands and knees, combing through desks, cabinets, closets and the waste basket, searching high and low for the damn thing which had somehow vanished in plain sight, she sighed in defeat. Crestfallen, she wondered how she could have possibly been so careless. We did our best to console her, reminding her it was a blank booklet anyway, letting her know it wasn't her fault, that these goddam MCAS people had sticks up their asses. She nodded and thanked us for our time and wiped her eyes and blew her nose and slumped in her chair. We stayed to comfort her, saying we didn't mind looking further if that would make her feel any better. It was like searching for someone's wallet: we were all relieved it hadn't happened to us.

Wednesday, May 14

At 11:15, I gathered up the last of the math MCAS materials and hurried them downstairs. After the kids went off to recess, I ate lunch at my desk and thought about the Bruins' seventh game against the Canadiens at the Garden tonight. Would they have enough left to advance? I hoped the afternoon would pass quickly, as, having expended themselves academically and emotionally, 6D was now under the mistaken impression that they were off the hook and could do whatever they wanted for the next three plus hours. When they returned from the cafeteria they were characteristically themselves, exploding into the room, ignoring my stern gaze and plopping into their seats with a bang and a sigh.

You don't expect us to do anything, do you? We had the MCAS all morning! We're exhausted! You can make us do no work!

Heads resting on their arms, they complained of migraines and upset stomachs and assorted ailments too numerous to name, all brought about from the morning's tribulation. They demanded I turn off the lights, pull down the shades and declare nap time for the rest of the day. The few stragglers, lacking excuses for their tardiness, wandered in, rebounding off desks as if they were balls in a pinball game. I corralled them and told everyone to take out a book and read, an activity I considered a compromise, agreeing to shut off the lights and allowing them to keep their heads down. They groaned and reluctantly fired up their Kindles, or opened their plain old hardcovers or paperbacks, the morning's effort having pushed them to the brink of maximum entropy.

Why do we have to do anything? Arya pleaded. *Why can't we just have fun for once?*

I ignored her and took out my own book.

Just think how lucky you are, I told them as I removed my book marker. *It wasn't that way when I was a kid.*

Yeah, we know, interrupted Ivan. *Your teacher made you read all the old stupid boring stuff. You hated reading because of it.*

That's right, I said. *And that's why I let you read whatever you want.*

Because I encouraged 6D to browse a wide range of genres, choosing whatever interested them, I did my best not to judge their selections, though it wasn't always easy. Some years ago, for example, a kid brought into class *The Long Hard Road Out of Hell,* the autobiography of singer/artist Marilyn Manson and the one book he'd shown any interest in all year. I glanced at the cover, asked if I could read a few pages, then informed him the content was inappropriate for a sixth grader (*Rolling Stone* magazine described it as *appalling and disturbing.*) I was no prig, at first happy the kid had found a book he liked since he wasn't much of a reader. The book, of course, was bait. And naturally I took it. *My mother bought it for me*, he said when I confiscated it, telling him he could have it at the end of the day when he could bring it home for good. Needless to say, the other kids begged for a chance to borrow it. A waiting list circulated, all boys, all reluctant readers, all desperate to get their hands on this amazingly foul book which would make reading fun for once, the kind of response I'd always hoped for.

That night when I called his mother she informed me she had indeed purchased the book for her son and saw nothing wrong with his reading it in class. *This is censorship!* she cried, as if I was some zealot protecting the purity of young minds. She threatened to take the matter up with the school committee and, after a few more minutes of my explaining that while I understood Mr. Manson could write whatever he wanted, the subject matter of his prose might alarm and even frightened sixth graders (though the effect was closer to titillation). She finally agreed to have him read it at home. I thanked her profusely, and despised her too. Her son had enough going on without scrutinizing a blueprint for embarking on *an appalling and disturbing* lifestyle with her encouragement.

I wouldn't miss these types of parents. While most were supportive and listened to my suggestions, a few bristled whenever I called, questioning my intent before I'd had the words out of my mouth. So there I was, exhausted and ready for bed, parsing what I said as I defended myself, speaking in a calm sympathetic tone while my heart raced, feeling as if I'd done something wrong and ought to apologize, wondering why I'd bothered to call in the first place.

So 6D read, with heads down, lights off, shades pulled. And soon most of them were asleep, in recovery, having survived another bout of the MCAS.

Thursday, May 15

We moved the desks out of the way and rearranged chairs into rows for a showing of the movie *Tex*. Feeling extravagant, I granted my colleagues Adelle and Sheila the last two hours of the day off, telling them I'd monitor both classes. Since all we were doing was watching a movie, there was no need for them to be here unless they wanted to join us. They didn't and dashed off to the teachers' lunch room. Before I pulled the shades down I announced a five minute bathroom/snack break (both prohibited during film showings). I then proceeded to separate groups of friends (to much protest) and discreetly moved those with large heads to the back row (to ensure a clean line of vision). Before a movie about a book we'd read, there was always heightened speculation over whether Hollywood's adaptation would live up to the real thing. I'd primed them for days, telling them to tally the differences, to be prepared to *compare and contrast,* though not in writing but for a later discussion, for which they thanked me profusely. Would the movie adhere to the authenticity of the prose as Francis Ford Coppola's *The Outsiders* had (we hoped) or would the screenwriter take fantastical liberties as in *Tuckeverlasting*, offering Jesse and Miles up at the end as easy targets, their coats open to a triggerhappy bewildered sheriff–to no effect since they were changeless–instead of having them quietly slip away once freed by Winnie (we hoped not)?

Roger Ebert gave Tex four stars, I added before I pressed the start button. *He only gave The Outsiders two and a half and we all loved that movie. I hope you're as excited as I am!*

Who's Roger Ebert?

Ten minutes in, however, it was clear that *Tex*, starring Matt Dillon (who also played Dally in *The Outsiders*) and Meg Tilly, didn't grab them the way the novel had. They giggled at fashion sense (bell bottom jeans, platform shoes, polyester shirts, teased and lacquered hairdos) and winced at the seventies Oklahoma slang. Or perhaps Coppolla's moody realism of *The Outsiders* struck a cord that Tim Hunter's directorial debut in *Tex* missed. Whatever the reason, I was faced with an unexpectedly intolerable situation once attention began to flag in earnest. Blaine, one of the first to lose interest, crossed his legs and squeezed his eyes shut, an urgent hand flung in the air.

May I? It's an emergency.

I'm sorry. Class policy. Please watch the movie.

I have to go.

You missed your chance.

Three others then put their own hands down. Those watching told those who weren't to shut up. Those who weren't in turn told those who were to shut up. One of the bigheads accidentally on purpose went over backwards in his chair, landing with a loud clap that seemed to knock the wind out of him. He lay there unmoving while everyone burst out in hysterics. I stood up and issued a warning from my desk. *Please watch the movie!* Two minutes later I issued a second. I grabbed the remote and increased the volume. Then I marched to the front of the classroom. With my back to the whiteboard, I squinted into the dark, surveying the viewers like an irritated usher. I could have shut the movie off then and there except two-thirds of the group was still enjoying it. I deliberated punishing everyone for the tomfoolery of some, a tactic often employed in schools when nothing else works. But I was enjoying the movie too, dammit, charmed by those same bell bottoms and seventies slang which reminded me of my own misspent youth. And besides, had I summoned Adelle and Sheila an hour earlier than planned they would have understandably been pissed.

The only thing to do was throw myself at the audience's mercy. After hitting pause and turning on the lights, I explained how I'd gone to the Rowley Public Library *on my own time* to borrow the video and would have to trudge back there *on my own time* to return it. Did they understand how little spare time I actually had? They studied me for a moment.

I don't have the easiest of lives. I confessed, softening my tone for dramatic effect. *Someday when you have kids of your own you'll understand. When I got to the library it was pouring. I got soaked just getting out of my car. At first the librarian couldn't find the CD. She looked for almost an hour while I waited. Actually, I was on my way to the pharmacy to pick up a prescription for one of my kids who had an ear infection. Ever have one of those? But I couldn't go later because the library was closing. So my kid had to wait. I just wanted to let you all know.*

They nodded. They were sorry to hear about the ear infection and hoped she was feeling better. They thanked me for doing what I did for them. I nodded with an exaggerated swallow. In appreciation for their understanding, and if they were willing to do so in complete silence so as not to disturb other classes, I would grant an unprecedented mid-movie two minute bathroom break. After they returned, I turned off the lights, pressed play and watched the rest of it in peace from my desk.

Friday, May 16

With well over a hundred sick days left and only a month in which to use them, I elected to stay home and cut the grass. The time allotted in the collective bargaining agreement amounted to eighteen days (fifteen sick, three personal) per academic year. Some teachers felt obligated to use every one even when they weren't feverish with a flu bug or had no urgent business to attend to, a practice that riled Maggie, our union president, who reminded us that allocated days were a privilege and ought to be treated as intended. We all knew who abused them and after a while it became obvious to parents too. It irked me to have one of my own kids tell me she had a substitute again, as her teacher was off to Disney World with her family for the week to avoid the school vacation crowd, and in a month's time this same person would act as a bridesmaid at her niece's wedding at a dude ranch in Colorado and would be gone for another week. And it didn't help our image when one of our own was spotted at a local watering hole at high noon on a weekday downing an Old Fashioned or two, though she had every right on her personal day to do whatever she wanted, as it was nobody's business but hers, and maybe she'd just returned from hauling her cantankerous wheelchair-bound mother-in-law to the podiatrist to have her toenails clipped and needed a stiff belt or two to recover from the ordeal.

Held to a higher moral standard than those in other lines of work, we never failed to provide a boost to the news cycle whenever one of us got arrested. Nothing carried shock value like a third-grade teacher busted on a drug charge or a high school teacher accused of having sex with one of her students. In this regard we were like everybody else—susceptible to temptation—though in polls measuring loyalty and trustworthiness, we finished ahead of clergy, funeral directors and veterinarians. For all our faults, we were for the most part decent, hard working, trouble-free. Good under pressure, we performed the kind of work evoking accolades whenever strangers got wind of what we did for a living.

I wouldn't last two seconds in that line of work.

You must have the patience of Job.

How do you survive without speaking to another adult all day?

I'll be arrested for murder within ten minutes.

How many other jobs do you have?

Kids were unruly these days, so everyone said. Respect had gone the way of the manual typewriter. Toll collectors enjoyed more creative leeway. The pay stunk. Who would want to be a teacher anyway? I never brought up the possibility with my own kids, afraid of what they might say, or, depending on the day, what they might hear from Carla and me.

While I mowed the lawn I imagined the person behind my desk, wondering about the potency of his blood pressure medication. It took a special type of individual to be a substitute teacher. With plenty of other low paying jobs available with half the aggravation why would one seek it out? I had no idea. A kind of higher calling I guess.

Monday, May 19

Ryder found a 9mm shell casing in one of the plastic bins of paperbacks left behind by a collection of area SWAT teams using SES as a site for a weekend training exercise, the cops firing paintball caps at one another to simulate dealing with an active shooter inside the school. Flecks of yellow and blue paint still wet spotted the linoleum and the whiteboard. They promised us they'd leave the school the way they'd found it and for the most part they did.

After the Newtown massacre, the task of killing a lot of people inside a school building had proven far from challenging. The doors and windows of SES consisted of large panes of glass, not the thick bulletproof kind afforded politicians and other important types, but the kind easily smashed with one of the fist-sized beach stones lying ornamentally around the shrubbery in front of the entrance. Once shattered, these portals provided a hole big enough for an intruder to crawl (or even walk) through along with his collection of assorted weaponry and ammunition. So why then was a SWAT team wasting its time in a training session simulating the tracking down of shooters *inside* SES? Had they really wanted to prevent a shooting, they would have come armed with trowels, jointers, shovels, and mixing tubs, with bags of mortar and a pallet loads of bricks. Then they could set to work sealing up all those windows and doors to keep the crazies *outside* where they belonged.

Tuesday, May 20

Leland told me his father was homeless again. He and his two brothers were living back with his mother. The four of them had no money, no car, etc. *Oh,* I said. That was the extent of the enthusiasm I could muster as this cycle had gone on in one way or another since he'd entered school. His running around the room bugging everyone was how he distracted himself from traumatic episodes which were a regular part of his life. I'd given him the watch with the fob. That made him happy. He'd thanked me and planned to bring it home and do something or other with it. And it made me happy to see the joy this trinket brought him. But I didn't have much to say about his latest predicament. True to form, he wasn't expecting much, simply updating me, filling me in on the specifics, not expecting sympathy or a chance to use this latest upheaval as a reason to make unreasonable demands. I loved that about him. In a perverse way his traumatic life, being consistently traumatic, had become a normal life since he had no other life to compare it to, and so for both of us his daily existence had lost its shock value. Episodes that might crumble another kid were a minor tremor barely felt. His behavior was the same, as were his work habits, social interactions, etc. Life simply went on, trauma having hardened him to the point where he seemed incapable of being thrown for a loss.

Thanks for letting me know, I said. *I hope things work out for him.*

I pass the information along to our social worker, not expecting that she, or anyone, could do much about it.

Wednesday, May 21

In the Smartboard classroom next door twenty teachers gathered with a consultant to hash out details of our standards-based report card, this latest consultant being paid handsomely for helping us design a report card few parents understood and over which we'd been laboring for five years. Our revolving report card committee had achieved a goal which had escaped humankind since the dawn of time: immortality. Every new edition of the committee endeavored to leave its own imprint by trashing the findings of the previous one, deleting what they thought didn't deserve to be evaluated and adding what they deemed more essential. In fact, the committee had grown in size despite its inability to agree– or perhaps because of it. Now the emphasis seemed to have shifted away from a final product to that of sustaining a committee by adding new members, bringing in highly paid consultants, and adding even more pages of ambiguous language (e.g. writing subcategory: *uses a variety of forms for different audiences and purposes*) into a report card we all doubted we'd live long enough to see the final version of.

Thursday, May 22

For *field work*, the sixth grade visited the Parker River National Wildlife Refuge on Plum Island to observe a demonstration on banding. Small birds on their way to somewhere else stopping for a rest were caught in nearly invisible black netting strung between two poles which we ourselves had walked into without noticing. The captured birds were then gently slipped into aluminum cone-shaped cylinders, their little heads popping through the other end while bands were clipped around their delicate ankles. The kids crowded around, struggling to see over one another as the ranger carefully manipulated a small pair of pliers and described what he was doing and why. I did not have to tell anyone to pay attention. There wasn't a sound, as all eyes zeroed in on this exquisite creature which had come so far and yet still had a long way to travel.

How does it even know where it has to go anyway? Phoebe asked. *How can it fly all that way with those little wings and that tiny heart? Does it even have ears to hear with? What about thunder and lightning?*

Tanner announced he was going to make a net like that for his own backyard. A bird lover, he was enthralled by the goings-on. Why had he never come to this amazing place before? Why had I waited until the end of the year to bring him here? He pulled my arm with such urgency he refused to let go. I apologized, saying I'd never been here myself and was ashamed when a group of Japanese tourists disembarked from a coach bus with cameras dangling from their necks. They'd come halfway around the world to visit this bird migration area not fifteen minutes from our school.

Well, Tanner said, *you're lucky. Next year you can come here every single day.*

Later we took a stroll along a boardwalk extending east over the Great Marsh, a vast expanse of barrier beaches, sand dunes and salt marshes that kept us safe from storm surges. We headed out toward the sea holding the binoculars we'd been given to spot various species alighting on both sides of us. The kids remarked how peaceful and quiet it was out here, how radiant the blues and greens, how wonderful the ocean smelled.

Look how big it is! Sierra said, as if noticing it for the first time.

We strolled and sniffed and listened and looked. On both sides the Great Marsh stretched north and south as far as we could see. Somehow all eighty of us managed to negotiate the boardwalk without tumbling off into the reeds. Somebody shouted about having to go to the bathroom and was instructed to hold it, as we were half a mile from the visitor's center. The person indicated that he was fine, he could wait, no problem, and wasn't this one of the best field trips ever? *Field work*, I corrected.

Friday, May 23

We went to the book fair in the school library today. Kids with no money received a five dollar coupon, like food stamps for books. The bright displays of fiction and nonfiction books, action figure posters, and assorted low priced stationery items were immediately swarmed over. This twice-yearly week-long travelling fair did a steady business, with SES getting a cut of the profits before the metal shelves on casters were folded into boxes and rolled up a ramp onto a box truck waiting to head to its next destination. Superhero graphic novels were a hit with the boys, main-character-with-a-terminal-disease genre a winner with the girls, knock-offs of *Diary of a Wimpy Kid* a draw for the lousy readers, and all of the books at kid-friendly prices so many ended up buying two or three. The enthusiasm of Evelyn, our librarian, was the reason everyone loved and respected the library. As your librarian went, so went kids' zeal for books. If you were fortunate enough to have a no-nonsense competent one who was receptive to the various needs of her readers, who imparted the notion that the library was a sacred place while at the same time a comfortable, welcoming sanc-tuary from the stress and tedium of the rest of the school day, then your job as a teacher was made easier. Once a week, after our library period, kids would return to class excited about their choices (the library being one of the few places where they had choices), wanting to sit and read, *just read,* and I was always happy then, seeing them escape into the world of books, just having them sit for half an hour or more, all of them silent, unmoving, lost in their selections, and me not having to do anything except check out something a kid couldn't wait to share.

Monday, May 26

Memorial Day-no school

My first male teacher was just doing us a favor. At least that's what it seemed to me. He descended on Saint Brendan's School to teach eighth grade two years before I had him, pulling up in a burgundy 1965 Pontiac Catalina convertible he parked along the curb under the classroom window. Well-groomed and hinting of Old Spice, dressed in a tweed sport coat, paisley tie with Windsor knot and polished wingtips, he slung a leather briefcase onto his desk every morning, snapping it open and keeping it that way until he departed at the end of the day, his red ballpoint evident for all of us to see. Mr. Cartelli didn't particularly care for kids but his aloof style never interfered with the job he was hired to do. He was organized and consistent and treated us not as children in a parochial school trained to behave as if Jesus was watching but as young adults who didn't need to be babysat, whether from someone like him or a divine force with the power to condemn us to hell. At times he left us alone, announcing he was going for a cup of coffee and a cigarette in the teacher's room and would return in fifteen minutes. As young adults, we were worthy of his trust, he reminded us, so long as we did nothing to break it. We agreed, knowing a thing or two about faith and guilt. And if he decided to stay away longer, what would that matter? It wouldn't, we replied.

And he would then return to the same studious atmosphere he'd left behind.

The men I knew weren't comfortable around kids, sometimes not even their own, either keeping their distance or chasing us out of backyards. We were a nuisance, a distraction, an unmanageable fact of life better left to the care of women. Cartelli, on the other hand, understood we could be reasoned with, be civilized without being brutalized. All of us accepted being hit at home by parents wielding leather belts and wooden spoons and in school by nuns twisting ears or poking ribs with the rubber tip of a pointer. The worst of Cartelli's offenses was lobbing a piece of chalk in the direction of Billy McKenna who'd fallen asleep in the middle of our taking turns reading aloud Kipling's *Captains Courageous*.

Occasionally Cartelli offered us snapshots of his life, though hardly enough to satisfy our curiosity. Did he have a girlfriend, a boyfriend? What about family, friends, goals and desires? He never let on. But what he did give us was the understanding we were old enough to look after ourselves and offered us plenty of chances to prove it.

I was a less-than-solid C student and remember sleepless nights anticipating the results of math tests (lower than sixty requiring a parent signature). But I liked him simply because he didn't live in the convent a stone's throw from our school. On weekends he partook of the bachelor nightlife, we imagined, driving to nightclubs in New York City or even Montreal. With a car like his, he told us, half the fun was getting there. Weeknights he relaxed and sipped cognac before a roaring fire while grading our history exams. Unimpressed by my less than stellar ability, he informed my mother I was nothing special and she shouldn't waste the money she didn't have on college tuition. It wasn't until years later she told me this, adding that any person who couldn't look her in the eye wasn't worth the ground he stood on. Still, to me Cartelli represented escape, the chance of a thriving existence beyond the confines of an insular Boston Irish Catholic neighborhood. No men I knew were teachers. None had even gone to college. Guys I knew hung from telephone poles, cut sheet metal, ran numbers, sorted mail on third shift, operated backhoes and jackhammers, drove cabs, delivery vans, buses. There were other options, I came to realize, and Mr. Cartelli was a living proof of them.

Tuesday, May 27

We had an election today to vote new members onto our Leadership Council. Teachers received a small stipend to meet with administration once a month concerning school issues and policies. As building representative, my job was to monitor the voting which I intended to do with more scrutiny than I had last year after reports surfaced about ballot stuffing. Taking for granted the integrity of my colleagues, I'd left a stack of paper ballots unguarded on a desk outside of my classroom. Throughout the day people came and went, some quickly casting a ballot while other milled around chatting. I'd sworn I'd seen a few come and go more than once. But that couldn't be, and I dismissed the illusion as a result of late day fatigue. Now, to eliminate any chance of fraud, I personally handed each teacher a list of candidates' names, then checked the name from the master list and watched as she filled out the ballot and slipped it through the slot in the wooden box affixed with a tiny lock (a kid had made it for me years ago as a classroom suggestion box and I still had the key). At the end of the school day I tallied the votes a couple of times, wrapped the ballots with an elastic band and carried them around in my briefcase in the event a recount was requested. The possibility of chicanery seemed like a long shot but given how little say teachers had in the running of their own school the urge for change might be powerful enough to override one's principles.

Wednesday, May 28

Today was eighty-five degrees, fifteen degrees warmer than it had been all spring. Only last week I'd given my portable heater to Adelle. Next year she would have two portable heaters going, a double violation of fire code. Windows were supposed to stay closed because of the non-existent AC. Vanquished by the sultry conditions I opened them on the scant chance of catching a breeze. Because of their size, they were drafty and icy to the touch in winter and functioned as magnifying glasses right now, desiccating a stack of vocabulary quizzes I'd left on the sill. Warm air flowed into the room but at least it was moving. The kids groaned and protested. *Shut them windows! Are you trying to kill us?* I left them open. The worksheets I'd distributed they folded into fans to wave under their chins. *You can't make us work in this heat! It's hotter in here than it is outside! We can't even breathe!* They had me and they knew it. In their eyes I was the one person responsible for the misery we found ourselves in. In response to their silent accusations I hated every one of them. The depth of my loathing frightened me. Engaging in debate would only serve to make them more indignant and piss me off even further. The heat had shrunk the room to a shoebox and amplified body odor so that it was even tougher to draw a breath. With two hours to go before dismissal and no one coming to save us, we were in serious trouble.

Suddenly, as happens in desperate moments when everything is lost, nature, the divine, or just plain dumb luck intervened. Something flew through the window. Something big and scary looking. Whatever it was glided in slow figure eights between the two rows of ceiling lights. Charcoal black with a greenish tinge, Ping-Pong ball sized with translucent wings, this creature climate change had delivered from the Amazon river basin droned around the room as if cruising beneath a jungle canopy. Corbin noticed it first and dove on the floor. The rest of them screamed and threw themselves under their desks for cover, pleading to be rescued. I watched in amazement while going on about how every sentient being served a purpose on this earth and had a right to exist, the same speech I gave whenever anything flew or crawled into 6D and was about to be annihilated.

Not this one! cried Brynn. *You have to kill it, Mr. D.!*

She was truly terrified. And whatever the creature was, it seemed equally frightened of us, keeping its distance, climbing up near the ceiling tiles and staying there in a holding pattern. I grabbed the broom in an attempt to redirect it back out into the world. Slow and lumbering, the cargo plane of the insect world, it at first outmaneuvered my efforts though I did manage to nudge it from behind with the bristles so that it dipped and rode the warm current carrying it back into the wild. Tanner jumped up and raced to slam shut every window in the room. Everyone cheered. *How did you do that, Mr. D.? How did you tap it on the butt like that?* They regarded me with awe. I shrugged. I had no idea. Only one teacher, they cried, would know what to do in a situation like that. *That teacher is you, Mr. D.!* I bowed. I loved them. I truly did. They were only twelve years old, so unbelievably young and new to this life, and how was it reasonable to expect much from them–anything really–when they were doing the best they could at their tender ages? My heart softened, maybe from the heat, maybe from the drama. But it softened. I asked were they okay? They nodded. I then declared a truce, though I never used the word lest they think we were equals. As a class we discussed what had just happened. It was only some sort of weird bug on steroids was all, minding its own business when its GPS screwed up. How about we write a story pretending we were that bug who'd just flown into a classroom full of crazy kids. What did it see, hear, smell, think? That would make one heck of a story, wouldn't it? They thought so.

And can we draw what it looked like too? Flynn asked me.

Thursday, May 29

I sat through an IEP review meeting on Calvin who I couldn't say I'd done much for this year. He was a nice enough kid though given his processing issues–he'd been labelled as having Asperger's Syndrome–he'd confounded me all year long. At times he'd look at me without responding when I said his name, or outright ignore me, or mumble what sounded like insults under his breath, making him impossible to read. His parents had brought along an advocate who made it clear that to address Calvin's academic and emotional woes he would need more services than were available at the middle school. After a few minutes it wasn't hard to decipher her pitch for a private placement which would end up costing the district a fortune. She inquired about services present and future, what exactly would be at his disposal next year, asked to see recent assessments, etc., all in an effort to make the case that what we had to offer clearly wasn't adequate. And she was right. Many of the kids on IEPs were in the same boat, as how could any public school district which endured a budget crisis every spring supply all the personnel required to see to the needs of these children? The SPED teacher, speech therapist, and the liaison took turns going on about how Calvin *was* having his needs met. The position of the district was to emphasize that point, and then to reemphasize it, to say whatever it took to keep the kid here, otherwise we'd go broke paying for a private placement for every child whose parents employed an advocate to press their case. While this back-and-forth discussion was going on, I stayed out of it. Though I sympathized with the parents' plight, as a taxpayer the idea of forking over a hundred grand a year for a private school made me nuts, especially when there was no guarantee Calvin would be better off.

Friday, May 30

I took a personal day to inch through Boston's nationally recognized Central Artery traffic in hopes of covering the sixty miles to the South Shore before nightfall to see about water seeping into my parents' basement. After more than two hours on the road I arrived in the center of Scituate where seniors slumped on park benches along the sunlit harbor while others hobbled on canes in and out of the pharmacy. Not one, as far as I could tell, looked young enough to hail from my generation, we baby boomers having decided to work ourselves into the grave to spare us from having to eat subsidized lunches at the senior center. What happened to the three day work week we'd been promised in elementary school, our labor replaced by robots that would make life in the 21st century one big picnic? While citizens in the rest of the world knew enough to call it quits at an age when getting out of an armchair was still a one person job, here in this country, retirement, for all the years we spent dreaming and talking about it, was a daunting prospect, given stagnant investments, monthly bills for kids' college loans, second homes, cars, boats, and other sundry acquisitions we cherished. Better to toil right to the end to pay off those bills rather than have to survive on a pared down budget and endure the stress of having all those days of freedom stretching out ahead of you.

And yet here I was, not fifty-nine years old, with two kids in high school and one in middle school, placing all my chips on a teacher's pension. *Was I completely insane?* What if I should survive another twenty or thirty years? My parents, in their mid-eighties, were still active and living independently. In all likelihood, thanks to them, I'd keep on going, growing more impoverished by the decade, until I was reduced to eating cat food, though as a vegetarian that wasn't an option either. Nevertheless I had to leave teaching and try something else. I could no longer suppress my guilt about the role I played in keeping kids locked up all day. They weren't allowed to act in their best interests, to assemble freely, to have a say in the way the school was run, or even given enough time to eat lunch. And I certainly was a part of the reason for that, despite my proclivity for placing the blame elsewhere.

Monday, June 2

Today was *Meet and Greet*, our annual trip to the middle school to give sixth graders district-wide the chance to mingle, challenge, and gossip about one another before they matriculated here in the fall. After a tour of the building, the kids from the three elementary schools were split into teams to play games supervised by parent volunteers. Without much to do, I stretched out on a patch of grass in the shade of the bleachers along with a group of elementary teachers. Someone wanted to know what we thought of all those contrails from commercial jetliners passing over us. In the clear blue sky streaks of brilliant white crisscrossed in skewed tic-tac-toe grids, the earlier ones dissipating from tight parallel lines into loose vapor clouds. Until that moment I hadn't given a second thought to those contrails, though my colleague was certain the United States government was dispensing a chemical specifically designed to manipulate our thoughts and emotions without us even knowing it. With renewed wonder we all lay there examining the sky. Contrails *were* more abundant nowadays, she said, many more than in the old days. There was your proof right there. But wait, someone asked, weren't there also more people flying than ever before?

That's all part of the plan, she noted with calm conviction. *More planes only gives the government more opportunity to dispense this mind controlling substance.*

She'd done her research; this government program was not only real but so nefarious we didn't realize our minds had been altered. And now it was too late to do anything. Unbeknownst to us we'd all been turned into a pack of zombies. But wouldn't the very same people who wanted to control us be affected by this fallout mixing with the air they had to breath too? Wouldn't they need gas masks which would tip us off as to what they were up to? We were laughing by then, though I was wondering about it myself. Such crazy talk—and yet could it be true? We didn't trust our leaders, would put nothing past them, but in the end considered this scenario a bit too sci-fi even for the U.S. government. Nonetheless, it was agreeable to lie on the warm grass on a sunny day and listen to conspiracy theories from someone I'd known for years. Her sincerity and depth of knowledge regarding this bizarre topic made me appreciate her even more.

Tuesday, June 3

For a good hour I sat with Mr. B. and Marcia going back and forth over her subpar formative evaluation. Her *artifacts* (a component of the new system requiring the teacher to compile pieces of information as proof of the obvious: that she'd existed as a teacher over the past year. Anything could be designated an *artifact* –a thank you note from a parent, a photo of your class notes from your whiteboard, a copy of a letter you'd written to a newspaper editor bemoaning budget cuts, etc.) had yet to be uploaded and here was Marcia's evaluation already signed, sealed, delivered. Well, Mr. B. said, despite the artifacts nothing would change the outcome. In the stifling conference room we sat around the table avoiding eye contact and speaking in awkward tones as if we hadn't known one another for ages. Next year would be a probationary period with more observations to see whether Marcia would fall in line or not. Where it went from there I had no idea, but it wouldn't matter for me anyway.

Wednesday, June 4

June was the cruelest month, at least for teachers. A schoolwide field day had been planned but would not happen for two weeks. Until then our only exposure to natural light and fresh air was restricted to our once a day recess allotment. All over America kids were growing obese before our eyes. Soon they would be wedged behind their desks unable to escape during a fire drill. Would schools do anything to reverse this epidemic they themselves were contributing to? No way. Until the last day we would stick to the usual routine. If it was good enough for September it was good enough for June.

The weeks before summer vacation, as anyone whoever attended a public school could attest (private schools already done for the year), meant running out the clock. Teachers and kids squared off yet wanted to be left alone, all of us cloistered in 750 square feet of space where the temperature had risen fifteen degrees over the last five days. Even less capable of listening, kids ignored whatever requests teachers made of them.

No one does anything this time of year! they proclaimed. *It's summer! We've been doing this same old stuff forever!*

There is still important material left to cover! I would tell them. *We have to get through these chapters! I need your attention!*

And so it went, with me warning them I was holding grades until the last possible day—*You can still flunk right up until the very end!* — though in truth grades had been finalized a week ago. Hostility continued on the part of kids as their natural inclination was to be outdoors this time of year. In response, I amped up the threats, both of us digging in for what would be the toughest stretch on the calendar.

Thursday, June 5

As a retiring teacher I was asked to present the annual SES scholarship for graduating seniors from Salisbury during an awards ceremony in the high school gym packed with kids, parents, grandparents, etc. all waiting to see who would walk away with a cut of the loot. The program listed pages of scholarships, most five hundred to a thousand dollars with one for fifteen thousand sponsored by a local car dealership. Lots of kids got something but most got nothing, it being the nature of these things, those unlucky recipients not only considered less deserving but having to endure a two hour assembly in sultry conditions, or perhaps the beneficiaries had applied for the scholarships while their counterparts hadn't bothered. In spite of donor generosity everyone would have to go out and procure loans anyway, the buoyant prospect of college life concealing the financial elephant until it was squatting on your chest. With college loans easy to get, no one thought twice, the borrower eighteen years old and not knowing any better, the parents figuring the more expensive the school the better chance for status. Both parties would try to forget that elephant until delinquent payments prevented the kid from renting an apartment or buying a car. With his zero credit score he would return to the couch in the basement and the dusty video games he'd left behind four years ago.

Friday, June 6

I bought a short sleeve avocado knit shirt at T.J. Maxx to wear with black slacks and shined my black loafers for the SES retirement party at a restaurant on Salisbury Beach where I was roasted by nine female colleagues, my *sister wives* as they called themselves. When it was my turn to speak I said I'd been given the job fifteen years and four principals ago after a five minute interview and a handshake just a week before the start of school. We'd just moved to the area, Carla had taken a leave to stay home with Beatrice, and I was tired of commuting to Woburn. With SES desperate for any male teacher who'd passed his CORI, I'd come along at the right time. And for that opportunity, I added, I was forever grateful.

The short speech I'd committed to memory, drafting what I wanted to say then walking around the house reciting the finished product until I grew hoarse. During dinner I meditated between tiny forkfuls so I could fool everyone and appear as a normal and relaxed person, though I'd had a few sleepless nights imagining myself too terrified to open my mouth.

After the festivities a few of us lingered, downing cocktails and chatting about summer plans until a dour waitress in canvas high tops vacuumed around our feet and drowned out our voices. I hoped Carla was okay to drive because I wasn't. Everyone was going to miss me, they said, the drinks taking hold, the school just wouldn't be the same, but you could come back and sub anytime.

Monday, June 9, 2104

Mr. B. emailed me on Friday saying he would not attend the retirement party (besides me, two other colleagues were also feted) as he would be attending one of his kid's soccer games. The choice between drinking beer with colleagues and watching six-year-olds chase a soccer ball around would not be a difficult one for me. Once upon a time administrators never missed these events—or any social gatherings—jumping at the chance to have a few drinks and relax, we teachers doing the same, all of us, supervisors and underlings, sharing stories and gossip and rumors about kids, parents, and anyone else not in attendance who drove us nuts. This mingling bred conviviality, the sense that we were all suffering together, albeit suffering for the right reasons, and afterwards all of us feeling recharged and tighter from this non-work time together. But those days seemed to be slipping away, the current model more of a business approach–bosses and workers not fraternizing so as not to blur the chain of command. This unspoken edict led to suspicion and mistrust on both sides. Communication amounted to taking orders and kowtowing to those who issued them, a practice that seemed on the rise in public schools these days, as I'd heard the same stories from friends who taught elsewhere.

Tuesday, June 10

Today was my last trip to Boston's Museum of Science as a teacher–and likely forever. I claimed the back seat as usual before the bus rumbled south down Interstate 95 well under the speed limit, gears grinding, radio blaring, windows down. The kids shouted at one another to converse and bounced up and down, rapturously, while teachers called out, perfunctorily, *Please stop all that shouting and sit down!* The wind funnelled down the aisle and made my eyes water. A painful jolt shot through my left eyeball, the precursor to a migraine I hoped to stave off but probably couldn't. I cupped my socket and lowered my head as if I'd been sucker-punched. Though I'd looked forward to field trips as a break from the classroom routine, ten minutes on a school bus left me feeling like the guy who'd posed for *The Scream*.

Once we arrived in the lobby of the museum (my migraine staved off for now), I collected half a dozen boys, members of The Hyperactivity Hall of Fame, in order to spare the chaperones who'd given up their day for us, then proceeded to lay down the one and only ground rule. Huddling to be heard about the din, I instructed us to stay together.

No matter what! I warned. *Building collapse? Stick together. Have to pee? We go as one. See your cousin from another school? Wave hello. If by chance you do get separated? Go directly to Lost and Found. We will claim you.*

To cement the agreement we grasped hands before charging off. The museum, so packed with kids, teachers and parents that with a turn of the head you lost your group, featured exhibits robust enough to withstand the relentless poundings visited upon them. Despite the chance to wreak further havoc, my group shot off in the opposite direction to scamper up and down the escalators, earning a rebuke from a glum heavy-set bespeckled guide in a red jacket. I apologized, saying it wouldn't happen again. As he lectured me on safety protocol, he pointed behind me to the kids who'd already returned to those enticing escalators.

At eleven o'clock the cafeteria opened. We were the first in line. Carrying trays of cheeseburgers, French fries, mini pizzas and astronaut ice cream we seized a table by the window and consumed our food with no effect on our rate of conversation. I looked away from this gustatory display toward the Longfellow Bridge and its granite salt and pepper shaker towers spanning The Charles. The sight of it brought me back to a sunny morning in May when I gazed down from the top floor of the Hyatt Regency Hotel where the previous night the Burlington High School senior class of 1994 had held their prom. Carla and I had been dating for six months and as class advisor she'd been given the room as a courtesy. Along with the rest of the couples we had our photograph taken under a latticed arch festooned with red and white roses. Later we aided and consoled an inebriated junior until an ambulance arrived. She'd slammed her face on the edge of a bathroom sink, breaking four perfect teeth and bleeding all over her coral gown. I was thirty-eight years old, had never been to a prom myself, and while I understood the event represented a rite-of-passage, I also understood why a kid might feel the need to get bombed to make it through the hyped-up tension and expectations of the evening.

After lunch it was off to the museum's Omni theater where we watched a movie about the Lewis and Clark Expedition. The theater was one of those steeply pitched, surround-sound deals with thunderous audio and overhead screens inducing vertigo. Within two minutes my head was spinning. Closing my eyes, I leaned back and fell straight to sleep, jerking myself awake at the end with an embarrassing twitch.

Last year when we'd visited Boston's Museum of Fine Arts I spent a taxing day shielding priceless works of art from exploring fingers, guarding marble sculptures and oil paintings against horseplay, reminding kids a million times that they were supposed to *whisper* and they in return saying *We are whispering!* which to them was a couple of decibels below a lawn mower. They intended to be heard, MFA docents be damned. At the end of the day as we boarded the bus I glanced back in relief that we'd escaped without an incident worthy of the evening news.

But the Museum of Science was different. Free to roam and play, the kids responded by keeping track of one another in the mobbed exhibit halls. In their enthusiasm they would grab my arm and pull me to a display I just had to see, according to them. They would patiently explain some science fact, breaking it down to get me to understand, repeating themselves because I didn't teach science and by my own admission was never any good at it.

Wednesday, June 11

At Calvin's follow-up IEP meeting his advocate continued to press for a private out-of-district placement, telling us the program offered at the middle school wasn't sufficient to address his social and emotional issues. As he wasn't particularly quick on the uptake in terms of peer interaction, he gave his lunch away to anyone who asked for it and had a tough time making and keeping friends. Imagine, the advocate asked, life for Calvin at the middle school with its transitioning between classes, locker combinations to decrypt, materials to keep organized, and three times the number of kids asking for his lunch. She presented a solid case and there was no doubt that Calvin's future would not be an easy one, but why should the district be responsible for the cost of a private school which could run upward of a hundred grand per year? His parents appreciated what I'd done though acknowledged he would have made more progress with a lower student-teacher ratio in a school tailored to his specific needs (*What kid wouldn't have?* I wanted to say). But private placements weren't necessarily the answer either. As a taxpayer I was hardly objective to the cost of this arrangement and remembered the time my special education colleague Kate went on a site visit to observe one of our kids enrolled in a residential school, only to find him fast asleep on a hallway bench. Well, she told me, he could just as easily sleep his day away here and for a lot less money. Assigning a paraprofessional to follow Calvin around was a possible solution, though of course his parents didn't want an adult trailing him around all day, as he had enough issues with peer acceptance as it was, which was why they'd called the meeting in the first place. The problem, of course, was the rigid setup of the middle school, not just for Calvin but for many other kids. That situation wouldn't be resolved any time soon.

Thursday, June 12

Wrapping up my tenure as building representative, I sat through two more meetings with teachers and Mr. B. and Ms. G. regarding evaluations. I didn't say much and left both meetings with a predictable headache. If anyone else asked me to meet with her evaluator–at this point in the year I hoped it wouldn't happen–I'd tell her to take the results and hope for better luck next year. All along our bosses had let it be known they'd wanted things done their way. That was hardly a crime. Some of us had managed to pull it off, others not so much. It all came down to insisting everyone *be on the same page*, which of course is how public schools are run, with consequences meted out for anyone turned to a different page, much like the kids, when they are on a different page and we teachers are not okay with it because that is not the way everyone else is doing it.

Friday, June 13

At the end of the day at the kids' request we made Father's Day cards, an activity I usually steered clear of given the relationships many in 6D had with the men in their lives. *Make a card for your dad, grandfather or any guy who's done something for you,* I told them, hoping I wouldn't be the recipient of one. They went for those cutting boards, markers, construction paper, glue sticks, adult scissors and started in while I moseyed around checking progress, not saying much as I stole a glance over their shoulders (*to Dad who is always there for me even when he isn't. You always have my back!*). Some kids didn't bother with a card at all, their arms folded in silent protest, while others kept messing up and starting over so they wouldn't have a finished product along with the pressure of having to decide who to give it to. In the end, to my relief, I didn't get one, and they complied when I asked them to clean up the mess. Next year having one less male in the building would make the lack of role models even more dire. We were an endangered species, so unusual that many of the younger kids were startled by the sight of us in the hallways and shied away, or else regarded us as they would a horse, having seen horses from a distance but never quite knowing how close to get or act around one. As far as I could tell hiring more male teachers wasn't a priority, but since men had little interest in teaching elementary school anyway, the effort required to procure such a scarce commodity could be redirected elsewhere.

Monday, June 16

The kids' names went into a beach pail for our classroom raffle. Assorted gewgaws and trifles, stuffed animals, laminated posters, and any other odds and ends I'd collected over the years filled two tables at the front of the classroom. Everyone got a chance to win, with plenty of prizes for a second round. My collection of eight little marble Buddhas went first, followed by a plastic green spiral wind chime, our big floppy teddy bear named Teddy, the 2014 Boston Marathon poster with my name on it (along with the names of 36,000 other runners), the heat shield blanket I'd kept from the same race, a stuffed cardinal (a bird, not a church dignitary), an assortment of wind-up toys, the two large bass (not taxidermal) suspended over the whiteboard with pushpins. Gone from my desk were all personalities who'd lived there for the past fifteen years, the ones kids picked up and enjoyed conversing with.

Where did you get this little alligator guy?
What's this penguin's name? He's adorable.
Can I have this windup Godzilla on the last day of school?
Woody Pride is my absolute favorite!

This really was the end, I told myself, with all my little action figures departing for new homes where they would receive much love and attention. Now I had a plain old ordinary no-nonsense teacher desk like everyone else.

Tuesday, June 17

With two days of school left, where were those feelings other than relief? Where was the emotional wave I'd been bracing for over the course of my last week? Why was I so ready to leave when I had no idea what I would be doing for the rest of my life, when the structure which had held me together for the last fifty years was all but gone? Having soundly repressed feelings of loss and insecurity which accompany a transition like retirement, I was on the giddy high one gets while standing on the platform of a bungee jumping tower or the crest of the highest hill on a roller coaster ride. Whatever awaited me down below, one decision was clear: I would never return to teaching. I was done faking it. Not in the sense of lacking enthusiasm but a worse kind— faking it with enthusiasm, as in trying to be someone I wasn't for the sole purpose of maintaining the existing state of affairs, something I'd done for too long. I couldn't see myself entering a classroom again, and figured this was a sure sign of improving mental health.

Wednesday, June 18

For some reason the sixth grade commencement ceremony was called *Forget Me Not*, the term *graduation*, indicating the completion of a course of study, apparently not aligning with what the kids had done over the past six years. By 6 p.m. every seat in the cafeteria was taken. Those without seats lined the walls and spilled out into the foyer. The kids were all done up, the boys in collared shirts, pressed slacks or cargo shorts, buffed dress shoes or new sneakers, along with a liberal application of Axe, the girls in tottering heels and layers of makeup and expensive hairdos, everyone of them transformed and nearly unrecognizable. A week ago we'd sent a memo home explaining that the hiring of limousines would not be tolerated (the fact that we had no power to enforce such a ban did not stop us). As some kids had a relative or two who operated such a business and were willing to transport a bunch of sixth graders to an elementary school graduation for a nominal fee, the front of the school had at one time resembled the entrance to the Dolby Theatre on Oscar night.

We sixth grade teachers sat on stage staring out at the audience. Our administrators and superintendent joined us, as did the chief of police, for a reason that was not clear to me. We'd rehearsed with the kids after lunch, warning them not to shout, whistle, chap or hoot when they weren't supposed to but we'd neglected to ask the parents to do the same. When Mr. B. called me to the podium to read off my students' names he mentioned I was retiring. His announcement set off a standing ovation, either because everyone was glad I was leaving or because I'd survived fifteen years with their kids. Having never received one, I was at a loss how to respond, nodding my head while gripping the sides of the lectern, a red-faced dummy looking at the back of the house while the applause tapered off and the audience sat back down. In the deafening silence, I cleared my throat and tried to think of something poignant to say while everyone fanned themselves, mopped their brows and stared back at me. Under the glare of the stage lights, I swallowed hard, cleared my throat, and spit out a *Thank you, that was wonderful.* With plenty of ceremony still to go and the temperature close to ninety, no doubt all were relieved by the brevity of my speech.

Later, after dignitaries and families had departed, we stacked the chairs on dollies while a DJ set her equipment up onstage. Volunteer mothers had decorated the cafeteria walls in a South Beach motif, taping up inflated palm trees, flamingoes and beach balls. They brought in cases of soda and water, cartons of chips and pretzels, stacks of pepperoni pizzas, paper plates and napkins, along with a gigantic blue and white sheet cake arriving on a cart. The social ran for ninety minutes, during which the girls danced together while the boys sprinted around them flinging water at one another. The volume was, of course, earsplitting. At the end of the night there was a dance-off to *Timber*. A large circle allowed plenty of room for you to jump into the center and show off your moves. A fair number of kids, too terrified to express themselves publicly in this most natural of human activities, clung to the wall. This fear, sadly, would likely follow them for the rest of their lives (unless they were drunk enough to chance it). Really, was anything more heartbreaking than a collection of twelve year old wallflowers? Being that dance was an artform, an expressive form of exercise, and a central ingredient in our social celebrations, why wasn't the skill addressed in the Massachusetts state standards? Plus, it was fun and made you feel good (that sealed it as a definite no-no).

The performers, sweat-soaked and exuberant, cheered the DJ, a mother whose kids had gone to SES. Some kids even charged the stage for a hug. We sixth grade teachers were also exuberant, having been treated to a side of the kids we never saw since dancing was pretty much prohibited in school.

Thursday, June 19

On the last day of my last year as a teacher, I distributed report cards, one of my final bookkeeping tasks. I'd gone easy, wanting to send 6D off in a good mood. Some proclaimed it was their best report card ever, others didn't bother to look, a few (those who'd done little or no work) merely shrugged in resignation. Another term down, two dozen more to go, all of it ending, with luck, in the granting of a high school diploma. There was profound happiness on this last day, as there was every year, all having been promoted (no one repeated sixth grade, to the relief of teachers and kids, kids' fear of the prospect worse than the fear of going blind, according to a study). All of 6D was game for a new start. But before that start stretched endless days of beach going and camping out and lots of time doing nothing. All vowed to do their middle school summer reading so as to get off on the right foot, though likely no copies would be left when they found their way to the town library a few days before Labor Day.

Once I'd collected the textbooks, the kids emptied the contents of their desks with uncontained glee into the over-flowing trash basket. I dispatched Ivan to find Tom and get us some larger industrial strength bags. With the room a disaster, I attempted to recruit volunteers to clean it up.

What trash? asked Barrett, standing in the middle of the pile. *I don't see any trash!*

He and the rest of 6D then raced off to the cafeteria to get their yearbooks signed with the other sixth grade classes. Joining them, I found a low stool connected to a table on wheels where I'd eaten my free lunch back in September. I wrote notes in those yearbooks until my hand hurt. *Congrats on a great year! We had a lot of fun together! Good luck in seventh grade!* etc. As dismissal approached, we struggled with the emotion of departure, knowing this was it—we were never coming back to SES. While 6D was bound for the middle school where they would forget their locker combinations, encounter eighth graders who shaved and vaped, and take orders from more teachers than they'd ever had before—some, purportedly, who'd been thrown out of the military for losing their temper—I had no idea where I was headed.

An hour later we returned to the classroom for the last time as we awaited the dismissal announcement. *You have nothing to worry about,* I told a bunch of teary girls who broke from their group hug to pose for a photograph with me. The boys, meanwhile, flung a Nerf football around the room, ignoring my request not to aim for one another's heads. Thad, a member of the pencil-sharpening-around-the-wastebasket trio, sat on his haunches under the ledge of the whiteboard. All year long his mother had clung to her decision, albeit reluctantly, not to treat his ADHD, her reasoning being that daily medication would eventually lead him into the world of addiction as there was a history of drug abuse and mental illness in the family. Perhaps she was right. Anyway, he was a skinny, florid-faced, pleasant kid with prominent ears who goofed around constantly and never left me alone. I could have easily spent my entire day chatting with him, as he possessed a wealth of knowledge he loved to impart as a way to avoid the distasteful chore of learning to read and write. He said hello to me every morning and asked if he could move his seat closer to his friends (to which I always said no which made him smile). Now when I attempted to console him, he kept his head down and shooed me away. I tried a second time, crouching down and whispering a few words about the difficulty of life's transitions (as if I was some expert). He shook his head. Forget about it. Those endless days of not working, not listening, squabbling with peers, fooling around, hanging out in the bathroom, gazing out the window, visiting the nurse for a cough drop, roaming around the room, and interrupting me while I held forth had finally come to an end and he was devastated. All I could do was squeeze his shoulder and tell him he'd be okay. He wiped a wet cheek. He wasn't buying. It was over for me too but unlike Thad I was still faking it, keeping my emotions in check with minutes remaining in my teaching career.

At 11:40, after the lower grades had gotten their usual five minute head start to the buses, the sixth grade was released. A flood of kids filled the stairwell, surged through the lobby and poured out the front doors. As was our custom, we teachers gathered along the preschool sidewalk to wave goodbye. Except no one was going anywhere as the lead driver had lost her key. Frantic, she raced up and down the sidewalk, in and out of her bus. How could this have happened? She'd just driven her bus here five minutes ago for crying out loud!

Did anyone see a key ring with a purple bottle opener attached to it? she called out.

We shrugged. Where was it then? Where had it gone to? Hands on hips in concentration, she seemed to be visualizing its whereabouts. She wore a sleeveless Bruins tee shirt and white capris. What looked like a dolphin tattoo adorned her right shoulder down to her elbow. She dug her cell phone out of her back pocket to call headquarters about a spare. A few of us volunteered to jump start the bus, laughing at the idea of a bunch of middle-aged teachers shouldering the rear bumper to get it moving. But we were game. We wanted them gone. *Go already!* At last she remembered she'd left the key on the office counter, ran to retrieve it and off the convoy went, horns blaring and kids hanging out windows screaming and crying and shouting *We love you!* and us blowing kisses and waving and shouting *We love you too!* and *Happy Summer!*, relieved as all hell the year was over, the younger teachers not as used to this sort of thing wiping away tears. The rest of us, having given another pound of flesh from an ever diminishing supply, were dry-eyed and delighted to see the parade advancing at last. Many of us would move into another line of work over the next ten weeks, the desperate or addicted signing on for six weeks of summer programming with the same population who'd pushed us to the brink all year long.

After the last bus followed the others down the long driveway toward Route 1, we strolled in threes and fours toward the cafeteria for a small ceremony for the retirees. Once the staff had assembled, my friend Pam stood up and read something she'd written describing a list of my accomplishments from high school on– information secretly supplied by Carla–which, as straightforward as it was, touched me and made me think it would make a good eulogy. She added she'd miss me and wished me good luck. Mr. B. then stood up, saying what he would remember most was my request some years back that he not assign teachers tasks simply for the sake of assigning them. This novel idea he took to heart, vowing then and there that whatever he asked us to do would have a purpose behind it. He wished me the best and shook my hand. From the social committee I received an envelope of donations, tens and twenties colleagues handed over to kids who had come to their classroom doors. When it was my turn I thanked everyone for their generosity and told a story about a student I'd had two years ago, a big sullen kid who had managed to get himself banned for life from riding the school bus as a third grader. Though I'd done my best to give him a fair shake, he didn't want anything to do with me, one time coming at me in a rage before pulling up. By the end of the year I was happy never to see him again. An eighth grader now, he'd spotted me after Apphia's middle school graduation two days ago. Dressed in a collared shirt, cargo shorts and Keds, he weaved his way through the crowd. At first I didn't know what to think. When he reached me he smiled and stuck out his hand.

I heard you were retiring. Best of luck. Thanks for all the help and advice you gave me.

All the help and advice I gave him? What I held firmly in my head was something else entirely–that he was going no-where, that he was a punk who'd end up in prison (his mother had told me herself he'd be there before he turned fifteen), that he was the type who saw teachers as obstacles to get around. And that he'd despised me. I'd spent considerable time with him, his desk close to mine, trying to shore up his reading skills, to teach him to behave himself, to get to know him, but in the end concluding my energy had been wasted. Clearly I'd misjudged him. That was the point I was trying to get across, though many of those listening no doubt stuck with their own impressions of him.

Later I gathered up some boxes and brought my car around to the back of the building. In the office I updated the cumulative folders we filled out on the last day, the ones that had followed the kids grade to grade and were kept in file cabinets next to the mailroom. At the small table by the front window, I transferred information from the report cards, averaging academic grades and totalling attendance figures. A few feet away two red and silver fish in the aquarium on the bookcase studied me as if they'd never seen a human being before. Stock still, noses pressed to the glass, they were enthralled by the dexterity of my clerical work. Barbara and Clare, our office secretaries, asked was I doing okay, figuring I'd be a wreck. They'd been a great help over the years, courteous, tolerant and helpful no matter what degree my manic state. I'd intended to finish and hurry out of the building to avoid running into anyone, but those damn fish wouldn't leave me alone, their curious interest releasing a weight that sank into the pit of my stomach.

Is this really the end? the two fish asked me. *Are you ready for that big scary world out there? Are you sure?*

After saying goodbye to those I'd worked with and wouldn't see again, lingering made the awkwardness worse. I gathered up the pile, each of the twenty folders an individual history an inch thick with assessments, report cards, tests results, work samples and all the other crap kids didn't see until graduation when the lot was handed over to them—to keep, trash or torch. I placed 6D's pile in a cardboard box with the rest of the six grade to be shipped off to the middle school.

Finally, after hugs from Barbara and Clare, I returned to my classroom. Tom had instructed us to sketch a schematic on the whiteboard to indicate where desks, chairs, tables and cabinets belonged after the furniture was removed and floors polished. I didn't bother. No one would occupy this classroom next year, the fifth grade population too small to justify replacing me.

The desks and chairs were stacked against the cubbies, the floor covered with debris that hadn't made it into the plastic bags (spiral notebooks, markers, pencils, rulers, scissors, tattered folders, loose leaf binders, a pair of headphones, candy/gum wrappers, a blue sock, an empty bottle of Listerine, a copy of *The Hunger Games*), the date I'd written in cursive still in the top left corner of the whiteboard. While I swept the mess into a bag, I thought again about the kid I'd seen at the graduation ceremony two days ago. How many others had I misread over the years, cementing opinions because I was certain I was right? How many had I dismissed when they didn't live up to what I expected of them?

As a teacher you sat behind your desk and watched kids file in the morning and hang up their coats and backpacks and you might ask how they were doing, perhaps recalling what it was like when you were twelve and hoping a teacher might ask you the same. Maybe because of you the classroom was a place kids where wanted to be or at least could tolerate. Or maybe you saw the kid as someone other than who he was because he didn't pay attention or mumbled under his breath or did his work in five seconds flat or no work at all. And though he may have a very good reason, the partiality of school and your own thinking prevented you from seeing. By contrast, if you could free yourself from those limitations and see each interaction as a chance for your own redemption, you might see the kid not as the school expected you to see him (lousy reader, juvenile delinquent, over/underachiever, loner, etc.) but someone like yourself who only wanted to be appreciated and considered unique.

Whatever good I achieved grew out of those times when the fog lifted as I listened to a kid read her story or update me on her sick beagle or her dad getting a job driving a tractor trailer or her elderly aunt relocating to Arizona on account of her COPD. If I paid attention I might notice she'd had her hair braided and say *Wow, who did your hair?* And she would smile and say *My mother's friend, the one I told you about who had the motorcycle accident but is doing hair again.* In my best moments the conversation was natural and unforced, the light in the kid's eye releasing me from the playacting of being a teacher. It took me years to feel comfortable doing this, to open up to spontaneous exchange–unstructured, stress free, illuminating–the type of thing normal human beings do all the time but which doesn't happen much between teachers and kids because of everything else shoved in the way.

Postscript

In September, I became a farmer. Behind the house I fenced in a quarter acre, burying chicken wire below grade to discourage woodchucks and rabbits. I built vegetable beds from scratch, each two feet by twenty-five, three rows of thirty-three, layering on the grass sheets of cardboard (procured from Dumpsters), wheelbarrows of aged horse manure (plenty available at no cost in Rowley), blankets of spent coffee grounds (hauled in five gallon buckets from Zumi's, a coffee shop in Ipswich), mounds of grass clippings, pails of kitchen compost, and piles of shredded leaves (chopped by my riding mower). I had no experience and had taken no classes on agriculture. I wasn't enrolled in a school where attendance was compulsory and where I was required to take two column notes from a whiteboard while being lectured to on how to plant, raise and harvest crops. I would take no assessments to determine where I stood among my peers cultivation-wise. What I did do was read blogs written by people doing what I wanted to do, borrow books from the Rowley public library (again, mostly memoirs by people who'd attempted to do the same), and quiz gardeners and farmers around town on the tricks of the trade. What drove me was desire and interest, a passion for growing my own food on my own land. No one was mandating I do it, or cared one way or another whether I succeeded or failed. Everyone thought my plan a great idea. What could be better than growing your own food?

By spring the beds would be ready for planting. As I toiled away, a mild late summer breeze ruffled the leaves of the maples and oaks. The ruckus of crows and blue jays high in the chokecherries provided something to listen to. Being outdoors and playing in the dirt felt like cheating. Like everyone at SES I'd left behind, I should be sitting behind a desk in a classroom. But after just one day the physical labor eased my mind and put me to sleep at night. I didn't miss school and wasn't lonely. Now that I was no longer teaching, I hoped to supplement my pension selling produce at local farmers' markets. With my hands gritty from loamy soil I was building myself and my voice on the mend, I imagined some day offering advice on everything from the most prolific varieties of kale to ways of outsmarting potato beetles. Yet as late summer slipped into fall, rather than feel relief about the ease of my transition, I was harried by guilt. Why hadn't I, with a year to go and free to do and say as I wanted, spoken up about kids having to sit all day through a curriculum that didn't interest them? Why hadn't I done something about the tight quarters, inflexible schedule, endless demands and unreasonable expectations placed on all of us? Why hadn't I gone ahead and built that snow fort, led exploratory hikes along the rail trail along the other side of the boundary fence, planned and set up that open classroom?

I didn't because I couldn't. As a product of more than half a century of indoctrination, my aptitude for championing the status quo scored in the superior range. Like any dutiful student, I did what I was told and kept quiet, suppressing any and all urges to take on what I believed the kids really needed. Simply put, I wanted to be liked. My biggest fear was being taken for a loudmouth and smartass whose ideas and actions went against the grain, whose unconventional suggestions made his colleagues bristle, someone who never shut up and was never satisfied. Now it was too late—I'd squandered my chance. As such, I was just as culpable as anyone in keeping the present system up and running.

Standing in the middle of my patch of earth, I took a breath and forgave myself. Any change was beyond the capacity of a single teacher anyhow. Something on a larger scale was needed, a national movement, an insurrection to reconfigure elementary education. A federal mandate for the welfare of children, similar to the Child Labor Law, would be a good place to start. Short of elementary schools seeing the same fate as underaged labor, a list of easy-to-implement entitlements ought to be posted in every classroom in America. Few would argue that kids, for their own health and well being, ought to be able to move about freely, indoors and out, to have enough time to eat lunch, to enjoy art, music, and PE classes daily, to learn about nutrition and sex and the environment, to know how to manage stress, to have the opportunity to connect with the wider community through volunteering, and, most importantly, to be free from the encumbrances of labels, assessments, and judgment.

Radical in their common sense, perhaps over the next fifty years these rights would find their way into public schools. I wasn't hopeful, given the track record of the last fifty. Anyway, going back into the house for lunch (I could eat when I was hungry) I stopped to look at something 6D had given me on my last day, a banner of sorts that hung on the back porch next to the kitchen door. Assembled entirely of rolls of Duct tape in a variety of colors, it contained all our names, with mine in larger letters at the top above *SIXTH GRADE* in case over the years I forgot what grade I'd taught. It was one of those crazy kid inventions involving intricate craftsmanship and employing the oddest of materials (inexpensive and readily available in bulk) whereby one kid improved on another's design and technique and so on. Created by Sierra and Lucy, who'd worked on other duct tape projects throughout the year which they displayed in class (wallets, handbags, briefcases), the project had taken hours of meticulous cutting, snipping and arranging, the names spaced and in rows, with the addition of little three-dimensional pencils, books, backpacks and–Bless them!–they had even found tape adorned with Patriots' helmets.

Anyone who came into the house would note the artistry and never think the same about Duct tape. What would I say when asked about the names on that banner, if I thought I'd made a difference in the lives of my students over the final year of my teaching career, or for that matter, any of the kids I'd taught? I'd begin by confessing I wasn't sure. Maybe to some but not others. Even the ones I was convinced I'd done little for had fooled me in the end. The results I'd expected weren't necessarily the ones I'd gotten.

Good teaching was nothing other than figuring out a way inside a kid's head. Simple enough, but tough to prioritize given that the running of public schools is about something else entirely–designed, as it were, to draw a teacher's attention *away* from kids. But if from the start you saw your job as the simple act of connecting with one child at a time and doing so without bias or appraisal, with an open heart and a clear mind, the outcome of your effort would be all the compensation you'd ever need.

Credits

The author would like to acknowledge the following, in which portions of this memoir first appeared, in slightly different form:

Teacher Magazine, January/February 2006, entitled Boys to Men.

Am I Teaching Yet? Stories from the Teacher-Training Trenches, edited by Molly Hoekstra, 2002 by Heinemann, entitled A Classroom Exchange.

Acknowledgements

Special thanks to Stevan V. Nikolic and the staff at Adelaide Books for claiming this manuscript from the slush pile and bringing it to the light of day.

I would also like to thank Carla Panciera, my wife (and author in her own right), for her careful reading, insightful suggestions and nearly bottomless patience. All three made this book so much better.

I was fortunate while teaching at SES to have developed many close friendships with dedicated and talented teachers and paraprofessionals. I owe them all a debt of gratitude for the motivation I needed to write this book.

About the Author

Dennis Donoghue retired as an elementary school teacher in 2014. His work had appeared in various journals, magazines, and anthologies, including Blue Lake Review, Brandeis Review, Broad River Review, Full Circle Review and Georgetown Review. He lives in Massachusetts.

The Final One Eighty, a day-by-day account of author's last year as a sixth grade teacher. The memoir reveals what it's like to teach in a public school these days, highlighting conflicts, frustrations and successes with humor and introspection, all from the point of view of someone who'd been at it for 37 years. Each of the 180 days is a stand-alone chapter, an essay really, with a particular anecdotes examined to reveal a deeper significance.

Written after a full career of over three and a half decades, its perspective differs vastly from typical teacher memoirs which tend to document the first year (or else are authored by journalists who teach for the purpose of producing a memoir about the experience). Certainly, new and veteran teachers would see themselves reflected in this work. And since most people have attended public schools and send their kids to them, they would also find it appealing, as it provides an intimate look at daily maneuverings of not only the teacher but everyone around him-- students, colleagues, administrators and parents.

Made in the USA
Middletown, DE
18 June 2020